Sage Sterling V.5

Integrated Accounting Software for DOS

User's Guide

Dexter J Booth and Denise Gallagher

PITMAN
PUBLISHING

PITMAN PUBLISHING
128 Long Acre, London, WC2E 9AN

A Division of Longman Group Limited

© Dexter J Booth and Denise Gallagher 1994

First published in Great Britain 1994

British Library Cataloguing-in-Publication Data
A catalogue record for this book is available from the British Library

ISBN 0 273 60631 X

Printed in England by Clays Ltd, St Ives plc

Contents

Introduction

The Sage Sterling Financial Controller V.5 is version 5 of Sage Sterling's leading accounts package. It is designed to run under DOS to provide a unique approach to automated book-keeping.

The purpose of this *Guide* is to introduce novice users to the Sage Sterling Financial Controller accounting system and, by leading them progressively through the package, to convert them into accomplished users.

This *Guide* accompanies *The Student Edition of Sage Sterling* software (adapted for education) and is also available as a stand alone text. It covers all the features of the software in *The Student Edition*, which are identical to the features of the non-educational version.

Working through this book

The book is divided into three parts: Elementary, Intermediate and Advanced, where each part builds upon the skills developed in the previous parts. Throughout the book comprehensive exercises permit each topic to be put into full working practice. Because some exercises require the use of accounting transactions from earlier chapters, it is recommended that all the exercises be worked through in the order in which they appear.

Icons used throughout the book

The bomb icon is used as a warning. Wherever you see this icon take especial care and read the information very carefully

The arrow icon indicates an exercise or activity.

The mouse

The Sage Sterling Financial Controller accounting system operates by presenting the user with a succession of screen views, each screen view being accessed by making the appropriate selection from a list of displayed options. The selections are effected by using either the mouse or the keyboard.

If you have a mouse installed then when you first enter the Sage Sterling Financial Controller accounting system you will notice a small rectangular graphic. This is referred to as the pointer and it can be moved around the screen by pushing the mouse across your flat table top. In this way specific screen items can be indicated by literally pointing to them by physically moving the mouse across your desktop.

On the top of the mouse are either two or three buttons. Within Sage Sterling the left-hand button is used to complete a selection. A screen item is pointed to and then the left-hand mouse button is first depressed and then released. This procedure is called clicking and results in the facility clicked being activated.

The keyboard

Whilst the mouse is an integral means of entering information into the computer the keyboard is an essential data input tool as you will see as we progress through the book. Indeed, in all instances where the mouse is used the keyboard could be used instead.

The company scenario

Throughout this book you will be dealing with the accounts of a company called Total Bedrooms Ltd. This is a company that supplies bedroom equipment to the hotel trade and it has decided that due to increased pressure of business it is time that the company automated its accounting and stockholding procedures. As you work your way through this book you will learn how to do this from the initial stages of setting up the nominal ledger accounts through to using the full system.

Getting started

The Sage Sterling Financial Controller accounting system is packaged on a pair of 3 1/2" diskettes. If your computer only has an external drive that takes 5 1/4" diskettes then the appropriate diskettes will be despatched on request. In addition to the diskettes there is a *User Manual* and a booklet describing the EC VAT regulations. The two diskettes contain the complete system and enable the system to be installed onto your computer's hard disk via an external floppy disk drive to run under MS-DOS.

In this book it is assumed that the Sage Sterling Financial Controller accounting system will be used to run from a hard disk under a previously installed version of DOS.

System requirements

To use Sage Sterling Financial Controller with DOS you will need:

- MS-DOS
- An IBM PC or compatible, PS/1, Apricot, RML Nimbus or Wang
- At least 512 KB of conventional memory
- A hard disk with at least 3 MB of free disk space
- A colour or monochrome monitor
- A printer
- A mouse may also be used.

Installing Sage Sterling Financial Controller

To install the Sage Sterling Financial Controller for DOS execute the following procedure:

1 Boot up your computer and display the DOS prompt:

   C : \ >

2 Place into the external drive A (or drive B, whichever is suitable to your computer) the Sage Sterling diskette marked:

   INSTALL

---

3   At the DOS prompt, depending upon which drive you are using, type

A: INSTALL *or* B: INSTALL and press Enter .

This will activate the Sage Sterling installation procedure which will cause the Install screen to be displayed.

```
Sagesoft              INSTALL           Version 5.1A

MSDOS Version 5.00

This installation program will copy from your SAGE
master disks and make a working copy of the program.
Appropriate amendments will be made to the system
file 'CONFIG.SYS'.

Ensure your SAGE master disks are write protected.




                  Press any key to continue
```

4   Follow the instruction at the bottom of the screen and press any key on the keyboard. The display will change to:

```
          Select which SAGE program you wish to install

              A).     Bookkeeper
              B).     Accountant
              C).     Accountant Plus
              D).     Financial Controller
              E).     Payroll II
              F).     Job Costing

Which option (A-F) ?
```

5 · Press the letter **D** to select the Financial Controller and then press Enter .

The screen display changes to:

```
          Select the type of install procedure required

        A).    Create completely new working program installation
        B).    Update program files only, saving existing data

Which option (A-B) ?
```

As we wish to install the complete system select option **A** by pressing the letter **A** and then pressing Enter. The screen display then changes to:

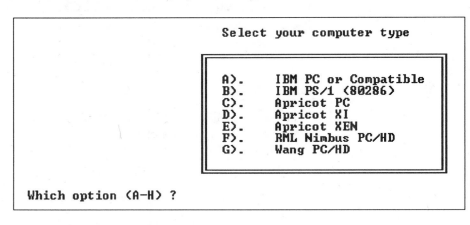

```
            Select the type of computer system

      ┌─────────────────────────────────────────────────┐
      │                                                 │
      │  A).    MS-DOS standalone PC                    │
      │  B).    MS-DOS network                          │
      │  C).    Concurrent DOS XM v6 or CDOS 386        │
      │                                                 │
      └─────────────────────────────────────────────────┘

   Which option (A-C) ? _
```

6   Select **A**. The screen display then changes to:

```
                    Select your computer type

            ┌───────────────────────────────────────────┐
            │                                           │
            │  A).    IBM PC or Compatible              │
            │  B).    IBM PS/1 (80286)                  │
            │  C).    Apricot PC                        │
            │  D).    Apricot XI                        │
            │  E).    Apricot XEN                       │
            │  F).    RML Nimbus PC/HD                  │
            │  G).    Wang PC/HD                        │
            │                                           │
            └───────────────────────────────────────────┘

   Which option (A-H) ?
```

7   Select the option that suits your particular computer system after which you will be required to select the drive configuration of your computer:

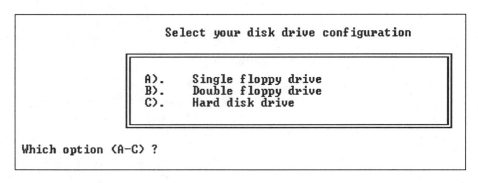

```
                Select your disk drive configuration

         ┌─────────────────────────────────────────────┐
         │                                             │
         │  A).    Single floppy drive                 │
         │  B).    Double floppy drive                 │
         │  C).    Hard disk drive                     │
         │                                             │
         └─────────────────────────────────────────────┘

   Which option (A-C) ?
```

8   Select option **C**.

Next you are asked to state where exactly on your hard disk you wish the program to reside:

```
Updating the FILES and BUFFERS parameters within CONFIG.SYS,
your existing version of this file will be saved as CONFIG.OLD

Your working program and data will be held on
a sub-directory of your hard (Winchester) disk.
No floppy disks will be needed.

Please select the default directory names unless you have
good reason not to.

Please enter your drive letter and subdirectory,
or press ENTER to select the defaults

Destination Drive [C] : _
```

9   Press **Enter** as we wish to adopt the default destination drive.

The screen then displays the default directory as:

    C:[\SAGE]

10   Press **Enter** to accept this default.

When you have done this you are asked to type in the name of the company that is
to use the Financial Controller system. Enter the name and address of the company
as follows:

```
    Please enter the name and address of your new company
    Note that this will be printed on statements, payslips
    etc, so be sure to enter it correctly

Name ?              TOTAL BEDROOMS LTD
Address Line 1?     SLUMBER LODGE
Address Line 2?     57 HALIFAX ROAD
Address Line 3?     HUDDERSFIELD
Address Line 4?     WEST YORKSHIRE
```

When this is complete the installation procedure will then proceed to copy files from
the INSTALL disk to your hard disk, displaying as it does so the names of the files
that it is copying. During this process you will be asked to swap the INSTALL disk in
your external drive with the PROGRAM disk and then back again. After a number of
files have been transferred to your hard disk you will be asked to designate your
type of printer and after that you are presented with the following screen display:

```
    About to initialise your Financial Controller data files

    ┌──────────────────────────────────────────────────────┐
    │                                                        │
    │   Select your Nominal Ledger Account Structure :       │
    │                                                        │
    │ A). Copy the standard default layout                   │
    │ B). Enter your own layout at a later date              │
    │                                                        │
    └──────────────────────────────────────────────────────┘

Which option (A-B) ?
```

The Nominal Ledger is at the very heart of the accounting system and for the purposes of this *Guide* we shall be adopting the standard default layout.

11   Select option **A**.

When the installation is complete a warranty screen will be displayed:

```
SAGE Installation Complete

To run the program:

Ensure you are in the C:\SAGE subdirectory,
type SAGE and press ENTER

WARRANTY

Now that you have installed your SAGE software, you are entitled
to 90 days FREE subscription to Sagecover.

This means that you can use our telephone Helpline for any advice
or information that you might need. It also means your software is
fully guaranteed against faulty materials and workmanship for 90 days.

To take advantage of our 90 day FREE subscription period, simply
COMPLETE THE REGISTRATION FORM, AND RETURN TO SAGE.

Please quote your serial number in all contacts with SAGE.

C:\SAGE>_
```

At the bottom of this screen you will see the DOS prompt:

C:\SAGE>

which tells you that the Sage Sterling Financial Controller accounting system has been fully installed and is now ready for use.

Entering the Sage Sterling Financial Controller

To enter the Sage Sterling Financial Controller from the DOS prompt:

C:\SAGE>

 1   Type in the command:

SAGE

followed by Enter.

Before you gain access into the system you are presented with the Copyright screen:

```
S A G E S O F T   F I N A N C I A L   C O N T R O L L E R  -  V5.1A
                Copyright (C) The Sage Group plc 1985-1992
                       Telephone (091) 201 0600
                        Single User Version

    This copy of the program has been licensed to, and only for the use of :


                        TOTAL BEDROOMS LTD
                        SLUMBER LODGE
                        57 HALIFAX ROAD
                        HUDDERSFIELD
                        WEST YORKSHIRE


      If your company name does not appear above, please contact SAGE on

                            (091) 201 0600

                  who will then issue an authorised copy
```

At this point you can either wait a few seconds for this display to disappear or you can press Enter to clear it. You are then presented with the date. Press Enter and a request to enter a password is then displayed:

```
Password        : [_____]▒
```

The default password is LETMEIN and this is the one that is recommended to be used throughout this *Guide*.

2   Type in:

LETMEIN and press Enter .

Notice that as you type in the password all that appears on the screen is XXXXXXX. This is done to maintain the confidentiality of the password whenever a user enters it into the system. We have retained the default password throughout this *Guide* to avoid creating a distraction as you learn how to use the system. In a real live accounting system, of course, the confidentiality of the password is essential to maintain the security of your accounts. To cater for this Sage includes a separate utility program that permits a new password to be installed. In addition the password program permits different passwords for different parts of the accounting system to enable restricted access to the accounts. A full explanation of this utility can be found in the *User Manual* that accompanies the software under the heading Changing the Password.

When the password has been entered the screen then changes to the full display of the Sage Sterling Financial Controller screen displaying the Main Menu:

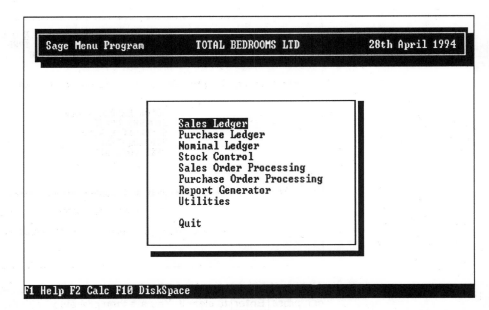

```
┌──────────────────────────────────────────────────────────────────┐
│ ███████████████████████████████████████████████████████████████  │
│ █ Sage Menu Program      TOTAL BEDROOMS LTD      28th April 1994  │
│ █████████████████████████████████████████████████████████████████│
│                                                                   │
│                                                                   │
│                ┌───────────────────────────────────┐             │
│                │ ███████████                        │             │
│                │ Sales Ledger                       │             │
│                │ Purchase Ledger                    │             │
│                │ Nominal Ledger                     │             │
│                │ Stock Control                      │             │
│                │ Sales Order Processing             │             │
│                │ Purchase Order Processing          │             │
│                │ Report Generator                   │             │
│                │ Utilities                          │             │
│                │                                    │             │
│                │ Quit                               │             │
│                │                                    │             │
│                └───────────────────────────────────┘             │
│                                                                   │
│ F1 Help F2 Calc F10 DiskSpace                                     │
└──────────────────────────────────────────────────────────────────┘
```

This screen is typical of the many screens that you will see as you use the system in that it has a number of features common to all such screens:

The title bar

Across the top of the Financial Controller screen is the title bar in which the name of the screen is displayed. This is common to all screens in the system.

The menu

In the body of the screen is a list of options where the first option - **Sales Ledger** - is highlighted. The highlight means that this option has been selected by default and can be activated by simply pressing the ⎡Enter⎤ key. To select an alternative option the highlight can be moved by using the up and down arrow cursor control keys ⎡↑⎤ and ⎡↓⎤. Alternatively, pressing the first letter of the option will select it.

3   Press the letter **Q** on the keyboard and the highlight instantly moves to the option **Quit**.

4   Press ⎡Enter⎤ to activate the option and at the bottom of the Financial Controller screen a question appears:

Do you want to back up your data files? : No Yes

We shall discuss backing up data files shortly. For now select the option **No** and the Financial Controller screen clears and returns the screen display to the DOS prompt.

Formatting a diskette

A diskette is a circular disk of plastic enclosed within a protective casing. The top and bottom surfaces of the plastic disk are coated with a chemical that is susceptible to magetisation. Information is placed on the surface of the plastic disk by means of a magnet in just the same way that sound is recorded on a cassette tape. Reading the information stored is then a matter of rotating the disk beneath a magnetic read head - again, just like the read head on a tape player.

When information is stored on the surface of the plastic disk it is placed in designated areas of the disk surface called sectors which have been previously marked out by a process known as *formatting*. When you purchase a diskette it is usually unformatted and before it can be used it has to be formatted by you.

 1   Display the DOS prompt:

   `C:\>`

2   If your external disk drive is the A drive then type in the command:

   FORMAT A:

   If your external disk drive is the B drive then type in the command:

   FORMAT B:

3   In either case, when you have typed in the command press Enter and the following message will appear:

   ```
   Insert new diskette for drive A: (or B)
   and press ENTER when ready...
   ```

4   Place the unformatted diskette in the drive and press Enter . Your computer will then proceed to format the diskette and when it has finished it will display the message:

   ```
   Format complete

   Volume label (11 characters, ENTER for none)?
   ```

   This message is displayed to permit you to give the diskette a name.

5   Type in:

   SAGE BACKUP and press Enter .

   The final message describes the storage capacity of the diskette and asks if you wish to:

   ```
   Format another (Y/N)?
   ```

6   Type **N** and press Enter

This completes the formatting process and the diskette is now ready for use. Take the diskette out of the drive and label the diskette SAGE BACKUP 1 and include the date. It is good practice always to have a number of such formatted diskettes on hand, suitably labelled.

Backing up

During your use of the Sage Sterling Financial Controller accounting system you will be entering the details of company transactions into the system and these will all be recorded in the appropriate files in the subdirectories of the **sage** directory on your hard disk. Because this storage is done automatically by the system and because hard disks are extremely reliable you will very soon come to accept the fact that the data is always there and ready to hand. However, you must always be aware of the fact that there is only one copy of your data and that is the copy stored on the hard disk which, though reliable, can become faulty thereby corrupting your data and making it useless. To safeguard against loss of information in this way it is essential that you adopt the practice of backing up your data onto a floppy diskette whenever you leave the Sage Sterling Financial Controller accounting system. We shall now do this.

 1   Place a formatted disk in the external drive.

2   Enter the Sage Sterling Financial Controller accounting system and display the Financial Controller screen. In order to practise backing up we shall now pretend that we have entered a number of transactions and are about to exit the system.

3   Select the **Quit** option to signal your intent to exit the system and at the bottom of the Financial Controller screen a question appears appears asking you if you wish to back up your data.

4   Select **Yes** to reveal the Backup Data Files screen:

```
Have you run Data Verification since your last
change to your data files? If not, you should
do so now before proceeding with Backup
```

We shall discuss data verification later in the *Guide*.

5   Press Enter and the question:

Do you want to back up your data files? :   No   Yes

is repeated at the bottom of this screen.

6   Select **Yes**.

If the disk already contains some files you will be prompted by the following warning:

```
Warning ! This disk already holds some other files
All floppy disks will be wiped clean before use
Do you want to OVERWRITE this information ? (Y/N)
```

SAOITEM.DTA - Sales Order Item File
Transferring...

7   Select **Y** and the warning in this box disappears to be replaced by the names of the various data files as they are copied to the floppy diskette in the external drive.

When the process of backing up all the data files is complete the screen display clears and returns you to the DOS prompt display. Your exit from the Sage Sterling Financial Controller is now complete.

8   Take the diskette out of the external drive and mark the label with the legend:

Backup of data files (include the date).

Setting the date

Any accounting system operates on historic data which means that most of the transactions that are entered into the system will have a reference date that precedes the date that they are entered into the system.

Your computer maintains a system date to which the Sage Sterling Financial Controller accounting system makes continual reference. For example, if you were to calculate a VAT Return then Sage Sterling automatically adopts the month of the system date as the default month of the calculation. Whilst, in this case, the default month can be amended to the appropriate month there are times when this is not possible. For example, If you were to review the historic data relating to your customers with a view to finding out who was behind time in paying their bills the computer's system date is automatically taken as the reference date and there is no option to change it during the course of your enquiry. In a live accounting system this causes no problem because the computer's system date will always be later than any transaction date and will give you a true picture of the state of your customers' indebtedness.

However, as you read this book you will see that the transactions that you are required to enter into the system have a date ranging from January 1994 to December 1994. This means that if you read the book during the year 1994 and follow the various instructions to enter transactions into the system the reference date of some of the transactions will be *later* than the system date recorded by your computer.

Alternatively, if you read the book in years subsequent to 1994 another problem will arise. All the transactions that you enter into the system will have a reference date that falls outside the company's current financial year which is taken from your computer's system date.

To prevent problems associated with the historic nature of the accounting presented in this book you will be required to ensure that the system date stored by your computer is always later than the reference dates of the transactions as you enter them into the system but is still within the financial year 1994. This involves changing the default system date recorded by your computer.

As you enter the Sage Sterling Financial Controller accounting system you are confronted with the current system date as stored by your computer. The date is displayed in the format:

DDMMYY

1   Type in the date:

010194   (As you type the existing date display will clear).

The system date of your computer has now been amended to 1 January 1994 which is the start date of all the financial transactions entered in the text of this book.

Part I

Elementary level

Finding your way around

The purpose of this chapter is to give you a limited appreciation of the range of facilities offered by the Sage Sterling Financial Controller accounting system and how those facilities are selected and activated.

To achieve this purpose, this chapter describes various features of the Financial Controller main menu and demonstrates its status as a home base from which all options within the system are selected. It also describes the status of the Nominal Ledger within the accounting system and concludes with the generation of a report that prints out the entire list of nominal account codes alongside their names.

1.1 The Financial Controller screen

 1   Enter the Sage Sterling Financial Controller accounting system from DOS and you are confronted with the Financial Controller screen:

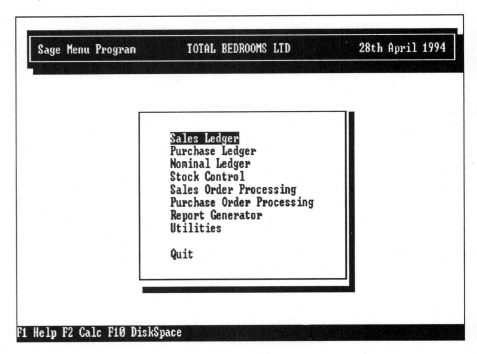

```
Sage Menu Program          TOTAL BEDROOMS LTD          28th April 1994



                    Sales Ledger
                    Purchase Ledger
                    Nominal Ledger
                    Stock Control
                    Sales Order Processing
                    Purchase Order Processing
                    Report Generator
                    Utilities

                    Quit



F1 Help F2 Calc F10 DiskSpace
```

This screen represents the starting point from which are accessed all the facilities that are available within the system. As you will see, the screen contains a display of nine options where each option serves as the entry point to a collection of facilities offered by the system - as described by their annotations. For example:

Option	Access to:
Sales Ledger	Customer sales procedures and the Sales Ledger
Purchase Ledger	Supplier purchases procedures and the Purchase Ledger

1.2 The ledger system

All companies have sales, purchases and monetary transactions and the purpose of the accounting system is to keep a record of the details and monetary value of each and every transaction, the information being recorded in a collection of accounts. This is done by using a method of recording transactions known as double-entry book-keeping.

Double-entry book-keeping

Recording transactions by double-entry book-keeping means that for every transaction there will be a debit entry and a credit entry which are equal. Within a manual book-keeping system double-entry book-keeping requires that each transaction be recorded twice manually. Within the Sage Sterling Financial Controller accounting system this is done automatically.

If the company buys a van to enable it to deliver its goods the total amount that is owed for the van will be recorded on the credit side of a supplier's account within the Purchase Ledger. The cost of the van before Value Added Tax (VAT) is added will be recorded on the debit side of a Nominal Ledger account called vans or motor vehicles. The related VAT will be recorded on the debit side of a Value Added Tax account, also in the nominal ledger. These entries into the various accounts will be carried out automatically by the Sage Sterling Financial Controller accounting system once the data has been initially entered into the system.

A further example occurs when the company sells a quantity of stock to a customer on credit. A customer account will exist within the Sales Ledger where the amount owed by the customer will be recorded on the debit side of the account. The value of the sales, before VAT is added, will be included on the credit side of a sales account within the nominal ledger and the related VAT on the credit side of the Value Added Tax account in the nominal ledger.

Ensure that the Financial Controller screen is on display.

The ledger accounts are grouped together as follows:

Sales Ledger

Each customer has an account within the Sales Ledger into which will be recorded the credit sales and cash received from this customer. These accounts are accessed via the **Sales Ledger** option.

Purchase Ledger

Each supplier has an account within the Purchase Ledger into which will be recorded the credit purchases and cash paid to this supplier. These accounts are accessed via the **Purchase Ledger** option.

Nominal Ledger

All accounts other than Sales and Purchase Ledger accounts are recorded in the Nominal Ledger. Typically, these accounts relate to items such as expenses (rent, insurance, salaries), bank payments and VAT paid and collected. These accounts are accessed via the **Nominal Ledger** option.

1.3   The Nominal Ledger screen

1   From the Financial Controller screen select the **Nominal Ledger** option thereby causing the Nominal Ledger screen to be displayed:

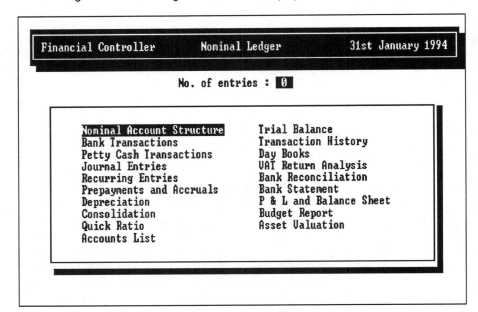

```
Financial Controller        Nominal Ledger        31st January 1994

                        No. of entries : 0

        Nominal Account Structure    Trial Balance
        Bank Transactions            Transaction History
        Petty Cash Transactions      Day Books
        Journal Entries              VAT Return Analysis
        Recurring Entries            Bank Reconciliation
        Prepayments and Accruals     Bank Statement
        Depreciation                 P & L and Balance Sheet
        Consolidation                Budget Report
        Quick Ratio                  Asset Valuation
        Accounts List
```

Just like the Financial Controller screen, this screen is typical of all such screens within the system. There is a title bar to tell you which screen you are looking at and below the title bar is a menu of further options that relate to aspects of the system that are contained within the Nominal Ledger.

Before we proceed to a more detailed view of the nominal ledger we shall see how to close a screen.

2   Press ⌐Esc¬

and immediately you exit from the Nominal Ledger screen and return to the Financial Controller screen.

Ensure that the Financial Controller screen is on display.

1   Display the Nominal Ledger screen and ensure that the highlight is on the **Accounts List** option at the bottom of the left-hand column of options.

2   Press Enter to reveal the Accounts List screen:

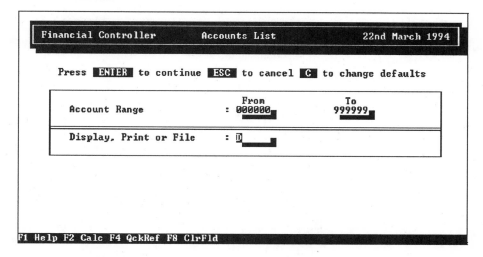

The default list of nominal accounts are numbered in the range 0010 to 9999. The range of account codes that is permissible is from 00000 to 99999 as can be seen in the **From** and **To** boxes in this screen. We can choose to display the list of account codes on the monitor screen, print them or send them to a file for access at a later stage. The default option, as seen here, is the **Display** option as evidenced by the **D** in the bottom box. From the list of instructions at the top of this screen we can press Enter to continue, press Esc to cancel and return to the nominal ledger screen or press **C** to change the defaults displayed. We shall accept all the defaults as displayed and proceed to display the account list.

3   Press Enter.

The screen then changes to a display of the first 15 account codes and their names:

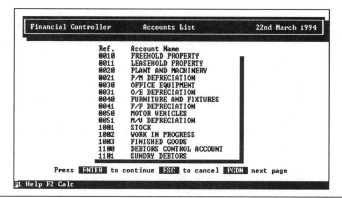

At the head of the list on the left-hand side is:

0010 FREEHOLD PROPERTY

This is telling you that any transaction involving freehold property must be posted using the Nominal Ledger Account Code 0010.

At the bottom of the list is a collection of instructions telling you how to access all the other accounts in the list.

4   Press | **Enter** | and the list of account codes and names scrolls to the next 15 accounts in the list.

5   Press | **PgDn** | and the same effect is observed again.

6   Press | **PgUp** | and the list of accounts scrolls in the opposite direction.

7   Press the other cursor control keys and you will see the corresponding effect on the displayed account list.

8   Press | **Esc** | and return to the Nominal Ledger screen.

By returning to the Nominal Ledger screen you have not seen the full extent of the Account structure so repeat this Activity and view all the Accounts. Make sure that when you have viewed all the Accounts and their codes you are back at the Nominal Ledger screen.

1.5   To produce a printout of the nominal codes

Whilst we can always view the list of nominal codes on the monitor screen we can only appreciate their full extent if we have a complete printed list to look at. We shall now proceed to produce such a list.

 1   From the Nominal Ledger screen re-select **Accounts List** to reveal the Accounts List screen.

From the instructions at the top of this screen we see that we can change the defaults if we press the letter **C** on the keyboard.

2   Press **C**.

Immediately a flashing cursor appears at the side of the first default value of **00000** under the heading **From**. We do not wish to amend this or the next default.

3   Press | **Enter** | twice to accept the first two defaults and to place the cursor on the letter **D** - the third default.

4   Type the letter **P** at the keyboard to change the default to the **Print** option.

5   Press ⎡Enter⎤ and a message appears:

```
Switch the Printer On and Press RETURN
```

6   Ensure that your printer is switched on and on-line and press ⎡Enter⎤.

The complete nominal ledger accounts list is then sent to your printer during which time a further message has appeared on the monitor screen:

```
Press ESC to pause printing
```

7   Press ⎡Esc⎤ and the printing stops.

The message on the monitor screen now changes to:

```
Press RETURN to abandon printing

Press C to continue printing
```

8   Press **C** to continue printing.

When the complete list has been printed you are returned to the Nominal Ledger screen.

1.6   The Chart of Accounts

We have seen that there is a large number of accounts in the nominal ledger. They are, however, not arranged at random but are grouped according to a predefined set of criteria. For example, those accounts that deal with sales are grouped within accounts 4000 to 4999 and those that relate to purchases are grouped within accounts 5000 to 5999. These groupings are collectively referred to as the Chart of Accounts and a printed list of the chart can be obtained via the **Nominal Accounts Structure** option on the Nominal Ledger screen.

1   Display the Nominal Ledger screen and select the **Nominal Accounts Structure** option to produce the Nominal Accounts Structure screen displaying the list of further options:

```
Account Names
Profit & Loss Structure
Balance Sheet Structure
Chart of Accounts Layout
```

2   Select **Chart of Accounts Layout** to reveal the Chart of Accounts Layout screen:

```
┌─────────────────────────────────────────────────────────────┐
│ ▛ Financial Controller   Chart of Accounts Layout   22nd March 1994 │
│                                                             │
│   Press ▊ENTER▊ to continue ▊ESC▊ to cancel ▊C▊ to change defaults │
│   ┌─────────────────────────────────────────────────┐      │
│   │   Display, Print or File     : D▊                │      │
│   │   Profit & Loss Structure    : Y▊                │      │
│   │   Balance Sheet Structure    : Y▊                │      │
│   │   Profit & Loss Format       : Y▊                │      │
│   │   Balance Sheet Format       : Y▊                │      │
│   │   Budget Report Format       : Y▊                │      │
│   │   Nominal Code Analysis      : Y▊                │      │
│   └─────────────────────────────────────────────────┘      │
│                                                             │
│ F1 Help F2 Calc                                             │
└─────────────────────────────────────────────────────────────┘
```

3   Accept the default in this screen and press Enter to produce a screen display of the chart.

You will immediately notice that this display is significantly different from all the other screen displays that you have seen so far. Indeed, the entire chart will not fit onto a single screen and you have to use the cursor control keys to range around the display in order to view its entire contents. A printed version is considerably better than this.

4   Press Esc and a small window appears in the centre of the screen containing a list of options:

5   Select the option **Print** by either using the down arrow cursor control key to move the highlight and pressing Enter or by pressing **P** followed by Enter.

6   Either way, you must ensure that your printer is switched on and on-line.

The resultant Chart of Accounts lists the nominal ledger accounts according to:

Sales
Purchases
Direct Expenses
Overheads

which collectively form the structure of the Profit and Loss Account report and

Fixed Assets
Current Assets
Current Liabilities
Financed by

which collectively form the structure of the Balance Sheet report. We shall be saying more about these two reports later in the *Guide*.

In addition to the Chart of Accounts, the formats of the Profit and Loss, Balance Sheet and Budget reports are also sent to the printer.

1.7 Summary

- Facilities within the Sage Sterling Financial Controller accounting system are accessed via the options displayed in the Financial Controller and subsequent screens.

- Information is entered into a screen by typing into designated areas of the screen.

- Any screen can be closed by pressing the $\boxed{\text{Esc}}$ key. This then reveals the previously displayed screen except that the Financial Controller screen cannot be closed in this way but requires the **Quit** option to be selected.

2   Amending and creating accounts

In this chapter we shall be concerned with the preliminaries of setting up the company ledger accounts and the details of the stock held by the company. In particular we shall amend existing and create new nominal ledger accounts and define specific departments within the company's accounts. Finally, we shall initiate sales and purchase ledger accounts by entering the details of both the customers and the suppliers.

2.1   Coding considerations

Every account in the Sage Sterling Financial Controller accounting system has a name and a short code. For example, the company's bank account has the name Bank Current Account and the short code 1200. The reason for the name is to describe to the user the purpose and nature of the account. The reason for the code is to enable the user to instruct the computer to access that account in a simple manner - it is more efficient for the user to refer to the account as 1200 rather than to type in the name. This brings to the fore the various problems associated with creating the coding.

The Sage Sterling Financial Controller accounting system contains a complete nominal ledger code list which can be adapted by a user. Coding for newly created accounts merely requires new numbers to be selected within the range 0001 to 9999 excluding, of course, those numbers already used that are required to be retained. We shall see later how to amend or delete default nominal accounts.

When it comes to coding the customers, the suppliers and the stock items there is a great deal of freedom. Because there are no default customers, suppliers or stock items there is no predefined coding to follow and it is left to the users to devise their own code subject to the restrictions that the code contain no more than 6 alpha-numeric characters in the case of suppliers or customers and no more than 14 in the case of stock.

The basic principle in devising any coding system is to ask why it is needed in the first place. Our coding is required to enable an account to be accessed accurately and efficiently. This means that the code must be short, easily remembered and must, in some measure, reflect the account to which it refers. A customer's code could begin with the first letter of the customer's name followed by a number. Alternatively, it could consist of the first part of the customer's name up to six characters or it could consist of some acronym that uniquely identifies that customer. For example, a customer by the name of Hot Rolled Steel Supplies could be coded as:

H001, HOT or HRSS

The choice of which code to use depends upon the circumstances of the company. If the company has few customers then the use of HOT may be sufficient to identify that particular customer. A company with a larger customer base may find more than one customer whose name begins with HOT in which case HRSS could suffice. However, in both of these situations the code is somewhat personal - it belongs to the person who devised it - and it works because the user is familiar with the names of the small number of accounts. In a company with a very large customer base with an accounting system that is to be used by more than one individual a code with a stricter logic behind it must be devised.

In addition to the problems associated with devising a code to identify accounts there are considerations concerning the interactive nature and linking of accounts. For example, we shall see that in Total Bedrooms' accounts a bed has three codes associated with it. Firstly, it has a stock code to identify its location in the inventory. Secondly, because it is a purchased item, it has a nominal code associated with its purchase. Thirdly, because it is also a saleable item, it has a nominal code associated with its sale. When the coding is devised it is desirable that this linkage also be taken into account.

The nominal ledger occupies a central role in the accounting system and for this reason we shall consider in detail the nominal codes first. This, however, presents a problem in that we need to possess information about our stock before we can sensibly discuss its relationship to the nominal ledger. At the same time we need to know how the default coding is arrayed within the nominal ledger before we can sensibly talk about stock coding.

Because Total Bedrooms Ltd is in the business of buying and selling stock, the company's activities are basically stock driven. Consequently, we shall initiate our devised code with the stock categories. We shall consider stock in greater detail in Chapter 3 but for now we shall simply state that we have seven categories of stock, coded as follows:

Category	Stock Item	Stock Code
1 Beds	Single bed	101
	Double bed	102
2 Furniture	Vanity unit small	201
	Vanity unit large	202
	Wardrobe (single)	203
	Wardrobe (double)	204
	Bedside table	205
3 Seating	Stool	301
	Chair	302
4 Lighting	Lamp (table)	401
	Lamp (standard)	402
5 Carpeting	Carpeting	501
6 Fabrics	Curtains (linen)	601
	Curtains (lace)	602

	Bedding (single)	603
	Bedding (double)	604
7 Sundries	Pictures (misc)	701
	Ashtrays	702
	Waste bins	703
	Decor pack (misc)	704

Notice the flexibility of this coding. Adding a new item of stock within a given category is a simple matter of selecting a code which begins with the category number and ends with a two-digit number representing that item's location within the category list. Further, adding a new category of stock is also straightforward.

Having devised the coding for the stock we are now in a position to consider the nominal ledger coding.

2.2 Amending existing nominal ledger accounts

As we saw in the previous chapter, when the Sage Sterling +2 accounting system is first installed it already contains a large list of nominal ledger accounts. However, despite the comprehensive nature of these accounts it is quite likely that new accounts need to be created. In particular, Total Bedrooms needs to keep track of its different purchases and sales. As far as sales are concerned you can see from the printout of nominal accounts that you obtained at the end of the last chapter that the different categories of sale can be catered for by using nominal accounts 4000, 4001, 4002, 4100 and 4101 which have names Sales Type A, B, C, D and E respectively. These will have to be amended to provide more meaningful information. For purchases, however, there are just two accounts that specifically mention purchases, namely 5000 Materials Purchases and 5002 Miscellaneous Purchases. These two latter accounts are insufficient for our requirements to keep a track of the different purchases made by Total Bedrooms so we shall have to create new accounts. But first, we amend an existing account.

Nominal ledger accounts are accessed via the **Nominal Ledger** option in the Financial Controller screen. Ensure that the Financial Controller screen is on display:

1   Select the **Nominal Ledger** option to reveal the Nominal Ledger screen.

2   In the Nominal Ledger screen select the option **Nominal Account Structure** to reveal a further list of options in the Nominal Account Structure screen.

3   Select the option **Account Names** to reveal the Account Names screen containing an empty form.

This form can be used to create new or amend existing nominal ledger accounts. In the box labelled **Account Reference** there is a flashing text cursor.

4   Type into the **Account Reference** box the account number:

5000 and press Enter .

The **Account Name** box then displays the name of this account as:

MATERIALS PURCHASES

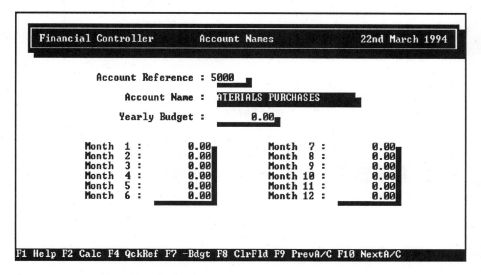

```
┌──────────────────────────────────────────────────────────────────┐
│ Financial Controller        Account Names        22nd March 1994  │
│                                                                    │
│         Account Reference : 5000                                   │
│             Account Name :  ATERIALS PURCHASES                     │
│             Yearly Budget :      0.00                              │
│                                                                    │
│      Month  1 :      0.00        Month  7 :      0.00              │
│      Month  2 :      0.00        Month  8 :      0.00              │
│      Month  3 :      0.00        Month  9 :      0.00              │
│      Month  4 :      0.00        Month 10 :      0.00              │
│      Month  5 :      0.00        Month 11 :      0.00              │
│      Month  6 :      0.00        Month 12 :      0.00              │
│                                                                    │
│                                                                    │
│ F1 Help F2 Calc F4 QckRef F7 -Bdgt F8 ClrFld F9 PrevA/C F10 NextA/C│
└──────────────────────────────────────────────────────────────────┘
```

Accounts are selected for display by entering the number of the account in the **Account Reference** box. The Account Names screen contains a form in which are displayed the details of the selected nominal ledger account 5000. Using this form it is possible to set a budget for this account.

We do not wish to amend this account.

5   Press F10 to display the next account:

5001

The **Account Name** then changes to:

MATERIALS IMPORTED

This account description is not required by Total Bedrooms. Instead, it will be used to accommodate purchases of category 1 stock.

6   Type in at the keyboard the new name for this account:

Purchases - Beds and press Enter

As you start to type the original account name clears leaving space for the new name to be entered. Notice the correlation between the 1 of 5001 and the 1 of 101 and 102. In all cases the 1 refers to the stock category 1 - beds.

You have now completed the amendment of the definition of this account - the relevance of all the other budget boxes will be discussed later in the book.

We now need to save this amended account to disk.

7   Press ⌷Esc⌷ and an annotation appears at the bottom of the screen:

```
Do you want to : Post  Edit  Abandon  Delete
```

We wish to save this information to the disk which means we wish to *post* the details to the ledgers.

8   Select **Post** and press ⌷Enter⌷.

The form now clears in readiness for a new account to be entered.

EXERCISE   1   Repeat this procedure and amend the following nominal ledger accounts:

5002 from Miscellaneous Purchases	to	Purchases - Furniture
5003 from Packaging	to	Purchases - Seating
4001 from Sales Type B	to	Sales - Beds
4002 from Sales Type C	to	Sales - Furniture

2   When you have saved these amended accounts to disk return to the Nominal Ledger screen.

2.3   Creating new nominal ledger accounts

Creating new nominal ledger accounts, just like amending existing nominal ledger accounts, is performed via the **Nominal Ledger** option in the Financial Controller screen. Ensure that the Nominal Ledger screen is on display.

    1   Access the Account Names screen displaying an empty account form.

2   With the flashing cursor in the **Account Reference** box type in at the keyboard the number:

5004 and press ⌷Enter⌷

At the bottom of the screen the following annotation appears:

```
Is this a new account : No  Yes
```

3   Select **Yes**, press ⌷Enter⌷ and the highlight moves to the **Account Name** box in readiness for a name to be entered.

4   Type into the **Account Name** box:

Purchases - Lighting and press Enter

You have now completed the creation of the definition of this account.

5   Press Esc and post this account definition to the ledger.

The form now clears in readiness for a new account to be entered.

EXERCISE   1   Repeat this procedure and create the following nominal ledger accounts:

5005 Purchases - Carpeting
5006 Purchases - Fabrics
5007 Purchases - Sundries

4003 Sales - Seating
4004 Sales - Lighting
4005 Sales - Carpeting
4006 Sales - Fabrics
4007 Sales - Sundries

Notice the correlation between the stock, sales and purchases codes.

2   When the last account has been posted to the ledger press Esc twice and you are returned to the Nominal Ledger screen.

3   Select **Accounts List** to reveal the list of nominal accounts and press Enter until the new and amended accounts appear to verify the fact that the system now has them installed.

4   Press Esc twice again to close the Nominal Ledger screen and to return to the Financial Controller screen.

2.4   Defining the company's accounting departments

To enable a proper analysis of the company's trading performance and to highlight the strengths and weaknesses of the various sections of the company's activities it has been decided to define three departments:

Sales
Purchases
Administration

The departmental structure is already in place within the Sage Sterling Financial Controller accounting system and assigning accounts to departments is a simple matter of designation in the various account setup procedures that we shall use as we progress through the book. What are not yet defined are the department names and this we shall do now. Ensure that the Financial Controller screen is on display.

1　Select the **Utilities** option to display the Utilities screen:

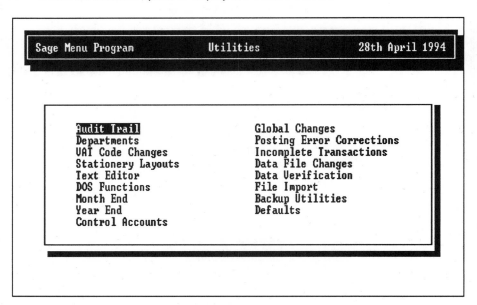

2　In the Utilities screen select the **Departments** option to reveal the Departments screen:

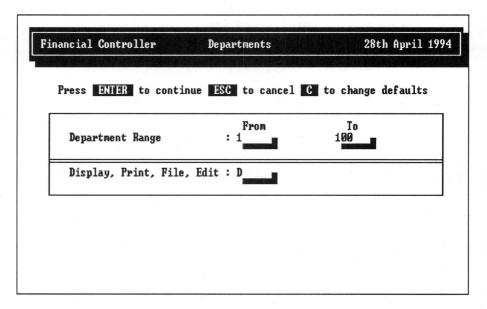

You will see from the information in this screen that there are 100 departments. The third default in the screen is **D** for screen display.

3　Press Enter to accept the defaults and to display the list of Departments:

```
┌─────────────────────────────────────────────────────────────┐
│  ▄▄▄▄▄▄▄▄▄▄▄▄▄▄▄▄▄▄▄▄▄▄▄▄▄▄▄▄▄▄▄▄▄▄▄▄▄▄▄▄▄▄▄▄▄▄▄▄▄▄▄▄▄▄▄▄     │
│  Financial Controller      Departments      22nd March 1994  │
│  ▀▀▀▀▀▀▀▀▀▀▀▀▀▀▀▀▀▀▀▀▀▀▀▀▀▀▀▀▀▀▀▀▀▀▀▀▀▀▀▀▀▀▀▀▀▀▀▀▀▀▀▀▀▀      │
│          No.   Department Name                               │
│                                                              │
│           1    UNUSED DEPARTMENT        ▐                    │
│           2    UNUSED DEPARTMENT        ▐                    │
│           3    UNUSED DEPARTMENT        ▐                    │
│           4    UNUSED DEPARTMENT        ▐                    │
│           5    UNUSED DEPARTMENT        ▐                    │
│           6    UNUSED DEPARTMENT        ▐                    │
│           7    UNUSED DEPARTMENT        ▐                    │
│           8    UNUSED DEPARTMENT        ▐                    │
│           9    UNUSED DEPARTMENT        ▐                    │
│          10    UNUSED DEPARTMENT        ▐                    │
│          11    UNUSED DEPARTMENT        ▐                    │
│          12    UNUSED DEPARTMENT        ▐                    │
│          13    UNUSED DEPARTMENT        ▐                    │
│          14    UNUSED DEPARTMENT                             │
│    Press  ENTER  to continue  ESC  to cancel  PGDN  next page│
└─────────────────────────────────────────────────────────────┘
```

If you use ▐PgDn▌ to scroll through all the departments you will find that they are all UNUSED.

4   Press ▐Esc▌ to return to the Utilities screen and re-select the **Departments** option.

5   Press **C** to change the defaults and move the cursor to the third default **D**.

6   Type in:

     E for Edit and press ▐Enter▌

This reveals the Department edit screen:

```
┌─────────────────────────────────────────────────────────────┐
│                                                              │
│    Department No.   :  ▐▅▅▅▅▅                                │
│                                                              │
│    Department Name  :  ▅▅▅▅▅▅▅▅▅▅▅▅▅▅▅▅▅▅▅▅▅▅▅▅▅            │
│                                                              │
└─────────────────────────────────────────────────────────────┘
```

7   Type into the box annotated **Department No.:**

     1

8   Type into the box annotated **Department Name:**

     Sales

9   Press ▐Enter▌ to post this information to the ledgers.

The details clear to enable the next department to be named.

10   Repeat this procedure and name:

Department 2 as Purchases
Department 3 as Administration

11   When all three Departments have been named press `Esc` to close the Departments screen and return to the Utilities screen.

12   Press `Esc` to close the Utilitties screen and return to the Financial Controller screen.

2.5   Creating sales ledger accounts

Having seen how to create nominal ledger accounts we shall now create the sales ledger accounts. The essential difference here is that there are no predefined sales accounts. We have to create them from scratch and so our first consideration is that of coding (see Section 2.1).

The coding that has been adopted for Total Bedrooms' customer accounts consists of the first letter of the customer's name followed by a three-digit number.

Creating the sales ledger accounts and entering the customer details into the accounting system is performed via the **Sales Ledger** option in the Financial Controller screen. Ensure that the Financial Controller screen is on display.

 1   Select the **Sales Ledger** option to reveal the Sales Ledger screen:

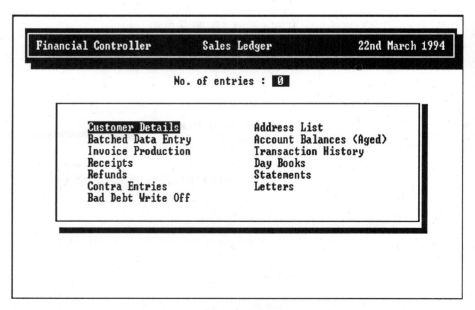

2   Select the **Customer Details** option to display the Customer Details screen:

```
┌─────────────────────────────────────────────────────────────┐
│ Financial Controller      Customer Details      22nd March 1994 │
│                                                                 │
│              Account Reference : ▮                              │
│                                                                 │
│                  Account Name :                                 │
│                     Address   :                                 │
│                        ..     :                                 │
│                        ..     :                                 │
│                        ..     :                                 │
│                  Credit Limit :                                 │
│                     Turnover  :                                 │
│                                                                 │
│ Telephone No. :                    UAT Reg Number  :            │
│ Contact Name  :                    UAT Country Code :           │
│ Discount Code :                    Default UAT Code :           │
│ Analysis Code :                                                 │
│                                                                 │
├─────────────────────────────────────────────────────────────┤
│ F1 Help F2 Calc F4 QckRef F8 ClrFld F9 PrevA/C F10 NextA/C      │
└─────────────────────────────────────────────────────────────┘
```

The Customer Details screen contains a blank form into which all the details
pertinent to a customer's account can be entered.

In the box labelled **Account Reference** there is a flashing text cursor. The cursor is
indicating where text will appear if you were to start typing and it is into this box that
you enter the customer code.

3   Type the code **B001** into this box and press │Enter│.

At the bottom of the screen the annotation appears:

        Is this a new account :   No Yes

4   Select **Yes** and the highlight immediately moves opposite **Account Name**.

5   Type into this box:

     Budget Hostelry Plc and press │Enter│

Now you see the rationale of the code. The customer's name begins with a B and it
is the first such one to be entered into the system.

6   Continue entering the customer's details as follows:

            Address   100 The Haymarket
               ..   Leith
               ..   Edinburgh
               ..   ED1 6TY
       Credit Limit   18000.00
          Turnover   leave blank

Telephone	031 342 5609	
Contact Name	Jane Dobson	
Discount Code		leave blank
Analysis Code	Chain	
VAT Reg Number	456 7832 89	
VAT Country Code	GB	
Default Tax Code	T1	

The Credit Limit and Discount Code entries tell us that this customer can possess an overdue account with Total Bedrooms up to a maximum of £18,000.00. In addition, sales to this customer will not be discounted.

Total Bedrooms' customers are either individual hotels or members of a chain of hotels. The particular type of customer is entered as either **Chain** or **Individual** against **Analysis Code** to permit analysis of customers to be done at a later time.

Note: You must take great care when entering data into this **Analysis** box because during analysis the system will look for the exact spelling, including capitals and lowercase.

The VAT Reg Number is the registered Value Added Tax (VAT) number as issued by Customs and Excise. The Tax Code of T1 means that all invoices to this customer will be charged at the standard rate of VAT which at the time of writing is 17.5%. The various tax options we shall discuss later in the *Guide*.

This completes the entry of Budget Hostelry's account details for the moment. You will note that we have not entered any information in the **Turnover** box. Indeed, at this stage it is not immediately possible to do so. Try it.

Next we must save this entered information to disk:

7   Press Esc and post these details to the ledger.

The account details are then saved to disk and cleared from the screen leaving a blank form in readiness for the entry of the next customer's details.

EXERCISE   1   Enter the details of the following customers into the Customer Details screen and save the details to disk. If at any time you make a mistake with your entry, try to correct it by overtyping. If that fails then press Esc and opt to **Abandon** the entry and start again.

Account Reference	G001	Account Reference	G002
Account Name	George Hotel	Account Name	Gibbert Arms
Address	75 Main Street	Address	34 Pellon Lane
..	Bradford	..	Halifax
..	West Yorkshire	..	West Yorkshire
..	BD1 3GH	..	HX1 8YJ
Credit Limit	5000.00	Credit Limit	3000.00
Telephone No	0274 349843	Telephone No	0422 456782
Contact Name	Helen Smith	Contact Name	Gary Mann

Analysis Code	Individual	Analysis Code	Individual
VAT Reg Number	23 7529 22	VAT Reg Number	774 3489 22
VAT Country Code	GB	VAT Country Code	GB
Default VAT Code	T1	Default VAT Code	T1

Account Reference	I001	Account Reference	M001
Account Name	Innkeepers Plc	Account Name	Main Line Hotels Plc
Address	123 The Stray	Address	200 Baker Street
..	Harrogate	..	London
..	North Yorkshire	..	
..	HR1 3ED	..	W1 6FT
Credit Limit	10000.00	Credit Limit	35000.00
Telephone No	0423 777744	Telephone No	071 334 1234
Contact Name	Andrew Armstrong	Contact Name	Peter Field
Analysis Code	Chain	Analysis Code	Chain
Analysis 2		Analysis 2	
VAT Reg Number	345 2945 12	VAT Reg Number	675 6382 22
VAT Country Code	GB	VAT Country Code	GB
Default VAT Code	T1	Default VAT Code	T1

Account Reference	Q001	Account Reference	T001
Account Name	Queens Hotel	Account Name	The Regency
Address	34 New Street	Address	12 Coppergate
..	Huddersfield	..	York
..	West Yorkshire	..	North Yorkshire
..	HD1 5DH	..	YO1 3TH
Credit Limit	14000.00	Credit Limit	3000.00
Telephone No	0484 537458	Telephone No	0904 458888
Contact Name	Ann Finlay	Contact Name	Patrick Gallaher
Analysis Code	Individual	Analysis Code	Individual
VAT Reg Number	345 8554 34	VAT Reg Number	096 5656 89
VAT Country Code	GB	VAT Country Code	GB
Default VAT Code	T1	Default VAT Code	T1

Account Reference	T002
Account Name	The Swallows Nest
Address	The Dalesway
..	Grassington
..	North Yorkshire
..	SK1 5RF
Credit Limit	2000.00
Telephone No	0535 238955
Contact Name	Howard Barnes
Analysis Code	Individual
VAT Reg Number	564 2387 12

VAT Country Code   GB
Default VAT Code   T1

When you have saved this last customer record:

2   Press Esc twice to close the screen and return to the Financial Controller
     screen.

2.6   **Entering the customers' opening balances**

When Total Bedrooms installed their computerised accounting system they had
already been trading for some years. Consequently, on the 1st January, when they
installed the system most of the company's customers had outstanding balances on
their accounts. These outstanding balances will now be entered into the customer
accounts before any further customer transactions are executed.

Ensure that the Financial Controller screen is on display.

    1   Select the **Sales Ledger** option to reveal the Sales Ledger screen.

2   Select the **Batched Data Entry** and reveal the Sales Invoices screen:

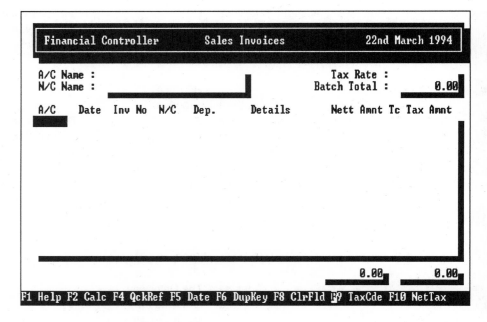

All invoices to customers are entered via this screen and because the opening
balances represent outstanding invoices they too are entered into this screen.
However, because the opening balances represent outstanding debts from the
previous accounting year they do not represent sales this year. Consequently, they
must not be analysed against a sales nominal account. Instead, they are analysed
against the nominal code 9998 for the SUSPENSE account. The effect of this will

become clear as we progress through the *Guide*.

The highlight resides under the heading **A/C** which stands for Account code.

3 Type in the account code for the Budget Hostelry account:

B001 and press Enter

The highlight moves to the next column.

4 Enter the **Date** as:

211093 and press Enter

This is the date of issue of the invoice.
Note: Sage Sterling uses the format DDMMYY for the date.

5 Enter the **Inv No** (invoice number) as:

1270 and press Enter

This is the number of the first outstanding invoice.

6 Enter the **N/C** (nominal code) as:

9998 and press Enter

This is the account number for the SUSPENSE account.

7 Enter the **Dep** (department) as:

1 and press Enter

This is the Sales Department.

8 Enter the **Details** as:

Opening Balance and press Enter

Because we are entering an opening balance it is essential that this entry is exactly as written here with capital **O** and **B**.

9 Enter the **Nett Amnt** as:

2398.31 and press Enter

Notice that this is the total invoice value: there is no necessity to separate the net invoice value and the VAT value because any VAT associated with this account would have been accounted for by Total Bedrooms in October. Total Bedrooms is now concerned with the total amount of the invoice that will be paid by the customer.

10 Enter the **Tc** (tax code) as:

T9 and press Enter

The tax code T9 represents a zero rated tax as evidenced by the **Tax Amnt** which is automatically entered by the system as **0.00**.

The details of this particular invoice are now complete. All that remains is to post the details to the ledgers.

11 Press Esc and post the invoice to the ledgers.

The Sales Invoices screen now clears of all the entered details in readiness for the entry of further invoices.

EXERCISE 1 Enter the following outstanding invoices as issued to Budget Hostelry Plc:

Date: 30/11/93
Invoice: 1319
Amount: 6754.11

Enter this invoice as an Opening Balance against nominal account 9998, Department 1 and with tax code T9. Do not post this invoice to ledgers just yet. Instead, on the next line enter the following invoice:

Date: 11/12/93
Invoice: 1329
Amount: 5196.86

When you come to enter **N/C** press F6 and the entry above will be duplicated below. Repeat this procedure for the **Dep**, **Details** and **Tc** entries.

Post both invoices together when they are complete.

2 Enter the following opening balances; again do not post them until you have filled the screen and use the F6 key to ease the entry.

If you are unsure of the account code for the customer when you come to enter it under **A/C** press F4 and a window opens with the complete list of customers and their codes:

```
B001      Budget Hostelry Plc
G001      George Hotel
G002      Gibbert Arms
I001      Innkeepers Plc
M001      Main Line Hotels Plc
Q001      Queens Hotel
T001      The Regency
T002      The Swallows Nest
```

Move the highlight to the particular customer whose invoice is being entered and press **Enter**. The account code is then automatically entered.

Note: The date of the Gibbert Arms opening balance must be entered as 091193 and not as 91193.

Customer	Invoice	Date	Value
Gibbert Arms	1300	09/11/93	2174.08
Innkeepers Plc	1306	21/11/93	1256.67
	1327	05/12/93	4306.82
Main Line Hotels	1258	11/10/93	3456.98
	1307	24/11/93	6732.56
	1321	17/12/93	6389.36
Queens Hotel	1315	29/11/93	6745.12
	1333	20/12/93	6887.01
The Regency	1320	01/12/93	1777.77
The Swallows Nest	1330	11/12/93	1616.13

3 Complete this activity with the Financial Controller screen on display.

2.7 Creating purchase ledger accounts

Creating the suppliers' accounts follows an identical procedure. Ensure that the Financial Controller screen is on display.

1 Select the **Purchase Ledger** option to reveal the Purchase Ledger screen:

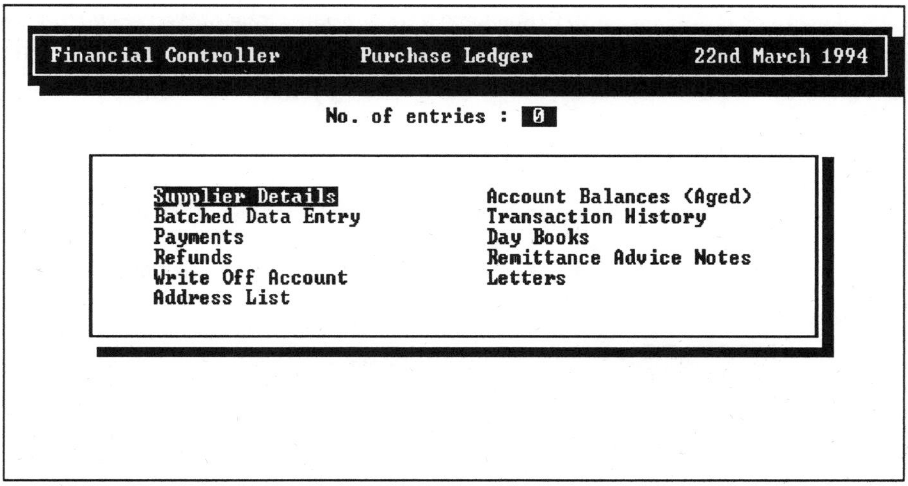

Financial Controller
Purchase Ledger
22nd March 1994
No. of entries : 0
Supplier Details
Batched Data Entry
Payments
Refunds
Write Off Account
Address List
Account Balances (Aged)
Transaction History
Day Books
Remittance Advice Notes
Letters

2   Select the **Supplier Details** option to display the Supplier Details screen.

You will see that this is identical to the Customer Details screen and the entry of a supplier's account details into this screen follows the identical procedure to that of entering a customer's account details into the Customer Details screen.

3   Type the code **ABC** into the box annotated **A/C** and press Enter .

At the bottom of the screen the annotation appears:

```
Is this a new account :   No   Yes
```

4   Select **Yes** and the highlight immediately moves opposite **Account Name**.

5   Type into this box:

ABC Fabrics and press Enter

Now you see the rationale of the code. The first name in the supplier's name is ABC.

6   Continue entering the customer's details as follows:

Address	Albion Mills	
..	St Andrews Road	
..	Bradford	
..	BD2 5TP	
Credit Limit	1000.00	
Turnover		leave blank
Telephone	0274 283017	
Contact Name	Peter Hartley	
Discount Code		leave blank
Analysis Code	Fabrics	
VAT Country Code	GB	
Default Tax Code	T1	

The Credit Limit and Discount Code entries tell us that Total Bedrooms can possess an overdue account with ABC Fabrics up to a maximum of £1,000.00. In addition, purchases from this customer will not be discounted.

Next we must save this entered information to disk:

7   Press Esc and post the details to the ledger.

The account details are then saved to disk and cleared from the screen leaving a blank form in readiness for the entry of the next customer's details.

EXERCISE   1   Enter the details of the following customers into the Supplier Details screen and save the details to disk. If at any time you make a mistake with your entry, try to correct it by overtyping. If that fails then press Esc and opt to **Abandon** the entry and start again.

Account Reference	ART
Account Name	Artwork
Address	23 Kensington High Street
..	Kensington
..	London
..	SW2 4SD
Credit Limit	1000.00
Telephone No	071 456 8320
Contact Name	Helen Brown
Analysis Code	Sundries
VAT Reg Number	
VAT Country Code	GB
Default Tax Code	T0

The tax code T0 means that ABC Fabrics are not registered for VAT and any invoices they issue will not contain VAT.

2 Continue entering supplier details as follows:

Account Reference	COMM
Account Name	Commercial Carpenters Ltd
Address	The Depot
..	Towngate
..	Hunslet, Leeds
..	LS8 7TY
Credit Limit	15000.00
Telephone No	0532 563920
Contact Name	Fred Smith
Analysis Code	Furniture
VAT Country Code	GB
Default Tax Code	T1

Account Reference	EEZEE
Account Name	EEZEE Beds Plc
Address	Slumber House
..	200 Featherstone Road
..	Leeds
..	LS17 5TH
Credit Limit	5000.00
Telephone No	0532 463896
Contact Name	Ron Jones
Analysis Code	Beds
VAT Country Code	GB
Default Tax Code	T1

Account Reference	FABRIC
Account Name	Fabrico
Address	The House
. .	The Park
. .	Roundhay, Leeds
. .	LS12 5RT
Credit Limit	3000.00
Telephone No	0532 238965
Contact Name	John Thompson
Analysis Code	Fabrics
VAT Country Code	GB
Default Tax Code	T1

Account Reference	FLASH
Account Name	Flash Lighting Ltd
Address	Lighting House
. .	17 Back Street
. .	Halton, Leeds
. .	LS5 9YX
Credit Limit	6000.00
Telephone No	0532 568340
Contact Name	Liz Jones
Analysis Code	Lighting
VAT Country Code	GB
Default Tax Code	T1

Account Reference	FOR
Account Name	Forward Bedding
Address	Pillow House
. .	Clifton Street
. .	Headingly, Leeds
. .	LS15 4EK
Credit Limit	1500.00
Telephone No	0532 347851
Contact Name	John Penn
Analysis Code	Fabrics
VAT Country Code	GB
Default Tax Code	T1

Account Reference	HAND
Account Name	Hand Craft Ltd
Address	25 York Road
. .	Pocklington
. .	York

..	YO3 2WS
Credit Limit	12000.00
Telephone No	0904 213421
Contact Name	Edward Singleton
Analysis Code	Furniture
VAT Country Code	GB
Default Tax Code	T1

Account Reference	KIDD
Account Name	KiddRugs
Address	346 Leeds Road
..	Huddersfield
..	West Yorkshire
..	HD4 3RG
Credit Limit	5000.00
Telephone No	0484 347591
Contact Name	Alan Kidd
Analysis Code	Carpeting
VAT Country Code	GB
Default Tax Code	T1

Account Reference	SEATS
Account Name	Seats and Things
Address	112 Batley Road
..	Huddersfield
..	West Yorkshire
..	HD5 7TC
Credit Limit	15000.00
Telephone No	0484 673298
Contact Name	David Peterson
Analysis Code	Furniture
VAT Country Code	GB
Default Tax Code	T1

Account Reference	SLEEP
Account Name	Sleepwell Ltd
Address	12 Wetherby Road
..	Acomb
..	York
..	YO5 7YA
Credit Limit	10000.00
Telephone No	0904 567778
Contact Name	Janet Feather
Analysis Code	Beds

VAT Country Code   GB
Default Tax Code   T1

Account Reference   SYKES
Account Name   Sykes Mills Ltd
Address   Sykes Mills
..   Fenay Bridge
..   Huddersfield
..   HD3 6PJ
Credit Limit   1000.00
Telephone No   0484 321987
Contact Name   Sarah Sykes
Analysis Code   Fabrics
VAT Country Code   GB
Default Tax Code   T1

Account Reference   WILM
Account Name   Wilminster Carpets Ltd
Address   Wilminster House
..   Kidderminster
..   West Midlands
..   KD3 6TH
Credit Limit   20000.00
Telephone No   0234 563420
Contact Name   David Walker
Analysis Code   Carpeting
VAT Country Code   GB
Default Tax Code   T1

When you have saved the last supplier record:

3   Press $\boxed{\text{Esc}}$ to return to the Purchase Ledger screen.

It is possible to check all your entries and, if required, to amend them.

4   Return to the display of the Supplier Details screen and enter the code **ABC** in the **Account Reference** box.

Immediately the ABC Fabrics account record details are displayed. At the bottom of the screen you will see:

```
F9 PrevA/C   F10 NextA/C
```

5   Press $\boxed{\text{F10}}$ and the display changes to the next account record.

You can browse at will through the account records using these two function keys.

6 Press Esc , select **Abandon** at the bottom of the screen to close the Supplier Details screen and return to the Financial Controller screen.

2.8 Entering the suppliers' opening balances

When Total Bedrooms installed their computerised accounting system they had already been trading for some years. Consequently, on the 1st January, when they installed the system most of the company's suppliers' accounts had outstanding balances. These outstanding balances will now be entered into the supplier accounts before any further supplier transactions are executed.

Ensure that the Financial Controller screen is on display.

1 Select the **Purchase Ledger** option to reveal the Purchase Ledger screen.

2 In the Purchase Ledger screen select the **Batched Data Entry** and reveal the Purchase Invoices screen.

This screen is identical to the Batched Data Entry screen that was accessed via the Sales Ledger and invoices can be entered into it in just the same way.

3 With the cursor located in the **A/C** box press F4 to reveal the Supplier List screen:

```
ABC         ABC Fabrics
ART         Artwork
COMM        Commercial Carpenters Ltd
EEZEE       EEZEE Beds Plc
FABRIC      Fabrico
FLASH       Flash Lighting Ltd
FOR         Forward Bedding
HAND        Hand Craft Ltd
KIDD        KiddRugs
SEATS       Seats and Things
SLEEP       Sleepwell Ltd
SYKES       Sykes Mills Ltd
```

4 Move the highlight to **ART Artwork** and press Enter .

The Artwork account code is then entered into the **A/C** box automatically.

5 Enter the remaining details as:

Date	101193	remember the format DDMMYY
Inv No	5044	
N/C	9998	We are analysing through the SUSPENSE account
Dep	2	Purchases
Details	Opening Balance	Remember the capital **O** and **B**
Nett Amnt	226.66	
Tc	T9	

There is just one outstanding invoice from Artwork from the previous financial year that has to be carried forward to this accounting year.

Notice again that, as in the case of the customer opening balances, the value entered under **Nett Amnt** is the total invoice value. This will not matter here because any VAT associated with this account will have been accounted for by Total Bedrooms in December. All that Total Bedrooms are now concerned with is the total amount of the invoice due to the supplier.

6   Press Esc and post this information to the ledgers.

EXERCISE

1   Enter the following opening balances using **N/C 9998**, **Dep 2** and tax code **Tc T9** (remember to use the F6 key):

Supplier	Inv	Date	Amount
Commercial Carpenters	4999	30/09/93	1265.98
	5021	23/10/93	3421.67
	5030	05/11/93	4571.56
	5065	19/12/93	1974.28
EEZEE Beds	5035	11/11/93	1278.34
	5060	12/12/93	2323.44
Flash Lighting	5047	01/12/93	4931.33
Forward Bedding	5050	02/12/93	998.49
Hand Craft	5015	15/10/93	791.35
	5027	02/11/93	5934.34
	5073	15/12/93	3953.25
Seats and Things	5061	13/12/93	719.55

It is only possible to enter 12 invoices at a time so post these to the ledgers and then continue entering the following invoices:

Sleepwell	5005	02/10/93	2223.67
	5040	23/11/93	3998.67
	5048	01/12/93	1268.66
Sykes Mills	5025	01/11/93	539.41
Wilminster Carpets	5031	11/11/93	8345.91
	5055	11/12/93	8232.80

2   Complete this activity with the Financial Controller screen on display.

2.9 Printing account lists

As an exercise to complete this chapter, print off two reports:

Customer balances
Supplier balances

Keep these reports available for reference as you progress through the book.

2.10 Backing up data to a floppy diskette

You have now completed Chapter Two and have entered data into the Sage Sterling Financial Controller accounting system which has been stored on your computer's hard disk. While the hard disk is a very reliable medium it is worthwhile reminding yourself that it is storing your only copy of the data and that the disk itself is not infallible. Data can be irretrievably lost if your hard disk fails. Therefore, it is advised that you back up your data onto a floppy diskette (refer to page xvi of *Getting started*).

 A word of caution. When backing up data to a floppy diskette from your hard disk, all the current information in the data files on your hard disk is copied to the floppy diskette. As a consequence, it is always best to back up using the Backup/Restore facility available within the Sage Sterling Financial Controller accounting system which backs up and restores *all* the data files. If you use any other method which enables you to select which data files to back up or restore you may be tempted not to back up or restore all of your data files. In such an event your data could very easily become corrupted and, therefore, worthless.

Remember to take the diskette out of the floppy drive and to store it in a safe place.

3　Setting up stock details

Total Bedrooms is in the business of providing complete bedrooms for the hotel trade. To enable it to do this the company purchases various bedroom components from a variety of suppliers. To maintain an efficient sales and installation operation the company finds it necessary to have a warehouse and hold stock. When a sale is made an invoice must be produced and the Sage Sterling +2 accounting system permits invoices to be issued against stock. This means that whenever an item is invoiced it can be automatically deducted from stock. This enables the company to keep a track of the physical stock and when stock items require reordering.

To enable invoicing from stock, the details of the stock held by the company must be recorded by the accounting system. In this chapter we shall enter the details of the opening stock. Quantities purchased and sold will be entered later.

Before entering the details of individual items of stock we must remember that the company has categorised its stock. For example, the company buys and sells two types of bed and four types of bedroom linen. To enable an efficient analysis of stock purchases and sales, it is necessary to summarise individual stock codes into categories. There are in total seven categories of stock:

    Beds
    Furniture
    Seating
    Lighting
    Carpeting
    Fabrics
    Sundries

3.1　Naming the stock categories

Stock categories are already accounted for within the Sage Sterling +2 accounting system, as were Departments. What is required is for us to give names to the various numbered, predefined categories. Ensure that the Financial Controller screen is on display.

1　Select the **Stock Control** option to reveal the Stock Control screen:

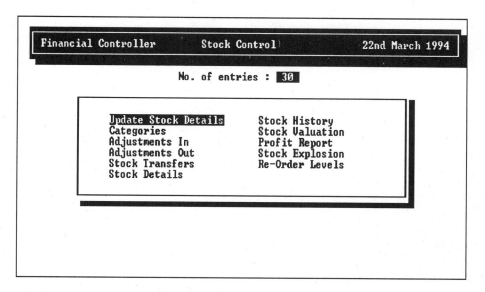

```
Financial Controller        Stock Control)        22nd March 1994

                    No. of entries :  30

        ┌──────────────────────────────────────────┐
        │  Update Stock Details     Stock History   │
        │  Categories               Stock Valuation │
        │  Adjustments In           Profit Report   │
        │  Adjustments Out          Stock Explosion │
        │  Stock Transfers          Re-Order Levels  │
        │  Stock Details                            │
        └──────────────────────────────────────────┘
```

2   Select the **Categories** option to reveal the Categories screen:

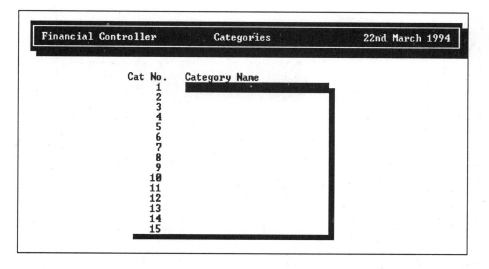

```
Financial Controller        Categories        22nd March 1994

            Cat No.    Category Name
               1
               2
               3
               4
               5
               6
               7
               8
               9
              10
              11
              12
              13
              14
              15
```

This screen is entirely analogous to the Departments screen encountered in the previous chapter. As expected, the naming of categories follows the identical procedure to the naming of Departments.

3   With the highlight opposite the category number 1, type in the name of the first category as:

Beds and press ⌐Enter¬

The highlight moves to the next category.

EXERCISE   1   Enter the remaining stock categories as follows:

Category	Name
2	Furniture
3	Seating
4	Lighting
5	Carpeting
6	Fabrics
7	Sundries

2　When you have named all the categories press `Esc` to save the category details to disk and to return to the Stock Control screen. Retain this screen display as we now need to enter the details of the individual stock items.

3.2 **Entering the details of stock items**

Entering the details of the individual stock items is analogous to entering customer and supplier account details. Ensure that the Stock Control screen is on display.

 1　Select the **Update Stock Details** option to reveal the Update Stock Details screen:

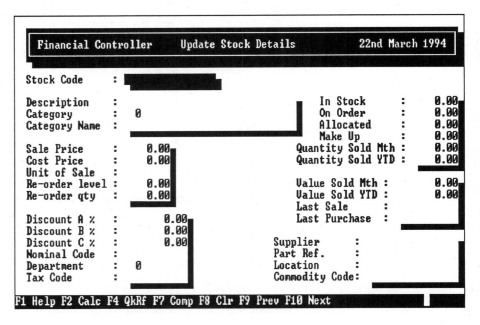

This screen display is divided into a number of boxes and the text cursor is located in the box labelled **Stock Code**.

2　Enter the code **101** and press `Enter`

The codes that have been devised for stock consist of three numbers. The first number is the category number and the second two numbers represent the item number in that category. The code that we have just entered indicates that we are going to enter the details of a bed.

3   Continue by entering the following:

Description	Single bed	
Category	1	
Category Name	Beds	Entered automatically
Sale Price	60.00	
Cost Price		We cannot enter anything here
Unit of Sale	Each	
Re-order level	30	
Re-order qty	100	
Discount A		Leave blank
Discount B		Leave blank
Discount C		Leave blank

4   With the cursor in the **Nominal Code** box press $\boxed{\text{F4}}$ to reveal the Nominal Code List window. Move the highlight in this window to enter the **Nominal Code**:

Nominal Code	4001	Sales - beds (use the $\boxed{\text{F4}}$ key)
Department	1	Sales
Tax Code	T1	

When you press $\boxed{\text{Enter}}$ after entering the **Tax Code** as **T1** the cursor moves to **Make Up**. We shall leave this blank for now.

5   Press $\boxed{\downarrow}$ again and the cursor moves to **Supplier**.

We are not going to enter any more information into this record at the moment.

It is not possible for us to enter any information relating to amount in stock, on order, allocated or relating to quantities and values sold. These are entered by the system automatically as stock is purchased and subsequently sold.

6   Press $\boxed{\text{Esc}}$ and post these stock details to the disk.

When the information of this item of stock has been saved to disk the form clears in readiness for the details of another item of stock to be entered.

7   Press $\boxed{\text{Esc}}$ to return to the Stock Control screen.

At the moment we do not wish to enter another item of stock. Instead we wish to complete the information relevant to the last item whose details we have just entered, namely the quantity already in stock and the cost price. We do this via the **Adjustments In** option in the Stock Control screen.

8   Select the **Adjustments In** option in the Stock Control screen to reveal the Adjustments In screen:

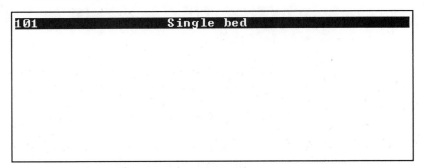

```
┌─────────────────────────────────────────────────────────────────┐
│ Financial Controller      Adjustments In        22nd March 1994  │
│                                                                   │
│                                                                   │
│    Stock Code      :                                              │
│    Description     :                                              │
│    Quantity        :      0.00        Qty in Stock  :     0.00    │
│                                       Qty Allocated :     0.00    │
│    Cost Price      :      0.00        Qty On-Order  :     0.00    │
│    Sale Price      :      0.00                                    │
│                                                                   │
│    Narrative       :                                              │
│                                                                   │
│    Reference       :                  Last Sale     :            │
│    Date            :                  Last Purchase :            │
│                                                                   │
└─────────────────────────────────────────────────────────────────┘
```

9   Locate the highlight in the **Stock Code** box and press F4 to reveal the Stock Code List window:

```
┌─────────────────────────────────────────────────────────────────┐
│ 101                        Single bed                            │
│                                                                   │
│                                                                   │
│                                                                   │
│                                                                   │
│                                                                   │
│                                                                   │
└─────────────────────────────────────────────────────────────────┘
```

The Stock Code List window contains a single highlighted item.

10   Press Enter and the code **101** automatically appears in the **Stock Code** box along with some of the details that you had previously entered.

11   Enter the **Quantity** as:

     120 and press Enter

12   Enter the **Cost Price** as:

     40 and press Enter twice to place the cursor in the **Narrative** box.

13   Press F7 and the narrative **Opening Stock** is automatically entered.

14   Enter the **Reference** as **O/Bal** and press Enter.

15   Enter the **Date** as:

010194

This completes the opening stock record for this item.

16   Press $\boxed{\text{Esc}}$ and post the details to the ledgers.

EXERCISE   1   Enter the following items of stock into the Update Stock Details screen and then use the Adjustments In screen to enter the opening stock quantities and the cost price. Use the date 010194 when entering the opening stock. If at any time you make a mistake with your entry, try to correct it by overtyping. If that fails press $\boxed{\text{Esc}}$ and select to **Abandon** the entry and start again.

Stock Code	102		Stock Code	201
Description	Double bed		Description	Vanity unit - small
Category	1		Category	2
Category Name	Beds		Category Name	Furniture
Sales Price	90.00		Sales Price	70.00
Unit of Sale	Each		Unit of Sale	Each
Re-Order Level	50.00		Re-Order Level	30.00
Re-Order Qty	100.00		Re-Order Qty	60.00
Nominal Code	4001 Sales - Beds		Nominal Code	4002 Sales - Furniture
Department	1		Department	1
Tax Code	T1		Tax Code	T1
In Stock	105.00		In Stock	70.00
Cost Price	60.00		Cost Price	50.00
Date	01/01/94		Date	01/01/94

Stock Code	202		Stock Code	203
Description	Vanity unit - large		Description	Wardrobe - single
Category	2		Category	2
Category Name	Furniture		Category Name	Furniture
Sales Price	129.00		Sales Price	200.00
Unit of Sale	Each		Unit of Sale	Each
Re-Order Level	30.00		Re-Order Level	30.00
Re-Order Qty	50.00		Re-Order Qty	60.00
Nominal Code	4002 Sales - Furniture		Nominal Code	4002 Sales - Furniture
Department	1		Department	1
Tax Code	T1		Tax Code	T1
In Stock	102.00		In Stock	55.00
Cost Price	80.00		Cost Price	150.00
Date	01/01/94		Date	01/01/94

Stock Code	204	Stock Code	301
Description	Wardrobe - double	Description	Stool
Category	2	Category	3
Category Name	Furniture	Category Name	Seating
Sales Price	280.00	Sales Price	18.00
Unit of Sale	Each	Unit of Sale	Each
Re-Order Level	30.00	Re-Order Level	25.00
Re-Order Qty	60.00	Re-Order Qty	50.00
Nominal Code	4002 Sales - Furniture	Nominal Code	4003 Sales - Seating
Department	1	Department	1
Tax Code	T1	Tax Code	T1
In Stock	77.00	In Stock	119.00
Cost Price	180.00	Cost Price	10.00
Date	01/01/94	Date	01/01/94

Stock Code	302	Stock Code	401
Description	Chair	Description	Table lamp
Category	3	Category	4
Category Name	Seating	Category Name	Lighting
Sales Price	140.00	Sales Price	20.00
Unit of Sale	Each	Unit of Sale	Each
Re-Order Level	25.00	Re-Order Level	50.00
Re-Order Qty	50.00	Re-Order Qty	100.00
Nominal Code	4003 Sales - Seating	Nominal Code	4004 Sales - Lighting
Department	1	Department	1
Tax Code	T1	Tax Code	T1
In Stock	63.00	In Stock	147.00
Cost Price	100.00	Cost Price	10.00
Date	01/01/94	Date	01/01/94

Stock Code	402	Stock Code	501
Description	Standard lamp	Description	Carpeting
Category	4	Category	5
Category Name	Lighting	Category Name	Carpeting
Sales Price	50.00	Sales Price	18.00
Unit of Sale	Each	Unit of Sale	Metre
Re-Order Level	30.00	Re-Order Level	850.00
Re-Order Qty	60.00	Re-Order Qty	1000.00
Nominal Code	4004 Sales - Lighting	Nominal Code	4005 Sales - Carpeting
Department	1	Department	1
Tax Code	T1	Tax Code	T1
In Stock	131.00	In Stock	1789.00
Cost Price	30.00	Cost Price	10.00
Date	01/01/94	Date	01/01/94

Stock Code	601		Stock Code	602
Description	Curtains - Linen		Description	Curtains - Lace
Category	6		Category	6
Category Name	Fabrics		Category Name	Fabrics
Sales Price	60.00		Sales Price	10.00
Unit of Sale	Pair		Unit of Sale	Pair
Re-Order Level	60.00		Re-Order Level	35.00
Re-Order Qty	120.00		Re-Order Qty	70.00
Nominal Code	4006 Sales - Fabrics		Nominal Code	4006 Sales - Fabrics
Department	1		Department	1
Tax Code	T1		Tax Code	T1
In Stock	166.00		In Stock	178.00
Cost Price	40.00		Cost Price	5.00
Date	01/01/94		Date	01/01/94

Stock Code	603		Stock Code	604
Description	Bedding - single		Description	Bedding - double
Category	6		Category	6
Category Name	Fabrics		Category Name	Fabrics
Sales Price	30.00		Sales Price	40.00
Unit of Sale	Set		Unit of Sale	Set
Re-Order Level	50.00		Re-Order Level	50.00
Re-Order Qty	100.00		Re-Order Qty	100.00
Nominal Code	4006 Sales - Fabrics		Nominal Code	4006 Sales - Fabrics
Department	1		Department	1
Tax Code	T1		Tax Code	T1
In Stock	149.00		In Stock	157.00
Cost Price	20.00		Cost Price	30.00
Date	01/01/94		Date	01/01/94

Stock Code	701		Stock Code	702
Description	Picture		Description	Ashtray
Category	7		Category	7
Category Name	Sundries		Category Name	Sundries
Sales Price	25.00		Sales Price	5.00
Unit of Sale	Each		Unit of Sale	Each
Re-Order Level	34.00		Re-Order Level	75.00
Re-Order Qty	70.00		Re-Order Qty	150.00
Nominal Code	4007 Sales - Sundries		Nominal Code	4007 Sales - Sundries
Department	1		Department	1
Tax Code	T1		Tax Code	T1
In Stock	99.00		In Stock	317.00
Cost Price	15.00		Cost Price	2.00
Date	01/01/94		Date	01/01/94

Stock Code	703		Stock Code	704
Description	Waste bins		Description	Decor pack
Category	7		Category	7
Category Name	Sundries		Category Name	Sundries
Sales Price	15.00		Sales Price	30.00
Unit of Sale	Each		Unit of Sale	Set
Re-Order Level	20.00		Re-Order Level	25.00
Re-Order Qty	40.00		Re-Order Qty	50.00
Nominal Code	4007 Sales - Sundries		Nominal Code	4007 Sales - Sundries
Department	1		Department	1
Tax Code	T1		Tax Code	T1
In Stock	77.00		In Stock	89.00
Cost Price	10.00		Cost Price	20.00
Date	01/01/94		Date	01/01/94

2   When you have entered the details of all the stock items press ⌑Esc⌑ to return to the Stock Control screen.

It is possible to check all your entries and, if required, to amend them.

3   Display the Update Stock Details screen where you will be able to browse through all the stock records which are now complete with In Stock quantities as well as the Cost Price.

4   Press ⌑Esc⌑ to return to the Financial Controller screen.

3.3   Printing the stock list

EXERCISE   As an exercise, to complete this chapter, print off the report:

Stock History

Keep this report available for reference as you progress through the book.

3.4   Backing up data to a floppy diskette

You have now completed Chapter Three and have entered data into the Sage Sterling Financial Controller accounting system which has been stored on your computer's hard disk. While the hard disk is a very reliable medium it is worthwhile reminding yourself that it is storing your only copy of the data and that the disk itself is not infallible. Data can be irretrievably lost if your hard disk fails. Therefore, it is advised that you back up your data onto a floppy diskette (refer to page xvi of *Getting started*).

A word of caution. When backing up data to a floppy diskette from your hard disk, all the current information in the data files on your hard disk is copied to the floppy diskette. As a consequence, it is always best to back up using the Backup/Restore facility available within the Sage Sterling Financial Controller accounting system which backs up and restores *all* the data files. If you use any other method which enables you to select which data files to back up or restore you may be tempted not to back up or restore all of your data files. In such an event your data could very easily become corrupted and, therefore, worthless.

Remember to take the diskette out of the floppy drive and to store it in a safe place.

Amending records and accounts

Amending accounts

Accounts can be amended at any time during the operation of the Sage Sterling Financial Controller accounting system but care must be taken when doing so. This is because many of the accounts interact with each other so that amending one account may adversely affect the contents of another account. Problems of this nature and their resolution we shall discuss later in the book. What we wish to consider here is the simple amending of an account name.

Total Bedrooms sell either bespoke bedrooms where the customer selects items from a list or suite bedrooms which are predefined collections of items and are automatically taken out of stock. To cater for suite sales that are made up from stock we shall allocate such sales to nominal ledger account 4000. This is currently defined as Sales Type A. We shall now change the name of this nominal account to reflect this.

1   Ensure that the Financial Controller screen is on display.

2   Select the **Nominal Ledger** option to reveal the Nominal Ledger screen.

3   Select the **Nominal Accounts Structure** and then the **Account Names** option in the Nominal Accounts Structure screen.

4   Enter the **Account Reference** as:

   4000 and press $\boxed{\text{Enter}}$

The **Account Name** box then displays **Sales Type A**.

5   In the **Account Name** box overtype the current name with:

   Suite Sales and press $\boxed{\text{Enter}}$

6   Press $\boxed{\text{Esc}}$ and post these amended details to the ledgers.

The form clears in readiness for the entry of a new account. Do not enter anything into this form. Instead:

7   Press $\boxed{\text{Esc}}$ twice and return to the Nominal Ledger screen.

When we entered the sales and purchase ledger opening balances we stated that because they related to invoices issued in the previous financial year it was not possible to analyse them against sales made this year. As a consequence they were analysed against the nominal ledger account 9998 - the SUSPENSE account.

We have already stated that the principle of double-entry book-keeping is that for every debit in the nominal ledger there must be a counterbalancing credit and vice versa. This requirement that is placed upon entries into the nominal ledger is taken care of automatically within the Sage Sterling Financial Controller accounting system, as can be seen when we look at the trial balance.

1   Ensure that the Financial Controller screen is on display and select the **Nominal Ledger** option to display the Nominal Ledger screen.

2   From the Nominal Ledger Screen select the **Trial Balance** option and further select the display of the trial balance to appear on the monitor screen:

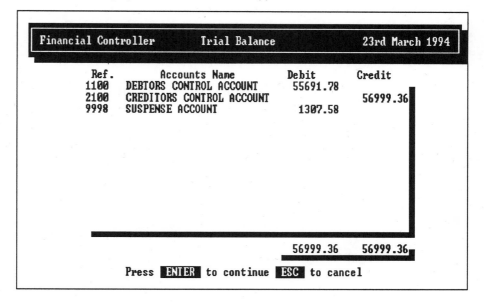

```
Financial Controller        Trial Balance           23rd March 1994

      Ref.        Accounts Name        Debit        Credit
      1100    DEBTORS CONTROL ACCOUNT    55691.78
      2100    CREDITORS CONTROL ACCOUNT              56999.36
      9998    SUSPENSE ACCOUNT            1307.58




                                       56999.36     56999.36

          Press  ENTER  to continue  ESC  to cancel
```

From this display you will see that all the opening balances entered into the sales ledger have also been entered as debits in the debtors control account and all the opening balances entered into the purchase ledger have also been entered as credits in the creditors control account. To maintain a balance of the entire nominal ledger each debit in the debtors control account is matched by a credit of an equal amount in the suspense account and each credit in the creditors control account is matched by a debit of an equal amount in the suspense account. This state of affairs can be viewed by looking at the transaction histories of these three accounts:

3   Ensure that the Nominal Ledger screen is on display and select the **Transaction History** option.

4   Accept all the defaults in the resulting screen and press [Enter] to reveal the Transaction History screen displaying the history of the Debtors Control Account:

```
┌──────────────────────────────────────────────────────────────┐
│  Financial Controller    Transaction History    23rd March 1994 │
│                                                                  │
│  A/C Ref. : 1100    CONTROL N/C    A/C Name : DEBTORS CONTROL ACCOUNT │
│                                                                  │
│  No. Tp  Date  Ref        Details      Value      Debit    Credit │
│   1 SI 211093 1270  Opening Balance    2398.31    2398.31         │
│   2 SI 301193 1319  Opening Balance    6754.11    6754.11         │
│   3 SI 111293 1329  Opening Balance    5196.86    5196.86         │
│   4 SI 091193 1300  Opening Balance    2174.08    2174.08         │
│   5 SI 211193 1306  Opening Balance    1256.67    1256.67         │
│   6 SI 051293 1327  Opening Balance    4306.82    4306.82         │
│   7 SI 111093 1258  Opening Balance    3456.98    3456.98         │
│   8 SI 241193 1307  Opening Balance    6732.56    6732.56         │
│   9 SI 171293 1321  Opening Balance    6389.36    6389.36         │
│  10 SI 291193 1315  Opening Balance    6745.12    6745.12         │
│  11 SI 201293 1333  Opening Balance    6887.01    6887.01         │
│                                                                  │
│                           Totals :    55691.78            0.00  │
│                           Balance :   55691.78                  │
└──────────────────────────────────────────────────────────────┘
```

Here you see that all the opening balances entered into the sales ledger are listed on the debit side of the Debtors Control Account. Notice that there are 13 of them.

5   Press `F4` to reveal a window displaying a list of nominal ledger codes:

```
┌──────────────────────────────────────────────┐
│ 1100      DEBTORS CONTROL ACCOUNT             │
│ 1101      SUNDRY DEBTORS                       │
│ 1102      OTHER DEBTORS                        │
│ 1103      PREPAYMENTS                          │
│ 1200      BANK CURRENT ACCOUNT                 │
│ 1210      BANK DEPOSIT ACCOUNT                 │
│ 1220      BUILDING SOCIETY ACCOUNT            │
│ 1230      PETTY CASH                           │
│ 2100      CREDITORS CONTROL ACCOUNT           │
│ 2101      SUNDRY CREDITORS                     │
│ 2102      OTHER CREDITORS                      │
│ 2109      ACCRUALS                             │
└──────────────────────────────────────────────┘
```

6   Use the cursor control keys to move the highlight in this screen to account **2100 Creditors Control Account** and press `Enter`:

```
┌──────────────────────────────────────────────────────────────┐
│  Financial Controller    Transaction History    23rd March 1994 │
│                                                                  │
│  A/C Ref. : 2100    CONTROL N/C    A/C Name : CREDITORS CONTROL ACCOUNT │
│                                                                  │
│  No. Tp  Date  Ref        Details      Value      Debit    Credit │
│  14 PI 101193 5044  Opening Balance     226.66             226.66 │
│  15 PI 300993 4999  Opening Balance    1265.98            1265.98 │
│  16 PI 231093 5021  Opening Balance    3421.67            3421.67 │
│  17 PI 051193 5030  Opening Balance    4571.56            4571.56 │
│  18 PI 191293 5065  Opening Balance    1974.28            1974.28 │
│  19 PI 111193 5035  Opening Balance    1278.34            1278.34 │
│  20 PI 121293 5060  Opening Balance    2323.44            2323.44 │
│  21 PI 011293 5047  Opening Balance    4931.33            4931.33 │
│  22 PI 021293 5050  Opening Balance     998.49             998.49 │
│  23 PI 151093 5015  Opening Balance     791.35             791.35 │
│  24 PI 021193 5027  Opening Balance    5934.34            5934.34 │
│                                                                  │
│                           Totals :          0.00      56999.36  │
│                           Balance :                   56999.36  │
└──────────────────────────────────────────────────────────────┘
```

Here you see that all the opening balances entered into the purchase ledger are listed on the credit side of the Creditors Control Account. Notice that there are 11 of them in the opening display.

7   Press PgDn and you will see that there are a further 8 entries.

8   Display the transaction history of the account **9998 Suspense Account** and there you will see all the counterbalancing debits and credits.

Notice that the debits exceed the credits leaving the account in overall debit to the value of £1307.58.

From its very name the SUSPENSE account is a temporary holding account of debits and credits that balance appropriate credits and debits in other nominal ledger accounts. Because it is a temporary holding account it must never show anything other than a zero balance. To achieve this we must post a counter-balancing credit to this account to the value of £1307.58. However, because the overall balance of the nominal ledger must be zero this credit must be counterbalanced by appropriate debits and credits to the creditor and debtor control accounts. This is achieved by making what is referred to as a journal entry.

4.3   Journal entries

A journal entry consists of a number of transactions entered directly into the nominal ledger under the proviso that the balance of the entries is zero.

1   Ensure that the Nominal Ledger screen is on display and select the **Journal Entries** option to reveal the Journal Entries screen:

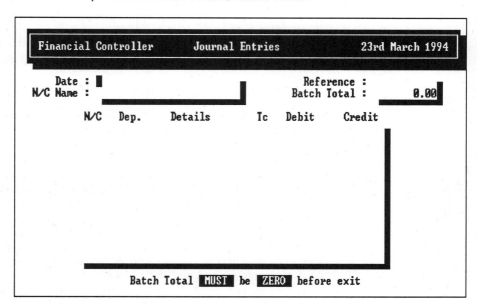

Notice the message at the bottom of the screen:

```
Batch Total MUST be ZERO before exit
```

This is essential to ensure that the overall balance of the nominal ledger remains zero. Indeed, despite the warning it is not actually possible to post a batch of entries that do not satisfy this condition.

2   Enter the **Date** as:

010194

3   Enter **Reference** as:

001 because this is the first journal entry we are about to make.

4   In the main box enter the following details:

N/C	Dep.	Details	Tc	Debit	Credit
1100	1	Opening Balance	T9		55691.78
2100	2	Opening Balance	T9	56999.36	
9998	0	Opening Balance	T9		1307.58

As you make the first two entries you will be presented with a warning window:

```
This entry will not be reflected in your
Sales/Purchase Ledger.
Do you wish to proceed ?   N
```

indicating that the entry will not be reflected in either the sales or purchase ledger accounts.

5   Press **Y** and Enter to clear this warning window and proceed with the entry.

Each of these entries will ensure that each account has a balance of zero. Notice that the **Batch Total** is now **0.00**.

6   Press Esc and post this journal entry to the nominal ledger.

7   Return to the Nominal Ledger screen and try to run a Trial Balance.

Nothing will happen because all the accounts in the nominal ledger each have a zero balance.

4.4   Setting up Nominal Ledger account opening balances

The zero balance that currently exists on the nominal ledger reflects the fact that Total Bedrooms have not entered any transactions resulting from trading during this current financial year. However, the company does have assets and liabilities carried forward from the previous financial year. For example, it possesses a bank account, motor vehicles and stock. These assets and liabilities must now be entered into the nominal ledger but, again, the eventual balance of all the debits and credits must be equal.

EXERCISE   1   Enter the following opening balances to the nominal ledger as a journal entry using:

Date	010194
Reference	002
Dep	3
Details	Opening Balance
Tc	T9

for each entry. Remember to use the $\boxed{\text{F6}}$ key where appropriate.

Account	0010 Freehold Property
Debit	50,000.00

Account	0040 Furniture and Fixtures
Debit	15,000.00

Account	0051 Motor Vehicles Depreciation
Credit	15,000.00

Account	3000 Ordinary Shares
Credit	50,000.00

2 When these four entries are complete press $\boxed{\text{Esc}}$ and post them to the ledger.

Notice that in this journal entry the Batch Total was zero for entries that were contained within the space of a single screen. When this does not happen the batch of entries will have to be saved in parts.

3 Continue entering the remaining opening balances as follows using:

Date	010194
Reference	002
Dep	3
Details	Opening Balance
Tc	T9

Account	0041 Furniture and Fixtures Depreciation
Credit	7,500.00

Account	0050 Motor Vehicles
Debit	30,000.00

Account	1100 Debtors Control
Debit	55,691.78

Account	1200 Bank Current Account
Debit	7,943.82

Account 2100 Creditors Control
Credit 56,999.36

Account 2201 VAT Liability
Credit 16,671.82

Account 2300 Loans
Credit 50,000.00

Account 3200 Profit & Loss
Credit 58,438.42

Account 5200 Opening Stock
Debit 95,539.00

Account 7103 General Rates
Debit 2,000.00

Account 7200 Electricity
Credit 515.00

Account 7304 Miscellaneous Motor Expenses
Credit 300.00

When this last entry has been made the screen if full and there appears to be no way of entering the last entry to make the Batch Total zero. At this stage we must post that part of the journal entry completed so far.

4   Press `Esc` and post the journal entries displayed on the screen.

The screen clears but you will notice that the journal entry Reference is still reading 3 and the Batch Total records a debit of 750.00. You have not yet exited the entry.

5   Enter the last credit:

Account 7504 Office Stationery
Date 010194
Dep 3
Details Opening Balance
Credit 750.00

When this last opening balance has been recorded you will notice that the Batch Total now reads 0.00. The journal entry is complete.

6   Press $\boxed{\text{Esc}}$ and post the details to the ledgers.

The screen now clears to leave a blank Journal Entry form.

7   Press $\boxed{\text{Esc}}$ to return to the Nominal Ledger screen.

4.5   Deleting accounts

Deleting an account follows a very similar procedure to that of amending an account except that an account can only be deleted if it has no transaction on it. Again, great care is required because of the interactive nature of the accounting system. We shall not delete an actual account here, but rather leave that procedure until later in the book.

4.6   Backing up data to a floppy diskette

You have now completed Chapter Four and have entered data into the Sage Sterling Financial Controller accounting system which has been stored on your computer's hard disk. While the hard disk is a very reliable medium it is worthwhile reminding yourself that it is storing your only copy of the data and that the disk itself is not infallible. Data can be irretrievably lost if your hard disk fails. Therefore, it is advised that you back up your data onto a floppy diskette (refer to page xvi of *Getting started*).

A word of caution. When backing up data to a floppy diskette from your hard disk, all the current information in the data files on your hard disk is copied to the floppy diskette. As a consequence, it is always best to back up using the Backup/Restore facility available within the Sage Sterling Financial Controller accounting system which backs up and restores *all* the data files. If you use any other method which enables you to select which data files to back up or restore you may be tempted not to back up or restore all of your data files. In such an event your data could very easily become corrupted and, therefore, worthless.

Remember to take the diskette out of the floppy drive and to store it in a safe place.

5   Sales processing

When Total Bedrooms receive an order for goods that are held in stock a well-defined sequence of actions is initiated:

- The customer's creditworthiness is checked and the stock records are checked to see if there is sufficient stock to fulfil the order.
- The customer request is written on an order form in duplicate and one copy of the order is sent to the warehouse, the other to accounts.
- At the warehouse the order is made up and packed ready for despatch.
- A despatch note is then prepared to accompany the onward transmission of the order to the customer.
- A copy of the despatch note is sent to accounts who check it against their copy of the order.
- Accounts issue an invoice for onward transmission to the customer and which records the details of the sale.
- Accounts amend their stock records to match their physically reduced stock.

In this chapter we shall be concerned with the last aspect of this sequence of events, namely the issuing of an invoice and the amendment of the stock records.

There are two distinct ways of approaching this aspect within the Sage Sterling Financial Controller accounting system. The first method is to issue an invoice via the **Batched Data Entry** option in the Sales Ledger screen and the second method, referred to as invoicing from stock, is achieved via the **Invoice Production** option, also in the Sales Ledger screen. In this chapter we shall consider both of these aspects.

5.1   Entering an invoice via batched data entry

On the 4th January 1994 Total Bedrooms sold 10 double beds and 6 single beds to Main Line Hotels. At the time of despatch an invoice with invoice number 1340 was issued from stock (we shall consider the numbering of sales invoices later in this chapter):

The details of the order are:

> Order for delivery to: Main Line Hotels
> Date: 4 January 1994
> Order: 10 double beds
> 6 single beds

From this order an invoice was issued by the accounting department using a standard typewriter. The details of this invoice are then entered into the Sage Sterling Financial Controller accounting system via the **Batched Data Entry** option in the Sales Ledger screen.

Ensure that the Sales Ledger screen is on display and that the system date has been set to 31 January 1994 (see *Getting started*).

1   Select the **Batched Data Entry** option and select **Sales Invoices** to display the Sales Invoices screen.

The text cursor is flashing in the box annotated **A/C** where **A/C** refers to the customer account code.

2   Press F4 to reveal the Customer Accounts window.

3   Select the account **M001 Main Line Hotels Plc** by moving the highlight.

4   Press Enter and the account code and account name are automatically entered into the Sales Invoice form.

5   Enter the date as:

040194

Remember to retain the date format as DDMMYY within Sage Sterling.

6   Enter the invoice number as:

1340

7   With the cursor immediately below the heading **N/C** press F4 to reveal the Nominal Ledger Codes window.

8   Select and enter the nominal account:

4001 Sales - Beds

9   Press Enter and the account code and account name are automatically entered into the Sales Invoice.

The text cursor is now flashing in the box beneath the heading **Dep**. Enter:

1 for Sales

10   Enter the **Description** as:

10 Double beds 102

This describes both the quantity and item to the customer and the stock code to you.

11   Enter the untaxed amount (**Nett Amnt**) as:

900.00

Here we see a problem with the smooth flow of creating this type of invoice. We need to know beforehand that each single bed sells for £90.00.

12   Enter the tax code **T1** for **Tc** and the **VAT Amount** is entered automatically.

13   Repeat this procedure and enter the 6 single beds, stock code 101, costing £60.00 each excluding VAT, in the next row.

14   Check that all the details on the Sales Invoice are correct and then press Esc and post the details of the invoice to the ledgers.

15   When the posting is complete press Esc three times to return to the Financial Controller screen.

Posting of this invoice to the ledgers involved:

●   Debiting the sales ledger account M001 with the gross amount thereby increasing the amount owed by the customer.
●   Debiting the nominal ledger's Debtors Control account 1100 with the gross amount thereby recording the increased amount owed by all customers.
●   Crediting the nominal ledger sales account 4001 with the net amount thereby increasing the amount of sales revenue for beds.
●   Crediting the nominal ledger's Sales VAT Tax Control account 2200 with the VAT amount thereby increasing the amount of tax due or collected against sales.

 Note: There is no facility within Sage Sterling Financial Controller for printing this invoice when this method of data entry is used. The purpose of entering the invoice details is to ensure that the sale is accounted for within the accounting system. It is assumed that the invoice has been produced by other means, hence the ability to know beforehand how much each item sells for.

5.2   Adjusting the stock

Having entered the details of the Main Line Hotels' invoice we have merely accounted for the transaction within the company's ledgers. We have not yet accounted for the transaction within the company's stock records. This we must now do.

Ensure that the Financial Controller screen is on display.

1 Select the **Stock Control** option in the Financial Controller screen to reveal the Stock Control screen.

There are two options that enable adjustments to the stock records. We wish to adjust the stock by taking stock out so we shall use the **Adjustments Out** option.

2 Select the **Adjustments Out** option to reveal the Adjustments Out screen:

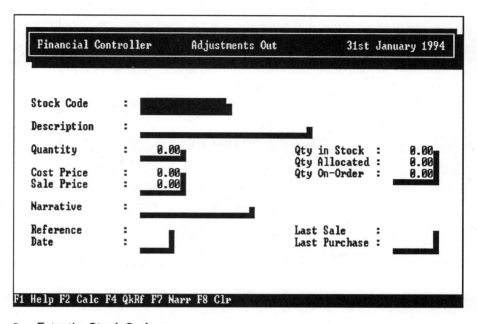

```
Financial Controller        Adjustments Out          31st January 1994

  Stock Code     :

  Description    :

  Quantity       :      0.00         Qty in Stock :      0.00
                                     Qty Allocated :     0.00
  Cost Price     :      0.00         Qty On-Order :      0.00
  Sale Price     :      0.00

  Narrative      :

  Reference      :                   Last Sale    :
  Date           :                   Last Purchase :

F1 Help F2 Calc F4 QkRf F7 Narr F8 Clr
```

3 Enter the **Stock Code** as:

102

4 Enter the **Quantity** as:

10

5 Enter the **Cost Price** as:

60.00

6 Enter the **Narrative**:

Removing Stock

by pressing the F7 key.

7 Enter the **Reference** as:

1340   the invoice number

8   Enter the **Date** as:

040194

The stock details are now completely entered.

9   Press | **Esc** | and post these details to the ledgers.

The details just entered are then cleared from the Adjustments Out screen in readiness for further stock abstraction.

10   Remove the **6 single beds** from stock (Cost Price 40.00) and complete this activity with the Financial Controller screen on display.

Having entered the details of an issued invoice and then having recorded the removal of the appropriate stock from the stock records it will be illuminating to view the effect on both the stock record and the sales ledger.

Ensure that the Financial Controller screen is on display.

1   Select the **Sales Ledger** option to reveal the Sales Ledger screen.

2   Select **Transaction History,** change the default values in the **Account Range** to:

From: M001
To: M001

and **Display** the Transaction History screen on your monitor:

```
┌─────────────────────────────────────────────────────────────────────────┐
│  ┌────────────────────────────────────────────────────────────────────┐  │
│  │ Financial Controller    Transaction History      31st January 1994 │  │
│  └────────────────────────────────────────────────────────────────────┘  │
│                                                                           │
│  A/C Ref. :    M001                        Balance      :    18059.40     │
│  A/C Name :    Main Line Hotels Plc        Amount paid  :        0.00     │
│  Credit Limit : 35000.00                   Turnover     :    17838.90     │
│                                                                           │
│  No.  Tp  Date    Ref       Details        Value      Debit     Credit    │
│    7  SI  111093  1258   Opening Balance   3456.98 *  3456.98             │
│    8  SI  241193  1307   Opening Balance   6732.56 *  6732.56             │
│    9  SI  171293  1321   Opening Balance   6389.36 *  6389.36             │
│   53  SI  040194  1340   10 Double beds 102 1057.50 *                     │
│   54  SI  040194  1340   6 Single beds 101   423.00 *  1480.50            │
│                                                                           │
│                                                                           │
│           Future    Current   30Days    60Days    90Days    Older        │
│  Aged :    0.00     1480.50   6389.36   6732.56   3456.98    0.00         │
│                                                                           │
└─────────────────────────────────────────────────────────────────────────┘
```

This screen records the **Turnover for the Year To Date (YTD)** as **17838.90** - the sum of the opening balances and the net value of invoice 1340 - the **Credit Limit** of **35000.00** and the **Balance** of the M001 account as **18059.40** which represents the opening balances plus the gross amount 1480.50 made up of the net amount 1260.00 plus the VAT 220.50 of invoice 1340.

This indicates that the details of the sale have been posted to the appropriate account in the sales ledger.

Notice that at the bottom of this screen is an **Aged** analysis showing the state of Main Line Hotels' debt to Total Bedrooms.

3   Press $\boxed{\text{Esc}}$ twice to return to the Financial Controller screen.

4   Select the **Nominal Ledger** option to reveal the Nominal Ledger screen.

5   Select the **Transaction History** option and view the transaction history of the **Debtors Control Account** number 1100.

You will see that the Debtors Control Account 1100 has been debited by the gross amount of the invoice - 1480.50 - to bring the account total to 55691.78.

6   Use the $\boxed{\text{F4}}$ key to enable you to view the transaction history of the Sales Tax Control Account 2200, confirming the tax code as **T**.

You will see that the VAT amount has been credited to this account - 220.50.

7   View the transaction history of the account 4001 Sales - Beds.

You will see that the net amount of the invoice has been credited to this account - 1260.00.

Here you see the double-entry system in operation. The debits in the nominal ledger equal the credits.

8   Press $\boxed{\text{Esc}}$ twice to return to the Financial Controller screen.

9   Select the **Stock Control** option to reveal the Stock Control screen.

10   Select **Stock Details**, accept the defaults in the Stock Details screen and display the Single bed stock record.

You will notice that in the **Stock Levels** region of the screen the **In Stock** box records **114** thus demonstrating that 6 beds have been abstracted from the opening stock of 120. Notice also that the **Last Purchase Date** and **Last Purchase Qty** are still blank. When an invoice is issued in this way these details are not recorded.

11   Press $\boxed{\text{F10}}$ to view the stock record of item **102 - Double bed** where you will see that the **In Stock** quantity has been reduced from the opening stock level of 105 to 95.

12   Press Esc to close the Stock Details screen and to return to the Stock Control screen.

13   Select the **Stock History** option to reveal the Stock History screen.

Accept the defaults to produce a display of the history of the single bed stock.

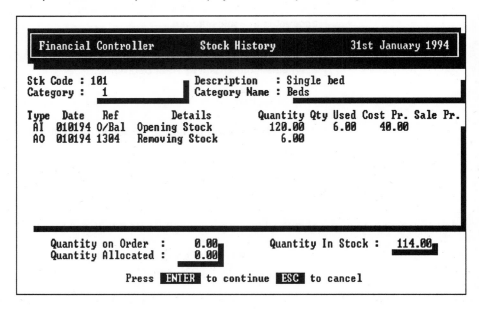

```
┌─────────────────────────────────────────────────────────────────────┐
│ Financial Controller        Stock History        31st January 1994  │
│                                                                      │
│  Stk Code : 101              Description   : Single bed              │
│  Category :   1              Category Name : Beds                    │
│                                                                      │
│  Type  Date   Ref       Details        Quantity Qty Used Cost Pr. Sale Pr. │
│  AI   010194 O/Bal   Opening Stock       120.00   6.00    40.00      │
│  AO   010194 1304    Removing Stock        6.00                      │
│                                                                      │
│                                                                      │
│       Quantity on Order  :     0.00      Quantity In Stock :  114.00 │
│       Quantity Allocated :     0.00                                  │
│              Press  ENTER  to continue  ESC  to cancel               │
└─────────────────────────────────────────────────────────────────────┘
```

14   Use F10 to view the history of the double bed stock.

You will see that for each item of stock both the opening amount and the amount abstracted are recorded. Under the heading **Tp**, for Type of transaction, you will see **AI**, which stands for adjustments in, and **AO**, which stands for adjustments out. Notice also that the **Sale Price** is not recorded. When an invoice is issued in this way there is no record of either the sale price or the profit made.

15   Press Esc twice to return to the Financial Controller screen.

5.4   Invoicing from stock

A much more convenient way of accounting for a sale is by entering the details of the transaction by selecting the **Invoice Production** option in the Sales Ledger screen. This procedure not only posts the transaction to the ledgers but it also prints a hard copy of the invoice and updates the stock records automatically.

On 9th January The Swallows Nest rang in an order to Total Bedrooms, the details of which are:

Order for delivery to: The Swallows Nest
Invoice number: 1341
Date: 9 January 1994
Order: 2 double beds
6 single beds
10 single wardrobes

Ensure that the Sales Ledger screen is on display and that the system date is still 31 January 1994.

1   Select the **Invoice Production** option in the Sales Ledger screen to reveal the Invoice Production screen:

```
Financial Controller      Invoice Production         31st January 1994


                      No. of entries : 50


                    ┌─────────────────────────────┐
                    │  Invoicing from Stock        │
                    │  Credit Note Production      │
                    │  Free Text Invoice           │
                    │  Free Text Credit Note       │
                    │  Display Index               │
                    │  Print Invoices              │
                    │  Update Ledgers              │
                    │  Delete Invoices             │
                    │                              │
                    └─────────────────────────────┘
```

2   Select **Invoicing from Stock** to reveal the Invoicing from Stock screen displaying the default date **310194**:

```
Financial Controller      Invoicing from Stock        31st January 1994

Customer   :                                    Invoice No. :      1
Address 1  :
Address 2  :                                          Date : 310194
Address 3  :
Address 4  :                                     Sales Ref :

Stock Code      Description          Quantity       Nett        VAT




Item No.    :    0 of    0          Totals :       0.00        0.00
Amount Paid :       0.00                  Total Gross :        0.00
F1 Help F2 Calc F3 Ord F4 QkRf F6 Skel F8 Clr F9 Foot F10 Paid
```

3   change the **Date** to:

     090194

4   Amend the **Invoice No.:** from **1** to **1341**.

5   With the cursor in the **Sales Ref** box press F4 and enter the code for The
     Swallows Nest.

The **Customer** name and **Address** details are then entered automatically.

6   Enter the stock code **101** beneath the **Stock Code** heading and press Enter
     to reveal the Stock Item window:

```
Stock Code              : 101
Description             : Single bed
Comment1                :
Comment2                :
_____

Quantity                :      1.00
Unit Price              :     60.00      Units : Each
Discount %              :       0.00
Tax Code                : T1              Tax % :        17.50
Nominal Code            : 4001
Department              :  1
_____

Nett                    :     60.00      Disc  :        60.00
VAT                     :     10.50
```

This window contains the details of stock item **101 - Single bed** and in the box
labelled **Quantity** is the number **1.00**. This is the default quantity.

7   Amend the default **Quantity** from **1** to **6**.

Notice that as you do this a warning message appears at the bottom of the screen
telling you that this invoice will cause The Swallows Nest debts to exceed their
credit limit.

All the other items in the Stock Item screen are left at their default values. You might
just peruse these to see exactly what they are.

8   When you are satisfied that the details in the Stock Item screen are correct
     press Esc .

You are returned to the Invoicing from Stock screen with all the details of the stock
item automatically entered and the text cursor located ready to enter the next item of
stock into the invoice.

9   Enter the other two items of stock required to fulfil the order, namely 2 double
     beds and 10 single wardrobes.

At the bottom of the Invoicing from Stock screen are 8 function keys, two of which are labelled **Ord** for Order and **Foot** for Footer. The key labelled **Ord** gives access to a facility to record details of the customer's order which is a facility we do not wish to use yet. We shall consider Order Processing in detail later in the book. The key labelled **Foot** gives access to a facility to enter details of carriage cost and settlement terms.

10   Press F9 , the **Foot** key, to reveal the Footer Details window:

```
          Carriage Values
Carriage : 0.00
Tax Code :                        Tax %  :          0.00
Nominal  :                        Tax    :          0.00
Departmt :     0                  Gross  :          0.00

          Settlement Values
Days     :     0        Early Payment   :       2984.50
Discount :         0.00

          Global values
Tax Code         :
Nominal Code     :                Tax %  :          0.00
Department       :     0
Description      :
          Balance       4600.63 > Credit Limit    2000.00
```

There are no separate carriage charges and there is no special discount applied to settlement of this account so leave the **Carriage Values** and **Settlement Values** boxes with their default entries.

In the **Global values** box there is a facility to override information that has already been entered on the invoice via the Stock Item screen. By entering a nominal code here, different nominal codes previously engaged during the creation of the invoice will be overridden and the entire invoice would be posted to the nominal code entered here. We do not wish to override anything we have previously entered on the invoice so leave all the entries at their default values. Press Esc to close the Footer Details window and to return to the Invoicing from Stock screen.

11 Press Esc and the following legend appears:

```
Do you want to : Save Edit Abandon Print Post
```

12   Move the highlight to **Post** and press Enter .

The details of the invoice are then posted to the ledgers and the details on the screen clear to leave an empty invoice form numbered 1342. We have yet to print the invoice number 1341.

13   Amend the invoice number to:

1341

A warning appears telling you that the invoice has already been posted. Press Enter and the details of the invoice that you have just entered re-appear.

14   Press Esc and this time select to **Print** the invoice after accepting each of the defaults by pressing Enter.

Complete this activity with the Financial Controller screen on display.

5.5   Security and control of documents

The confidentiality and accuracy of accounting data must be maintained at all times. Confidentiality because of the sensitive nature of the information within a highly competitive marketplace and accuracy because the information is used as the basis for the preparation of the business' financial statements. There must, therefore, be strict controls over the documents that are used as the basis for inputting data into the Sage Sterling Financial Controller accounting system. It is essential that a strict physical control be maintained over documents and that the data on the documents be accurately transferred into the accounting system so as to avoid data being lost, duplicated or erroneously entered.

In order to minimise the possibility of errors:

●   All outgoing documents of a given type must be given their own sequential numbering system. In the case of customer invoices, for example, this is a simple matter of leaving the numbering control to the computer system once the number of the first invoice issued has been entered. The Sage Sterling Financial Controller accounting system automatically remembers the number of the last customer invoice issued and then increments this by one for the next invoice. In the case of other documents it may be necessary to number each document manually prior to entering the data from the document into the system. At the same time a record of the numbering used must be maintained.

●   All incoming documents of a given type must also be given their own sequential numbering system. In the case of a supplier's invoice, for example, the existing invoice number will refer to the supplier's accounting system and will bear no relation to Total Bedrooms' system. Here, each supplier invoice must be re-numbered manually as it is received and then physically filed in numerical order, again a record of the numbering used being maintained. This will then enable controls on the handling and management of the document to be efficiently maintained.

●   Extensive use of the Sage Sterling accounting system's reporting facilities is advised after entering any data. For example, a printed list of sales invoices can be used to check that all such invoices have been entered and correctly entered. It may not be necessary to produce hard copy of the reports as a visual display on the computer monitor screen may be sufficient. In either event, the byword is check; always check that any data entered from a document is identical to the data contained in the document.

Entering further invoices

EXERCISE

1   As an exercise to familiarise yourself with the processing of invoices, generate an invoice from stock to account for the following sales order:

Order for delivery to: Innkeepers Plc
Invoice number   1342   (Notice that the updated number is
                                     automatically entered)
Date: 20 January 1994
Order: 10 stools
                        5 chairs
                        3 pictures

If you make an error when entering this order try to correct it by overtyping. If that fails then press ⟨Esc⟩ and select **Abandon** and start again.

2   When you have entered the details of the invoice post it to the ledgers and then print it.

3   Enter the following invoices:

Order for delivery to	Invoice	Date	Order
George Hotel	1343	23/01/94	100 metres carpeting
The Swallows Nest	1344	24/01/94	4 double beds 5 single beds 3 stools

A warning informs you that The Swallows Nest credit limit is exceeded. Press **Y**.

Gibbert Arms	1345	24/01/94	12 sets single bedding 8 sets double bedding
The Regency	1346	27/01/94	10 pictures
Main Line Hotels	1347	28/01/94	12 table lamps 2 double wardrobes

5.7   Entering a credit note

A credit note issued by Total Bedrooms to a customer is, in effect, a reverse invoice. It is issued by Total Bedrooms whenever an issued invoice overcharges a customer for goods received or the wrong or damaged goods are despatched. This can happen in a number of ways but it usually occurs when goods are rejected by the customer on delivery. Instead of recording money owed by the customer to Total Bedrooms as an invoice does it records money owed by Total Bedrooms to the customer. The credit note can then be used by the customer to reduce the amount due to Total Bedrooms.

The production and processing of a credit note follows the same sequence of actions as the production and processing of invoices.

When the order to Main Line Hotels arrived, against which invoice 1347 was issued, it was found that one of the 12 table lamps was damaged. Accordingly it was returned to Total Bedrooms who then replaced it in stock in the damaged goods section. To counter the fact that an invoice had been issued requesting payment for 12 table lamps when only 11 had been received a credit note was issued for the single lamp returned, dated 29 January 1994. We shall now enter the credit note transaction into the accounting system.

Ensure that the Financial Controller screen is on display and that the date is still set at 31 January 1994.

1   Select the **Sales Ledger** option in the Financial Controller screen to reveal the Sales Ledger screen.

2   Select the **Invoice Production** option in the Sales Ledger screen to reveal the Invoice Production screen.

3   Select the **Credit Note Production** option in the Invoice Production screen to reveal the Credit Note Production screen:

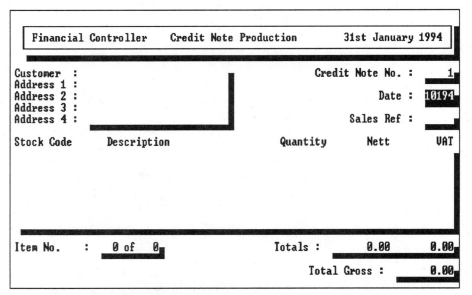

As you will see this screen is identical in format to the invoice form that appears in the Invoicing from Stock screen.

4   Enter the details of the returned table lamp by following exactly the same procedures that you performed for the entry of an invoice using **Credit Note No.: 1**. Post the details of this credit note to the ledgers and then print the credit note.

Complete this activity with the Financial Controller screen on display.

In a manual accounting system every sale is recorded in a sales ledger and a list of balances owing can be extracted. Within the Sage Sterling Financial Controller accounting system a printed list of customer account balances can be obtained via the system's reporting facility.

Ensure that the Financial Controller screen is on display.

1   Select the **Report Generator** option to reveal the Report Generator screen:

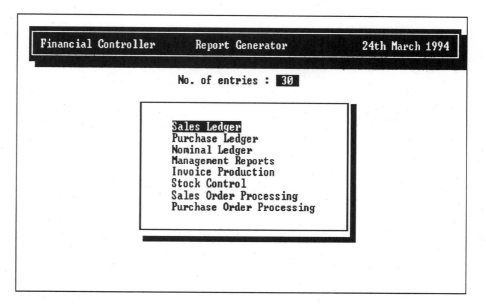

```
 Financial Controller      Report Generator       24th March 1994


                   No. of entries :  30


                  Sales Ledger
                  Purchase Ledger
                  Nominal Ledger
                  Management Reports
                  Invoice Production
                  Stock Control
                  Sales Order Processing
                  Purchase Order Processing
```

2   Select the **Sales Ledger** option to reveal the Sales Ledger reports screen:

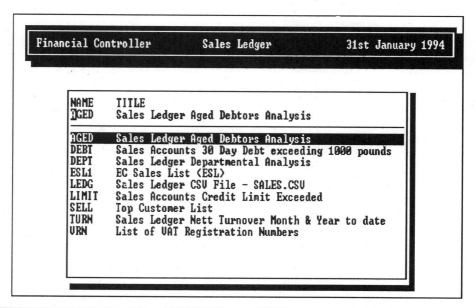

```
 Financial Controller       Sales Ledger       31st January 1994


   NAME   TITLE
   AGED   Sales Ledger Aged Debtors Analysis

   AGED   Sales Ledger Aged Debtors Analysis
   DEBT   Sales Accounts 30 Day Debt exceeding 1000 pounds
   DEPT   Sales Ledger Departmental Analysis
   ESL1   EC Sales List (ESL)
   LEDG   Sales Ledger CSV File - SALES.CSV
   LIMIT  Sales Accounts Credit Limit Exceeded
   SELL   Top Customer List
   TURN   Sales Ledger Nett Turnover Month & Year to date
   VRN    List of VAT Registration Numbers
```

3 Select the report coded as **AGED** by highlighting it.

4 Press Enter and select to send the report to the printer.

5 When the report printing is complete press Esc twice to return to the Financial Controller screen.

From the printed report you can see, in the column headed **Balance,** the amounts outstanding that are owed to Total Bedrooms by the customers. You can also see from the **Current, 30 days, 60 days** and **90 days** columns the history of your customers' indebtedness.

5.9 Printing an updated stock report

EXERCISE As an exercise to complete this chapter, print off an updated Stock History report that is accessible from the Stock Control screen.

5.10 Backing up data to a floppy diskette

You have now completed Chapter Five and have entered data into the Sage Sterling Financial Controller accounting system which has been stored on your computer's hard disk. While the hard disk is a very reliable medium it is worthwhile reminding yourself that it is storing your only copy of the data and that the disk itself is not infallible. Data can be irretrievably lost if your hard disk fails. Therefore, it is advised that you back up your data onto a floppy diskette (refer to page xvi of *Getting started*).

 A word of caution. When backing up data to a floppy diskette from your hard disk, all the current information in the data files on your hard disk is copied to the floppy diskette. As a consequence, it is always best to back up using the Backup/Restore facility available within the Sage Sterling Financial Controller accounting system which backs up and restores *all* the data files. If you use any other method which enables you to select which data files to back up or restore you may be tempted not to back up or restore all of your data files. In such an event your data could very easily become corrupted and, therefore, worthless.

Remember to take the diskette out of the floppy drive and to store it in a safe place.

6   Purchase processing

When Total Bedrooms requires to purchase stock a well defined sequence of actions is initiated:

- The purchase order is written in triplicate. One copy of the order is sent to the supplier, one copy of the order is sent to the warehouse and one copy of the order is sent to accounts.
- When the goods arrive at the warehouse they are checked against the physical order and then placed in stock.
- A goods received note is then sent to accounts who check it against the purchase invoice that has been received from the supplier.

In this chapter we shall be concerned with the last aspect of this sequence of events, namely the accounting for a purchase invoice and the amendment of the stock records to account for the purchase.

This is achieved within the Sage Sterling Financial Controller accounting system via the **Batched Data Entry** option in the Purchase Ledger screen.

6.1   Entering a purchase invoice

On 4th January Total Bedrooms took delivery of 30 double beds and 20 single beds from EEZEE Beds. At the time of arrival of the goods a delivery note was received which was checked against both the physical stock and the original order. All was found to be correct and the order was accepted:

Purchase Invoice:	EEZEE Beds
Invoice:	5080
Date:	4 January 1994
Order:	30 double beds @ £60.00 each
	20 single beds @ £40.00 each

We shall discuss purchase invoice numbers later in the chapter.

It is now required to enter the details of the purchase invoice into the accounting system. Ensure that the Financial Controller screen is on display and that the system date is 31 January 1994 (see *Getting started*).

 1   Select the **Purchase Ledger** option to reveal the Purchase Ledger screen.

2   Select the **Batched Data Entry** option and from the Batched Data Entry screen select **Purchase Invoices** to reveal the Purchase Invoices screen.

We have already used this facility to enter the opening balances into the Purchase Ledger.

3   Use the `F4` function key to enter the account code (**A/C**) as:

EEZEE

4   Enter the invoice **Date** as:

040194

5   Enter the invoice number (**Inv No**) as:

5080

6   Use the `F4` key to enter the nominal code (**N/C**) as:

5001 (Purchases - Beds)

7   Enter the **Dep.** as **2** and the **Description** as:

30 Double Beds

The amount given on the purchase invoice for this item is £1800.00 made up of 30 beds costing £60.00 each. To check that this, or any other amount, is correct you can access the Sage Calculator window.

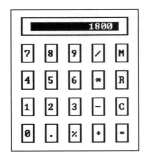

8   Ensure that the highlight is under the heading **Nett Amnt**.

9   Press `F2` and the Sage Calculator appears in its own window.

10   At the keyboard enter:

30

The number **30** appears in the calculator display.

11   Continue your calculation by entering:

* 60 =

The * means multiplication and the answer 1800 appears in the display.

12   Press `Enter` and this amount is automatically entered into the invoice closing the Calculator window simultaneously.

Notice the warning window that opens telling you that the credit limit is exceeded.

13   Press ⌈Enter⌉ to clear the warning window and enter the the default tax code in the **T/c** box as:

   T1

The **VAT** amount is automatically calculated and entered into the invoice.

The details of this invoice invoice item are complete but do not post the details to the ledgers just yet.

At the bottom of the Purchase Invoices screen is a function key ⌈F10⌉ labelled **NetTax**. This button can be used when a supplier issues an invoice in which the VAT is incorporated in the invoice total without being shown as a separate item. By using this key the invoice total can be separated into the net amount and the tax amount.

To demonstrate this:

14   Change the **NettAmnt** of **1800** to the gross amount of **2115** and place the cursor beneath **Tc**.

15   Press the ⌈F10⌉ key and the **2115** is changed to **1800.00** and the appropriate tax entered.

16   Repeat the above procedure and enter the next item on the invoice - the 20 single beds at 40.00 per bed.

17   When you are satisfied that you have entered all the details of the purchase invoice satisfactorily press ⌈Esc⌉ and opt to post the details to the ledgers.

The details of the purchase invoice are then cleared from the screen leaving a blank form in readiness for another purchase invoice to be entered. We do not wish to enter another purchase invoice at the moment.

18   Press ⌈Esc⌉ twice to return to the Financial Controller screen.

6.2   Adjusting the stock

Having entered the details of the EEZEE Beds' invoice we have merely accounted for the transaction within the company's ledgers. We have not yet accounted for the transaction within the company's stock records. This we must now do.

Ensure that the Financial Controller screen is on display.

1   Select the **Stock Control** option in the Financial Controller screen to reveal the Stock Control screen.

2   Select the **Adjustments-In** option to reveal the Adjustments In screen.

We have already used this facility to enter the opening balances into the Purchase Ledger.

3   With the highlight in the **Stock Code** box press F4 to reveal the Stock List screen.

4   Select the stock item:

101 and press Enter .

The stock item number and name are then automatically entered into the Adjustments In screen.

5   Enter the **Quantity** as:

20

The previous **Cost Price** of **40.00** appears automatically from the existing stock record. The cost has not changed so accept this default.

6   Enter the **Narrative** as the name of the supplier:

EEZEE Beds

Do not press F7 to obtain the default narrative.

7   In the **Ref** box enter the invoice number:

5080

8   Amend the default **Date** to:

040194

The details of this first item are now fully entered into the Adjustments In form.

9   Press Esc and post the details to the disk.

The Adjustments In form now clears in readiness for the next item to be entered.

10   Enter the details of the second stock item on the invoice:

Code   102
Quantity   30
Cost Price   60.00

11   Complete this activity with the Financial Controller screen on display.

Having entered the details of an accepted invoice and then having recorded the addition of the appropriate stock to the stock records it will be illuminating to view the effect on both the stock record and the ledgers.

Ensure that the Financial Controller screen is on display.

1   Select the **Purchase Ledger** option to reveal the Puchase Ledger sceen.

2   Select the **Transaction History** option to reveal the Transaction History screen:

3   Amend the default **Account Range** to read:

From: EEZEE
To: EEZEE

and display the EEZEE Transaction History on your monitor.

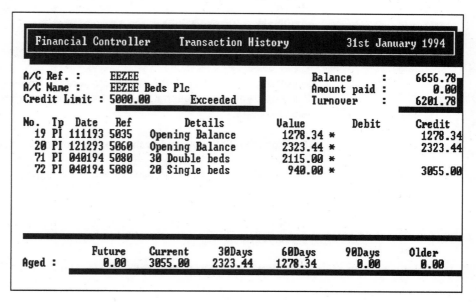

```
Financial Controller      Transaction History          31st January 1994

A/C Ref. :      EEZEE                              Balance     :    6656.78
A/C Name :      EEZEE Beds Plc                     Amount paid :       0.00
Credit Limit : 5000.00          Exceeded          Turnover    :    6201.78

No.  Tp  Date   Ref        Details          Value        Debit       Credit
 19  PI  111193 5035   Opening Balance     1278.34 *                1278.34
 20  PI  121293 5060   Opening Balance     2323.44 *                2323.44
 71  PI  040194 5080   30 Double beds      2115.00 *
 72  PI  040194 5080   20 Single beds       940.00 *                3055.00



              Future    Current    30Days    60Days    90Days    Older
Aged :         0.00     3055.00    2323.44   1278.34     0.00      0.00
```

This screen records the **Turnover for the Year To Date (YTD)** as **6201.78**, the **Credit Limit** of **5000.00** and the **Balance** of the EEZEE account as **6656.78**. Notice the * at the side of **Value**. This indicates that the balance has exceeded the credit limit. Notice the detailed **Aged** analysis of this account at the bottom of the screen.

4   Press Esc twice to return to the Financial Controller screen.

5   Select the **Nominal Ledger** option to reveal the Nominal Ledger screen.

6   Select **Transaction History** in this screen and view the Creditors Control Account 2100 transaction history.

You will then see in the information panel that the account 2100 has been credited by the gross amount of the invoice to give the account a total credit of 60054.36. You will also see that the Tax Control account 2200 has been debited with 455.00, the VAT amount of this invoice.

7   Press ⃞Esc twice to return to the Financial Controller screen.

8   Select the **Nominal Ledger** option and view the transaction history of the account **5001 Purchases - Beds**

Here you see the double-entry system in operation - the debits in the nominal ledger balance the credits.

9   Press ⃞Esc twice to return to the Financial Controller screen.

10   Select the **Stock Control** option to reveal the Stock Control screen.

11   Select the **Stock Details** option to reveal the Stock Details screen.

12   With the highlight in the **Stock Code** box, use the ⃞F4 key to view the stock details of the stock item:

101 Single bed

By comparing your copy of the printed stock report from Section 5.9 with the **In Stock** box, you will notice that 20 beds have been added to the stock to give a balance of 123.

13   Press the ⃞F10 key to view the next item of stock - **102 - Double bed.**

You will see that the **In Stock** quantity has also been increased, this time by 30 to 119.

14   Press ⃞Esc to close the Stock Details screen and to return to the Stock Control screen.

15   Select the **Stock History** option to reveal the Stock history screen.

16   Amend the **Stock Code Range** to read:

From: 101
To: 102

17   Accept all the other defaults and display the report on your computer monitor.

For each item of stock you can see a number of stock transactions recorded including the latest addition to stock. Under the heading **Tp**, for Type of transaction, you will see **AI**, **AO** and **GO** which stand for adjustments in, out and goods out respectively.

18   When you have perused this report return to the Financial Controller screen.

6.4   Entering further purchase invoices

EXERCISE   As the month of January progressed Total Bedrooms made a series of purchases. Enter the details of the purchase invoices received for stock deliveries accepted against the following orders. Ensure that the system date is 31 January 1994 (see *Getting started*).

Purchaser	Invoice	Date	Order	Price	N/C
Flash Lighting	5081	05/01/94	50 table lamps	10.00	5004
Hand Craft	5082	08/01/94	45 single wardrobes	150.00	5002
			10 double wardrobes	180.00	5002
Artwork	5083	12/01/94	28 pictures	15.00	5007

Remember that Artwork is zero rated for VAT.

Purchaser	Invoice	Date	Order	Price	N/C
Seats and Things	5084	18/01/94	46 stools	10.00	5003
			25 chairs	100.00	5003
Wilminster	5085	23/01/94	500 metres carpeting	10.00	5005
Forward Bedding	5086	25/01/94	20 sets single bedding	20.00	5006
			30 sets double bedding	30.00	5006

1   When you have completed the entry of all the purchase invoices ensure that the Financial Controller screen is on display.

Saving the details automatically updates the appropriate accounts but does not amend the stock. To do this you will have to account for the addition of the stock using the **Adjustments-In** option in the Stock Control screen accessed via the **Stock Control** option in the Financial Controller screen. Do this now and complete this activity with the Financial Controller screen on display.

6.5   Entering a purchase credit note

When the delivery of bedding arrived from Forward Bedding it was found that five of the sets of double bedding were damaged. Unfortunately, this fact was only made known to the accounts department after the details of the purchase order had been entered into the accounting system and the stock records had been appropriately updated.

The five sets of bedding were returned to Forward Bedding who then issued a credit note. It is now required to enter this credit note into the accounting system and to record the reduction in stock of the five sets of double bedding. As in the case of entering sales credit notes, the production and processing of a purchase credit note follows the same sequence of actions as the production and processing of a purchase invoice.

Ensure that the Financial Controller is on display and that the system date is 31 January 1994 (see *Getting started*).

1 Select the **Purchase Ledger** then **Batched Data Entry** and then **Purchase Credit notes** to reveal the Purchase Credit Notes screen:

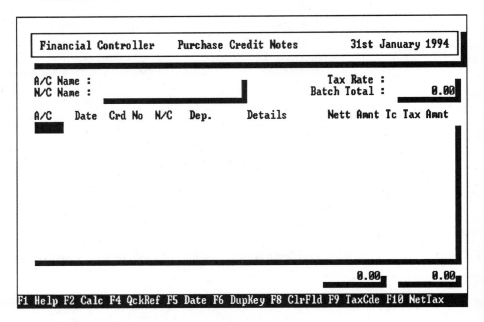

```
┌──────────────────────────────────────────────────────────────────┐
│ Financial Controller    Purchase Credit Notes      31st January 1994 │
│                                                                    │
│  A/C Name :                               Tax Rate :               │
│  N/C Name :                               Batch Total :      0.00   │
│                                                                    │
│  A/C    Date  Crd No  N/C  Dep.     Details      Nett Amnt Tc Tax Amnt │
│                                                                    │
│                                                                    │
│                                                                    │
│                                                                    │
│                                                              0.00        0.00 │
├──────────────────────────────────────────────────────────────────┤
│ F1 Help F2 Calc F4 QckRef F5 Date F6 DupKey F8 ClrFld F9 TaxCde F10 NetTax │
└──────────────────────────────────────────────────────────────────┘
```

As you will see this screen is identical in format to the invoice form that appears in the Invoice screen.

2 Enter the details of the returned bedding by following exactly the same procedures that you performed for the entry of an invoice. Use the nominal code **5006 Purchases - Fabrics**, enter the **Crd No** as **5086** - the same as the original invoice number - and enter the **Nett Amnt** as **150.00** and the **Date** as **26 January 1994**.

Complete this activity with the Financial Controller screen on display.

Posting the details automatically updates the appropriate accounts but does not amend the stock. To do this you will have to account for the abstraction of the stock using the **Adjustments-Out** option in the Stock Control screen accessed via the **Stock Control** option in the Financial Controller screen. Do this now and complete this activity with the Financial Controller screen on display.

Printing the purchase ledger balances

In a manual accounting system every purchase is recorded in a purchase ledger. It is also possible to print a purchase day book which is a list of purchases for a certain period. Within the Sage Sterling accounting system a printed list of supplier account balances can be obtained via the reporting facility of the purchase ledger. Ensure that the Financial Controller screen is on display.

1   Select the **Report Generator** option to reveal the Report Generator screen.

2   Select the **Purchase Ledger** option to reveal the Purchase Ledger reports screen:

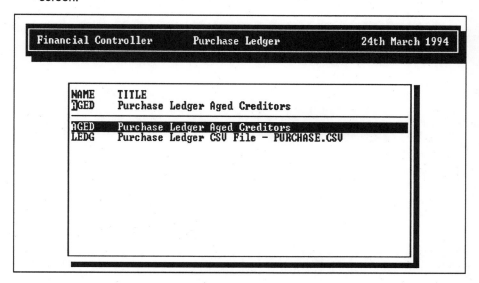

```
Financial Controller        Purchase Ledger        24th March 1994


        NAME    TITLE
        AGED    Purchase Ledger Aged Creditors

        AGED    Purchase Ledger Aged Creditors
        LEDG    Purchase Ledger CSV File - PURCHASE.CSV
```

3   Print the report:

AGED

4   When the report printing is complete press [Esc] twice to return to the Financial Controller screen.

From the printed report you can see, in the column headed **Balance**, the amounts outstanding that are owed by Total Bedrooms to the customers. In addition, under the columns **Current**, **30 days**, **60 days**, **90 days** and **Older** you will see the history of Total Bedrooms' indebtedness to their suppliers.

Backing up data to a floppy diskette

You have now completed Chapter Six and have entered data into the Sage Sterling Financial Controller accounting system which has been stored on your computer's hard disk. While the hard disk is a very reliable medium it is worthwhile reminding yourself that it is storing your only copy of the data and that the disk itself is not infallible. Data can be irretrievably lost if your hard disk fails. Therefore, it is advised that you back up your data onto a floppy diskette (refer to page xvi of *Getting started*).

A word of caution. When backing up data to a floppy diskette from your hard disk, all the current information in the data files on your hard disk is copied to the floppy diskette. As a consequence, it is always best to back up using the Backup/Restore facility available within the Sage Sterling Financial Controller accounting system which backs up and restores *all* the data files. If you use any other method which enables you to select which data files to back up or restore you may be tempted not to back up or restore all of your data files. In such an event your data could very easily become corrupted and, therefore, worthless.

Remember to take the diskette out of the floppy drive and to store it in a safe place.

Nominal ledger processing

Entering bank receipts

On 15th January, a cheque arrived from Main Line Hotels to the value of £3456.98 in settlement of their outstanding account. This was paid into the company's bank account on the same day and so this bank receipt must now be recorded in the company's accounting system.

Ensure that the Financial Controller screen is on display.

1   Select the **Sales Ledger** option to reveal the Sales Ledger screen.

2   Select the **Receipts** option to reveal the Customer Receipt screen:

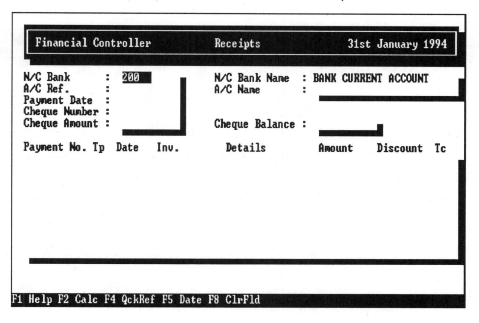

3   Press Enter to place the highlight against **A/C Ref.** and then use F4 to enter the customer account reference **M001**.

The **A/C Name** of the account fills in automatically as do the details of the opening balance and all outstanding invoices.

4   Enter the **Payment Date** as:

150194

5   Leave the **Cheque Number** box empty.

6   Enter the **Cheque Amount** as:

3456.98 and press ⌷ **Enter** ⌷.

Immediately the **Cheque Balance** box reads the same amount. The cheque balance refers to the amount of value left after a payment has been recorded. As no payment has yet been recorded the cheque balance is for the full amount of the cheque. Notice the legend that has appeared at the bottom of the screen:

```
Method of Payment : Automatic  Manual
```

7   Select **Automatic** and the highlight extends over the details of the first invoice numbered 1258 where the original Amount of 3456.98 has been replaced by 0.00 to indicate that the invoice has been paid.

The annotation FULL appears at the left-hand side of the invoice details to indicate that the invoice has been fully settled. Also, because the **Cheque Amount** was for just this amount the **Cheque Balance** now reads **0.00**:

```
┌────────────────────────────────────────────────────────────────────┐
│ Financial Controller          Receipts           31st January 1994  │
└────────────────────────────────────────────────────────────────────┘

 N/C Bank      : 1200        N/C Bank Name : BANK CURRENT ACCOUNT
 A/C Ref.      : M001        A/C Name      : Main Line Hotels Plc
 Payment Date  : 150194
 Cheque Number :
 Cheque Amount :     3456.98  Cheque Balance :       0.00

 Payment No. Tp Date   Inv.    Details         Amount   Discount  Tc
 FULL      5 SI 111093 1258  Opening Balance      0.00     0.00 T9
          6 SI 241193 1307  Opening Balance   6732.56     0.00 T9
          7 SI 171293 1321  Opening Balance   6389.36     0.00 T9
         49 SI 040194 1340  10 Double beds 102 1057.50    0.00 T1
```

8   Press ⌷ **Esc** ⌷ and post this payment to the ledgers.

The screen now clears in readiness for another another payment to be entered.

9   Press ⌷ **Esc** ⌷ twice to return to the Financial Controller screen.

Having entered Main Line Hotels' payment it will be instructive to see where it has had an effect.

10   Select the **Sales Ledger** option to reveal the Sales Ledger screen.

11   Select the **Transaction History** option to view the Transaction History screen.

12   Amend the default **Account Range** to read:

From: M001
To: M001

13 Display the transaction history of the Main Line Hotels account on your computer monitor.

Here you will see all the transactions that have been entered relevant to this account. In particular you will see that the customer receipt of 3456.98 has been recorded, thereby reducing the **Amount Outstanding**. Also, between the **Value** and the **Debit** columns, the marker * has been deleted alongside the first **Opening Balance** entry indicating that it has been paid.

14 Press Esc twice to return to the display of the Financial Controller screen.

By the end of January all those customers with an outstanding and due account had settled some of their outstanding debts. Enter the following customer payments as bank receipts using the date as 31/01/94 for each one:

Customer	Payment
Budget Hostelry	2398.31
George Hotel	2115.00
Gibbert Arms	2174.08
Innkeepers Plc	1256.67
Queens Hotel	6745.12
The Regency	1777.77
The Swallows Nest	1616.13

Conclude this activity with the Financial Controller screen on display.

7.2   Entering bank payments

On 17th January, Total Bedrooms sent a cheque to the value of £8345.91 to Wilminster Carpets Ltd in payment towards the outstanding balance. This bank payment must now be recorded in the company's accounting system.

Ensure that the Financial Controller screen is on display.

1 Select the **Puchase Ledger** option to reveal the Purchase Ledger screen.

2 Select the **Payments** option to reveal the Payments screen:

```
┌─────────────────────────────────────────────────────────────────┐
│  ┌───────────────────────────────────────────────────────────┐   │
│  │ Financial Controller      Payments      31st January 1994 │   │
│  └───────────────────────────────────────────────────────────┘   │
│                                                                   │
│  N/C Bank      : 1200         N/C Bank Name : BANK CURRENT ACCOUNT │
│  A/C Ref.      :              A/C Name      :                     │
│  Payment Date  :                                                  │
│  Cheque Number :                                                  │
│  Cheque Amount :              Cheque Balance :                    │
│                                                                   │
│  Payment No. Tp  Date   Inv.     Details      Amount  Discount  Tc│
│                                                                   │
│                                                                   │
│                                                                   │
│                                                                   │
│                                                                   │
│                                                                   │
└─────────────────────────────────────────────────────────────────┘
```

3 Press **Enter** and then use **F4** to enter the customer account **WILM** in the box labelled **A/C Ref.**

The **A/C Name** of the account fills in automatically as does the default date and all outstanding amounts.

4 Enter the **Payment Date** as:

170194

5 Enter the **Cheque Number** as:

1240

6 Enter the **Cheque Amount** as:

8345.91

The legend appears at the bottom of the screen:

```
Method of Payment : Automatic   Manual
```

7 Select **Manual** and press **Enter** to ensure that the highlight extends over the details of the first invoice numbered 5031 to the value £8345.91.

8 Press **Esc** and the following legend appears at the bottom of the screen:

```
Type of Payment : Full Part Discount Cancel
```

9 Select **Full** and press **Enter**.

The annotation FULL appears at the left-hand side of the invoice details and the Amount changes to 0.00 to indicate that the invoice has been fully settled. Also, because the **Cheque Amount** was for just this amount the **Cheque Balance** now reads **0.00**:

10   Press Esc and post this payment to the ledgers.

11   Press Esc twice to return to the Financial Controller screen.

Having entered Wilminster Carpets' payment it will be instructive to see where it has had an effect in the accounts.

12   Select the **Purchase Ledger** option to reveal the Purchase Ledger screen.

13   Select the **Transaction History** option and view the transaction history of the WILM account on your computer monitor.

Here you will see all the transactions that have been entered relevant to this account. In particular you will see that the **Supplier Payment** of **8345.91** has been recorded, thereby reducing the **Amount Outstanding**.

14   Press Esc twice to return to the display of the Financial Controller screen.

EXERCISE   By the end of January Total Bedrooms had paid money to all those suppliers with outstanding and due accounts. Enter the following supplier payments via the Payments screen using the default date 31 January 1994:

Customer	Payment	Cheque No.
Commercial Carpenters	1265.98	1241
Hand Craft Ltd	791.35	1242
Sleepwell Ltd	2223.67	1243

In addition to paying suppliers Total Bedrooms' VAT liability up to December 1993 is now due. This VAT liability was recorded as the opening balance of £16,671.82 in the account 2201 VAT Liability.

1   From the Financial Controller screen select the **Nominal Ledger** option followed by the **Bank Transactions** and then the **Bank Payments** options to reveal the Payments screen.

2   Pay HM Customs & Excise £16,671.82 as a bank payment:

N/C   2201
Dep   0
Date   280194
Cheque 1244
Details Last quarter 1993
Nett   16671.82
Tc   T0

At any time a listing may be required of suppliers and customers whose accounts have been settled or part settled. This can be obtained via the **Nominal Ledger** option in the Financial Controller screen.

Ensure that the Financial Controller screen is on display.

1　Select the **Nominal Ledger** option in the Financial Controller screen to reveal the Nominal Ledger screen.

2　Select the **Day Books** option to reveal the Day Books screen:

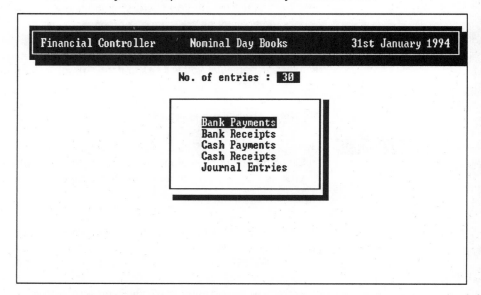

This **Day Books** option is a report that permits a listing to be obtained of all the transactions involving bank and cash payments and receipts over a specified period of time. It also permits a list of journal entries to be obtained.

3　Select the **Bank Payments** option to reveal the Bank Payments screen:

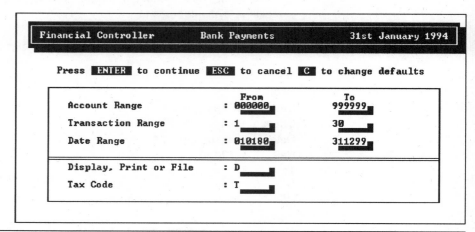

4   Accept all the defaults in the screen and produce a display on your computer monitor of all the payments made into the Bank Current Account.

5   Clear this display and obtain a printed version of the same report.

6   Repeat the above procedure to obtain first a screen display of the bank receipts and then a printout of the same report.

Conclude this activity with the Financial Controller screen on display.

7.4   Backing up data to a floppy diskette

You have now completed Chapter Seven and have entered data into the Sage Sterling Financial Controller accounting system which has been stored on your computer's hard disk. While the hard disk is a very reliable medium it is worthwhile reminding yourself that it is storing your only copy of the data and that the disk itself is not infallible. Data can be irretrievably lost if your hard disk fails. Therefore, it is advised that you back up your data onto a floppy diskette (refer to page xvi of *Getting started*).

 A word of caution. When backing up data to a floppy diskette from your hard disk, all the current information in the data files on your hard disk is copied to the floppy diskette. As a consequence, it is always best to back up using the Backup/Restore facility available within the Sage Sterling Financial Controller accounting system which backs up and restores *all* the data files. If you use any other method which enables you to select which data files to back up or restore you may be tempted not to back up or restore all of your data files. In such an event your data could very easily become corrupted and, therefore, worthless.

Remember to take the diskette out of the floppy drive and to store it in a safe place.

8   Trial balance

8.1   What is a trial balance?

At the end of each accounting period it is necessary to produce the company's financial statements which will give users information about the company's profit and state of affairs. Before these statements are produced it is advisable to ensure that the accounting information has been correctly entered into the ledger accounts. In a manual system it is necessary to calculate the balance on each ledger account and then list the debit and credit balances and ensure that the two columns agree. This list of balances is called a trial balance. The agreement of the trial balance will hopefully ensure that in the majority of cases the information has been correctly entered and can be used as the basis of the company's financial statements.

In the Sage Sterling accounting system this procedure is produced automatically either printed or displayed on the screen. This procedure is extremely simple to carry out so that it is possible to produce a trial balance at more frequent intervals than just at the end of the accounting period. This has the advantage of maintaining a continual check on the accuracy of the nominal ledger, thereby permitting an early warning of any errors occurring and enabling efficient error correction.

8.2   Printing a trial balance

Ensure that the Financial Controller screen is on display.

  1   Select the **Nominal Ledger** option in the Financial Controller screen to reveal the Nominal Ledger screen.

2   Select the **Trial Balance** option to reveal the Trial Balance screen:

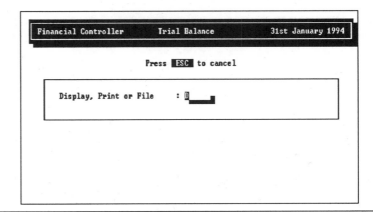

```
Financial Controller        Trial Balance           31st January 1994


                         Press  ESC  to cancel


      Display, Print or File      : D
```

3   Press [Enter] to accept the **Display** default and the Trial Balance is displayed
on your computer monitor

In the box in the centre of this screen you will see listed the first twelve of all those
nominal ledger accounts that have a non-zero balance. To see all the relevant
accounts you will have to use the [Enter] or [PgDn] key. Each account balance is
registered as either a credit or a debit and just below the information panel you will
see that the total debits add up to the same figure as the total credits.

From this information it is now possible to prepare financial statements from the
accounts by using the ledger as the basis for preparation.

EXERCISE   1   Press [Esc] and produce a printed version of this report.

Ref.	Accounts Name	Debit	Credit
0010	FREEHOLD PROPERTY	50000.00	
0040	FURNITURE AND FIXTURES	15000.00	
0041	F/F DEPRECIATION		7500.00
0050	MOTOR VEHICLES	30000.00	
0051	M/V DEPRECIATION		15000.00
1100	DEBTORS CONTROL ACCOUNT	44702.05	
1200	BANK CURRENT ACCOUNT	185.15	
2100	CREDITORS CONTROL ACCOUNT		70051.70
2200	TAX CONTROL ACCOUNT	2927.92	
2300	LOANS		50000.00
3000	ORDINARY SHARES		50000.00
3200	PROFIT AND LOSS ACCOUNT		58438.42
4001	Sales – Beds		2460.00
4002	Sales – Furniture		2560.00
4003	Sales – Seating		934.00
4004	Sales – Lighting		220.00
4005	Sales – Carpeting		1800.00
4006	Sales – Fabrics		680.00
4007	Sales – Sundries		325.00
5001	Purchases – Beds	2600.00	
5002	Purchases – Furniture	8550.00	
5003	Purchases – Seating	2960.00	
5004	Purchases – Lighting	500.00	
5005	Purchases – Carpeting	5000.00	
5006	Purchases – Fabrics	1150.00	
5007	Purchases – Sundries	420.00	
5200	OPENING STOCK	95539.00	
7103	GENERAL RATES	2000.00	
7200	ELECTRICITY		515.00
7304	MISC. MOTOR EXPENSES		300.00
7504	OFFICE STATIONERY		750.00
		261534.12	261534.12

Complete this activity with the Financial Controller screen on display.

End of Part I reports

Restoring data from a floppy diskette

At the end of each of the preceding chapters you have been advised to back up the data files in the Sage Sterling Financial Controller accounting system. If you have not done this then do so now, assuming that you have entered all the data up to and including Chapter Seven. (For backing up, refer to *Getting started* .)

Having backed up the data files to a floppy diskette, we now wish to demonstrate how they can be restored back to the hard disk.

1   Place the floppy diskette containing the backed up files in drive A or drive B, depending upon which drive is appropriate for your system.

2   Ensure that the Financial Controller screen is on display.

3   Select the **Utilities** option to reveal the Utilities screen:

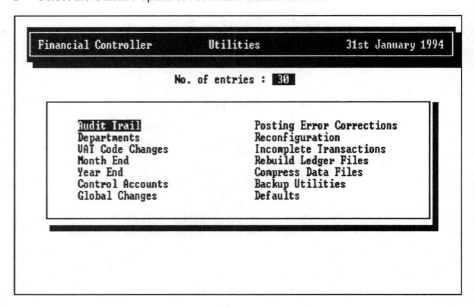

```
Financial Controller          Utilities          31st January 1994

                         No. of entries : 30

        Audit Trail                  Posting Error Corrections
        Departments                  Reconfiguration
        VAT Code Changes             Incomplete Transactions
        Month End                    Rebuild Ledger Files
        Year End                     Compress Data Files
        Control Accounts             Backup Utilities
        Global Changes               Defaults
```

4   Select the **Backup Utilities** option to reveal the Backup Utilities screen:

```
        Backup Data Files
        Restore Data Files
```

5   Select the **Restore Data Files** option to reveal the following annotation:

     Do you want to Restore your data files : No Yes

6   Select **Yes** and the following message appears:

     Restore files from drive A

7   If you are using drive B then amend this display and press Enter . If the display
     is correct then just press Enter .

A verification message appears:

> It is recommended that you run Data Verification after
>
> loading to check that the restored data is valid

8   Press Enter and a window opens up below the verification message and lists
     the files that are being restored as and when they are restored.

When the restoration is complete you are returned to the Backup Utilities screen.

9   Press Esc twice to return to the Financial Controller screen.

10   Take the diskette out of the floppy drive and store it in a safe place.

9.2   Data verification

In compliance with the warning that was issued in the Verification window just prior
to restoring the data files we shall now activate the verification program and verify
the files. This procedure cannot be performed from within the Sage Sterling Financial Controller as it is part of a separate utility program called the Disk Doctor.

 1   Ensure that the Financial Controller screen is on display and select the **Quit**
     option and leave the system, returning to the DOS prompt display:

     C:\SAGE>

2   Type in at the DOS prompt:

     DOCTOR and press Enter .

The Disk Doctor screen appears:

```
Financial Controller Terminated


C:\SAGE>doctor

Sagesoft  (R) Disk Doctor Utility - V5.1
Copyright (C) The Sage Group plc 1988-1992

Error    on ACCOUNT.DTA  : File does not exist
Warning on CATEGORY.DTA  : File does not exist
Warning on DEPARMT.DTA   : File does not exist

  1 error(s)   found
  2 warning(s) found

Attempt a reconstruction of the ACCOUNT.DTA file based on the existing
data in the other Ledger files - (Y/N) ? _
```

3   Type **Y** and the screen message adds the following:

```
You can select the Profit & Loss Report format or Balance Sheet format
options to create a new CATEGORY.DTA file. Alternatively, restore or copy
the CATEGORY.DTA file only from a backup disk. You may need to set up the
Monthly Accounts report formats again.

Press any key to continue
```

4   Press any key and the following message appears:

```
You can select the Departments option to create a new DEPARMT.DTA file.
Alternatively, restore or copy the DEPARMT.DTA file only from a backup
disk. You may need to set up the Department Names again.

Press any key to continue
```

5   Press any key and the ACCOUNT.DTA file is reconstructed:

```
*** Reconstruct ACCOUNT.DTA file ***

Reconstructing POSTING.DTA and STKCAT.DTA files
Reconstructing SALINDEX.DTA and SALES.DTA files
Reconstructing PURINDEX.DTA and PURCHASE.DTA files
Reconstructing NOMINDEX.DTA and NOMINAL.DTA files

Resetting Control Account Links

ACCOUNT.DTA File Reconstructed successfully

You MUST run the Disk Doctor program again to rebuild the Audit Trail
links. The reconstructed Ledger files are not yet correctly linked with
the transaction file.

Do you want to run the DISK DOCTOR again - (Y/N) ?
```

6   Enter **N** and you are returned to the DOS prompt.

To complete the Elementary section of this book we shall print a selection of reports
that can be used to give an overall view of what it is that we have done in this
section. The first report will describe the various transactions that have been

entered against accounts in the sales ledger.

9.3 Customer reports

Ensure that the Financial Controller window is on display and that the system date is 31/01/94.

1   Select the **Sales Ledger** option to reveal the Sales Ledger screen.

2   Select the **Transaction History** option to reveal the Transaction History screen.

3   Accept the **Account Range** defaults but amend the third default to **P** instead of **D** so that the report will be sent to the printer instead of the computer monitor.

4   Send the report to the printer.

Complete this activity with the Financial Controller screen on display.

5   Select the **Report Generator** option to reveal the Report Generator screen.

6   Select the **Sales Ledger** option to reveal the Sales Ledger Report screen.

7   Print the AGED report.

Complete this activity with the Financial Controller screen on display.

The next reports will describe the various transactions that have been entered against accounts in the purchase ledger.

9.4 Supplier reports

Ensure that the Financial Controller screen is on display and that the system date is 31/01/94.

1   Select the **Purchase Ledger** option to reveal the Purchase Ledger screen.

2   Select the **Transaction History** option to reveal the Transaction History screen.

3   Accept the **Account Range** defaults but amend the third default to **P** instead of **D** so that the report will be sent to the printer instead of the computer monitor.

4   Send the report to the printer.

Complete this activity with the Financial Controller screen on display.

5   Select the **Report Generator** option to reveal the Report Generator screen.

6   Select the **Purchase Ledger** option to reveal the Purchase Ledger Report screen.

7   Print the AGED report.

Complete this activity with the Financial Controller screen on display.

The third set of reports will describe the history and the current state of the stock. This will enable us to correlate the sales and purchase transactions to the stock history.

9.5 **Stock reports**

Ensure that the Financial Controller screen is on display and that the system date is 31/01/94.

 1   Select the **Stock Control** option to reveal the Stock Control screen.

2   Select the **Stock History** option to reveal the Stock history screen.

3   Print a copy of the stock **History** report.

Complete this activity with the Financial Controller screen on display.

4   Select the **Report Generator** option to reveal the Report Generator screen.

5   Select the **Stock Control** option to reveal the Stock Control Report screen.

6   Print the TRANS report.

Complete this activity with the Financial Controller screen on display.

By comparing these three sets of reports see if you can connect specific sales and purchase transactions with specific stock transactions. In this way you will increase your appreciation of the interconnectivity of the Sage Sterling Financial Controller accounting system.

9.6 **Nominal ledger reports**

The fourth set of reports we wish to generate describes the current state of the nominal accounts. However, as we shall see, a large number of accounts will not contribute to this report because they have not yet been activated.

Ensure that the Financial Controller screen is on display.

1   Select the **Nominal Ledger** button to reveal the Nominal Ledger screen.

2   Select the **Transaction History** option to reveal the Transaction History screen.

3   Accept all the defaults and send the report to the printer.

To complete this activity see if you can relate entries in this nominal ledger report with entries in the customer and suppliers' **Activity** reports.

Also look at the tax control account 2200. When a customer pays the company VAT against a sales invoice then the company holds that money for HM Customs and Excise. When the company pays VAT to a supplier against a purchase invoice then the company is entitled to claim that money back from HM Customs and Excise. From the information in the tax control account can you see whether the company owes money to HM Customs and Excise or whether HM Customs and Excise owes money to the company?

9.7   The audit trail

The audit trail is a report that lists every transaction that has been entered into the Sage Sterling Financial controller accounting system. The British Computer Society defines an audit trail as *a record of the file updating that takes place during a specific transaction. It enables a trace to be kept on files.* The audit trail gives the user the ability to trace input to output and vice versa. The audit trail will be used by auditors as part of their check of the computer system. It is available as a standard report via the **Utilities** option in the Financial Controller screen.

Ensure that the system date is 31/01/94 and print a copy of the audit trail report for transactions between 01/01/94 and 31/01/94 and correlate the entries in this report with all the entries in the customer, supplier and nominal reports that you have just generated.

Part II

Intermediate level

More nominal ledger processing

The principle of double-entry book-keeping is that the sum of all the account debits must equal the sum of all the account credits. In Chapter 8, where we produced a trial balance, we saw this principle in action when we displayed a balanced set of accounts.

This balance was achieved automatically because all our information input was under the double-entry processing control of the Sage Sterling accounting system. This meant that whenever a debit was entered into the system an appropriate corresponding credit was automatically entered by the system and vice versa.

There are occasions, however, when such double-entry book-keeping is not automatically available. Take, for instance, the company's purchase of a second-hand van to enable the collection of small items of stock to avoid excessive delivery charges. There is no purchase account in the name of the company from whom the van was purchased and so the automatic entry of the purchase transaction into the nominal ledger, normally done via an entry into the purchase ledger, is not available. Instead we must enter the details of the purchase directly into the nominal ledger taking account as we do so that *any debit must be counterbalanced by an appropriate credit and vice vers*a. Such entries are referred to as journal entries.

10.1   Journal entries

Ensure that the Financial Controller screen is on display and that the system date is 31 January 1994.

1   From the Financial Controller screen select the **Nominal Ledger** option to reveal the Nominal Ledger screen.

2   Select the **Journal Entries** option to reveal the Journal Entries screen with a Journal Entry form displayed:

```
┌─────────────────────────────────────────────────────────────┐
│  Financial Controller      Journal Entries      31st January 1994 │
│                                                               │
│       Date : ▮              Reference :                       │
│   N/C Name :                Batch Total :           0.00      │
│                                                               │
│         N/C   Dep.   Details    Tc   Debit    Credit          │
│                                                               │
│                                                               │
│                                                               │
│                                                               │
│                                                               │
│                                                               │
│           Batch Total  MUST  be  ZERO  before exit            │
└─────────────────────────────────────────────────────────────┘
```

Total Bedrooms have purchased a second-hand van for £8000.00 plus VAT at 17.5%, giving a total payment of:

£8000.00 + £1400.00 = £9400.00

You might like to check this using the Calculator that can be accessed via the F2 key.

Having checked the total cost of the van, this purchase must be entered into the Journal Entry form as:

9400 Credit to Nominal Code 1200 for Bank Current Account

This accounts for the payment out of the bank account for the total purchase and is balanced by the total debit comprising:

8000 Debit to Nominal Code 0050 for Motor Vehicles
1400 Debit to Nominal Code 2201 for Purchase Tax Control Account

3   Enter the **Date** as:

260194

4   Enter **Reference** as:

004 to identify the journal entry.

Numbering journal entries in this way means that any vouchers associated with the transaction can have the number written on them so that they can be stored in numerical sequence.

5 Enter the debits and credit as described in the following list using Department (**Dep.**) 3 for administration.

Notice that as you enter each item the **Batch Total** entry changes automatically. When you have entered the last item the **Batch Total** entry will be zero:

N/C	Name	Details	Tc	Debit	Credit
1200	Bank Current Account	Van Purchase	T9		9400.00
0050	Motor Vehicles	Van	T9	8000.00	
2200	Tax Control Account	VAT on van	T9	1400.00	

As journal entries are normally a transfer of amounts between nominal accounts that do not involve VAT, the tax code would normally be T9. Whatever code you use the program will not calculate the VAT for you, nor will it automatically post the VAT to the VAT control account. If, as here, there is an element of VAT associated with the journal entry then it must be included as a line in the entry with the appropriate debit or credit to the VAT control account. In this case we use the nominal account 2200 which is reserved for VAT and must be used whenever VAT is entered in this way.

6 Press Esc and post the details to the ledgers.

7 Press Esc to return to the Nominal Ledger screen.

You may now wish to look through the **Transaction History** reports available in the Nominal Ledger to see the effect of the posting that you have just made.

Complete this activity with the Financial Controller screen on display.

10.2 Prepayments

Prepayments are adjustments to the accounts to enable the preparation of an accurate set of final accounts. If you pay an expense in advance, the expense will be spread over the months to which it relates, rather than being accounted for in the month in which it was paid. For example, Total Bedrooms received a bill that was due on the 15th January for their premises insurance. The amount of the premium was £3534.00 and it gives insurance cover for a full year. Whilst the account was settled on the 15th January the benefit is felt throughout the year. Accordingly this payment was recorded as a prepayment spread over 12 months.

Ensure that the Financial Controller screen is on display.

1 Enter the payment of the insurance premium on the 15th January 1994 as a journal entry against Department 3 and with **Ref 005** by:

Crediting the account 1200 Bank Current Account with 3534.00
Debiting the account 7104 Premises Insurance with 3534.00

When the journal entry has been saved to disk:

2   Press ⌈Esc⌉ to display the Nominal Ledger screen.

3   Select the **Prepayments and Accruals** option to display the Prepayments and
     Accruals screen:

4   Select the **Prepayments** option to reveal the Prepayments screen:

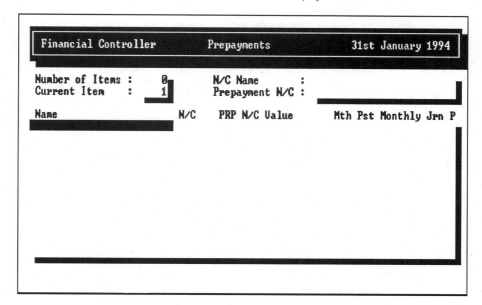

5   Enter the **Name** as:

Premium for 1994

The **PRP N/C** entry of **1103** is automatically entered by the system. This is the
nominal code for the Prepayments Account.

6   Use ⌈F4⌉ to enter the nominal code (**N/C**) entry as:

7104 - the code for Premises Insurance

7   Enter the **Value** as:

3534.00 - the amount paid

The next column headed **Mth** relates to the number of months over which this
amount must be spread, namely the full year.

8   Enter **Mth** as **12** and the **Monthly** (monthly amount) of **294.50** is automatically entered by the Sage Sterling accounting system.

Note: No entry can be made under **Pst** or **P** - for posted - at this time. The entry here is done automatically by the Sage Sterling accounting system when these details are posted to the ledgers during the month end routine.

9   Press $\boxed{\text{Esc}}$ to save this information to disk. No accounting is done as a result of saving this prepayment. The entry to the nominal ledger is only made when the Month End function is used. We shall say more about the recording of prepayments when we execute the month end procedures.

EXERCISE   1   Enter the following prepayment, having first made an appropriate journal entry against Department 3 with reference **006** and **Date 05/01/94** for postage and carriage:

Nominal code 7501 - Postage and Carriage at £235.00 over the next three months

10.3   Accruals

Accruals, like prepayments, are adjustments to the accounts to enable the preparation of an accurate set of final accounts. An accrual is an amount of money where you have incurred the expense, but the invoice has not yet been received. The most common accruals are gas, electricity and telephone bills. For example, Total Bedrooms expect to receive a bill for £1500 that will be due on the 20th April for their electricity consumption. Whilst the account will be settled on the 20th April the benefit is felt from January onwards. Accordingly this payment was recorded as an accrual.

Ensure that the Financial Controller screen is on display.

    1   Display the Nominal Ledger screen.

2   Select the **Prepayments and Accruals** option to display the Prepayments and Accruals screen.

3   Select the **Accruals** option to reveal the Accruals screen which, apart from the title, is identical in appearance to the Prepayments screen:

```
┌─────────────────────────────────────────────────────────────┐
│  ┌──────────────────────────────────────────────────────┐   │
│  │ Financial Controller      Accruals      31st January 1994│ │
│  └──────────────────────────────────────────────────────┘   │
│   Number of Items :   0     N/C Name    :                   │
│   Current Item    :   1     Accruals N/C :                   │
│                                                              │
│   Name                 N/C    ACR N/C Value   Mth Pst Monthly Jrn P │
│                                                              │
└─────────────────────────────────────────────────────────────┘
```

4   Enter the **Name** as:

Accrual for electricity

5   Use $\boxed{\text{F4}}$ to enter the nominal code (**N/C**) entry as:

7200 - the code for Electricity

The **ACR N/C** entry of **2109** is automatically entered by the system. This is the nominal code for the Accruals Account.

6   Enter the **Value** as:

1500

The next column headed **Mth** relates to the number of months to which the payment will relate, namely three.

7   Enter **Mth** as **3** and the **Monthly** (monthly amount) of **500** is automatically entered by the Sage Sterling accounting system.

Note: No entry can be made under **Pst** or **P** at this time. The entry here is done automatically by the Sage Sterling accounting system when these details are posted to the ledgers during the month end routine.

8   Press $\boxed{\text{Esc}}$ to save this information to disk. No accounting is done as a result of saving this accrual. The entry to the nominal ledger is only made when the Month End function is used. We shall say more about the recording of accruals when we execute the month end procedures.

1 Enter the following accrual:

Nominal code 7502 - Telephone at £1200.00 over the next three months

10.4 Depreciation

Depreciation is a reduction in the value of a fixed asset due to its use. This may be caused by wear and tear as in the case of a vehicle or it may be due to obsolescence as in the case of a computer used within the business.

Within the Sage Sterling +2 accounting system there are two ways of accounting for depreciation. The first is called straight line depreciation where the original cost of the asset is spread out over its useful life. For example, a car costing £8,000 with an estimated useful life of 4 years would have its cost of £8,000 spread evenly at £2,000 per year over the four years.

The second method of accounting for depreciation is called the reducing balance method where the asset loses a fixed percentage of its reduced balance each year. For example, office equipment may depreciate by 15% of its current value per year. This means that its value will never depreciate to zero. There will come a time, however, when its value will have reduced to such an extent that it is virtually worthless but still remains accounted for. When the asset is sold or scrapped this small amount will be removed from the Fixed Assets account.

Ensure that the Financial Controller screen is on display.

 1 Display the Nominal Ledger screen.

2 Select the **Depreciation** option to reveal the Depreciation screen:

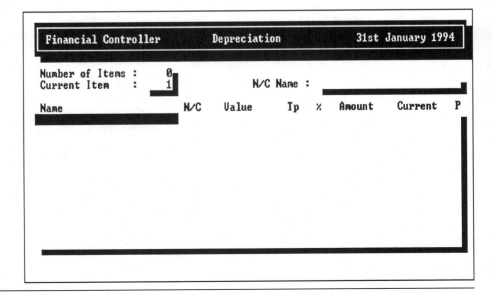

3   Enter the **Name** as:

Fleet depreciation

4   Use F4 to enter the nominal code (**N/C**) entry as:

0051 (Motor vehicles Depreciation)

5   Enter the **Value** as:

15000

You will notice that the value recorded for the motor vehicles in account 0050 is £30,000. A two-year depreciation of £15,000.00 has already been posted leaving a residual value of £15,000 whose depreciation is to be spread over a further two years.

The next column headed **Tp** relates to the type of depreciation.

6   Enter **Tp** as **S** for straight line depreciation.

This means that over two years the rate of depreciation must be 50% per year.

7   Enter the rate of depreciation (**%**) as:

50

The **Amount** of **625.00** is automatically entered by the Sage Sterling accounting system and is the monthly amount of depreciation that will be recorded in the accounts. Also recorded is the **15000** in the **Current** column which records the current book value of the asset.

Note: No entry can be made under **P** at this time. The entry here is done automatically by the Sage Sterling +2 accounting system when these details are posted to the ledgers during the month end routine.

8   Press Esc to save this information to disk. No accounting is done as a result of saving this depreciation charge. The entry to the nominal ledger is only made when the Month End function is used. We shall say more about the recording of depreciation when we execute the month end procedures.

9   Enter the following depreciation:

Nominal code 0041 - (Furniture/Fixture Depreciation) with a current value 7500 depreciating at 15% by reducing balance - coded as **R** under the heading **Tp**.

You have now completed Chapter Ten and have entered data into the Sage Sterling Financial Controller accounting system which has been stored on your computer's hard disk. While the hard disk is a very reliable medium it is worthwhile reminding yourself that it is storing your only copy of the data and that the disk itself is not infallible. Data can be irretrievably lost if your hard disk fails. Therefore, it is advised that you back up your data onto a floppy diskette (refer to page xvi of *Getting started*).

 A word of caution. When backing up data to a floppy diskette from your hard disk, all the current information in the data files on your hard disk is copied to the floppy diskette. As a consequence, it is always best to back up using the Backup/Restore facility available within the Sage Sterling Financial Controller accounting system which backs up and restores *all* the data files. If you use any other method which enables you to select which data files to back up or restore you may be tempted not to back up or restore all of your data files. In such an event your data could very easily become corrupted and, therefore, worthless.

Remember to take the diskette out of the floppy drive and to store it in a safe place.

11

Further ledger processing

Total Bedrooms have a large insurance commitment that covers all their employees, stock and public liability. This insurance cover is very expensive and to ease the burden of payment Total Bedrooms have negotiated with the insurance company an arrangement whereby they pay for their insurance cover monthly by direct debit, payable on the first day of the month. Such a payment, of a fixed amount each month, is referred to as a recurring payment and is entered into the accounts as such. To avoid the tedium of entering such regular payments every month there is a facility within the Sage Sterling +2 accounting system that permits automatic posting of recurring entries to the ledgers.

11.1 Recurring entries

Total Bedrooms have arranged to pay for their insurance commitment by direct debit on the 1st of every month and the currently agreed monthly amount is £456.75 exclusive of VAT. This payment recurs every month and to avoid having to enter the transaction into the Sage Sterling accounting system each month it can be automatically accounted for by recording the amount as a recurring entry.

Ensure that the Financial Controller screen is on display and that the system date is 31 January 1994.

  1   Display the Nominal Ledger screen.

2   Select the **Recurring Entries** option to reveal the Recurring Entries screen:

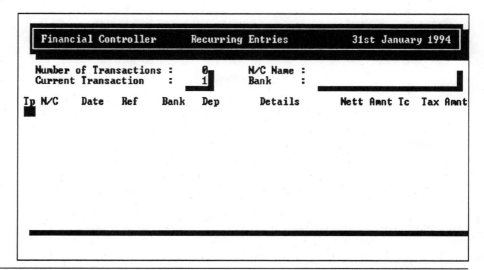

```
Financial Controller      Recurring Entries        31st January 1994

Number of Transactions :      0     N/C Name :
Current Transaction    :      1     Bank     :

Tp N/C   Date   Ref    Bank   Dep      Details      Nett Amnt Tc   Tax Amnt
```

The cursor is flashing in the box headed **Tp. Tp** stands for Type of transaction to be entered and the possible options are:

Bank payments coded	BP
Bank receipts coded	BR
Journal credits coded	JC
Journal debits coded	JD

3   Under **Tp**, enter the code:

BP for bank payment

4   Use F4 to enter the nominal code (**N/C**) entry as:

8204 - the code for Insurance

The next column headed **Date** refers to the day on which the entry is to be posted to the ledgers. Posting of recurring entries to the ledgers is activated as a procedure that is distinct from the current procedure of entering the details of the transaciton. We shall see later how this is achieved.

5   To enter the **Date** press F5 . The entry is displayed as:

TODAY

This means that when the recurring entry is posted then the date is automatically taken to be the current system date.

6   Enter the **Ref** as

001

7   The **Bank** code was automatically entered as:

1200

8   Enter the **Dep** as:

3 for Administration

9   Enter the **Details** as:

Insurance

10   Enter the **Nett Amnt** as:

456.75

11 Enter the tax code (**Tc**) as:

T0   at the time of writing insurance premiums are not liable to VAT.

12 Press Esc to save the details of this recurring entry to disk.

The details of the recurring entry have been saved to the disk but they have not yet been posted to the ledgers.

EXERCISE 1 Enter the following recurring entry with **Ref 002**:

Nominal Code 7901 - Bank charges; a non-taxable bank payment of £150.00 per month payable on the 28th of the month

Complete this activity with the Financial Controller screen on display.

11.2 Bank statements

Each month the bank sends Total Bedrooms a copy of their bank statement on which is recorded all Total Bedrooms' bank transactions that have passed through the bank's accounting system. In addition, any charges, standing orders and direct debits that may have been incurred or activated are also included.

Whilst this statement will represent a record of the bank's accounts at the date at which it was produced it will not represent a record of Total Bedrooms' accounts in their bank current account in the accounting system. There will undoubtedly be bank receipts and payments made that have been recorded in Total Bedrooms' accounts but which have not appeared on the bank's statement due to the time that it takes for a payment or receipt to be cleared by the banking system. Also, items such as bank charges may not have been included in Total Bedrooms' accounts as they will not know exactly what they are until they receive a statement from the bank.

As a result some reconciliation is necessary between the bank statement as issued by the bank and the existing state of Total Bedrooms' bank account. To effect this reconciliation it is first necessary to have a copy of the bank account produced from Total Bedrooms' accounts so as to be able to compare it with the bank statement produced from the bank's accounts.

11.3 Bank statement printing

Ensure that the Financial Controller screen is on display.

1 Display the Nominal Ledger screen.

2 Select the **Bank Statement** option to reveal the Bank Statement screen:

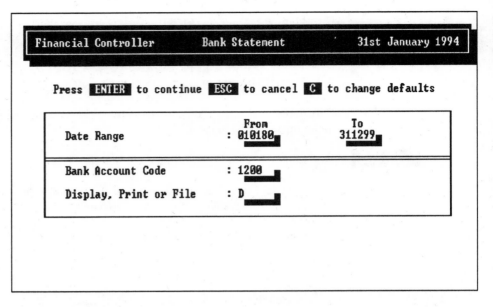

```
┌─────────────────────────────────────────────────────────────────┐
│  Financial Controller      Bank Statement        31st January 1994 │
│                                                                     │
│     Press ENTER to continue ESC to cancel C to change defaults     │
│    ┌──────────────────────────────────────────────────────────┐   │
│    │                              From           To            │   │
│    │   Date Range            : 010180▪       311299▪           │   │
│    │ ─────────────────────────────────────────────────────────│   │
│    │   Bank Account Code     : 1200▪                           │   │
│    │                                                           │   │
│    │   Display, Print or File : D▪                             │   │
│    └──────────────────────────────────────────────────────────┘   │
│                                                                     │
└─────────────────────────────────────────────────────────────────┘
```

3   Press **C** to change the defaults.

4   Change the bottom default from **D** to:

    P

5   Press **Enter** and send the bank statement to the printer.

The company's bank account as recorded by the company's accounts is then sent to the printer leaving the Nominal Ledger screen on display.

As yet no transactions have yet been reconciled so there are only unreconciled transactions listed.

We shall refer to this bank statement, which is simply a printout of Total Bedrooms' bank current account, as the nominal list of transactions to distinguish it from the bank statement produced by the bank. Notice that Payments and Receipts are recorded separately for convenience.

11.4   Adjustments to the nominal list of transactions

Reconciling the printout of Total Bedrooms' bank current account with the bank statement as issued by the bank is a matter of ensuring that those items on the bank statement are also included in Total Bedrooms' accounts. When the bank statement is received from the bank this may not be the case.

Before we can reconcile the nominal list of transactions in Total Bedrooms' bank current account with the bank statement as issued by the bank we need to make some adjustments to the list. We start by displaying the Bank Reconciliation - Bank Current Account screen.

1   From the Nominal Ledger screen select the **Bank Reconciliation** option to reveal the Bank Reconciliation screen:

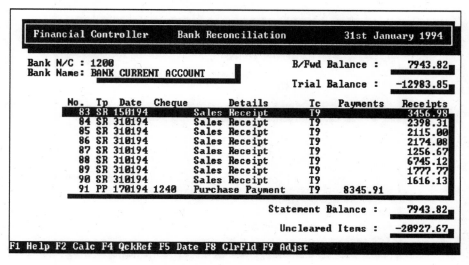

At the bottom of this screen are two totals:

Statement Balance recording   7943.82
Uncleared Items recording   -20927.67

Neither of these totals agrees with the final total balance on your bank statement of (12,552.50) received from the bank. This is not surprising as there are more transactions listed in the bank current account that you have just printed than are listed in the bank statement issued by the bank. However, all the transactions that are recorded on the bank statement are also recorded in the printed bank current account except for a bank service charge of 14.55 which represents charges for services in addition to those already paid for by standing order to the value of £150.00 per month. This charge, recorded on the bank statement, must now be added to the nominal list of transactions.

2   Press the **Adjustment** key F9 (labelled **Adjst**) to reveal the Adjustment screen:

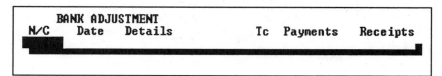

3   Use F4 to enter the nominal ledger account (**N/C**) as:

7901 the code for Bank Charges

4   Enter the **Date** as:

180194   the date the charge was levied according to your bank statement

5   Enter **Details** as:

Extra bank charges

6   Enter **Tc** as:

T0   0.00%

7   Enter **Payment** as:

14.55

8   Press **Esc** and post these details to the ledgers.

This transaction is now recorded in the ledgers as a cheque payment and appears at the bottom of the nominal list of transactions on your monitor screen.

9   Press **Esc** to reveal the following window:

```
Mark Transactions As Reconciled <Y or N> ? Y
```

10   Enter **Y** and press **Enter** to mark the selected transaction as reconciled and to return to the Nominal Ledger screen.

Note: Adjustments are written to the nominal ledger at this stage. If you subsequently abandon the reconciliation procedure the adjustments made will not be reversed.

11.5   Bank statement reconciliation

Finally, we must reconcile the final total recorded on your bank statement with the information in this screen by selecting items in this screen that are also on your bank statement. This is done by clicking them to highlight them in reverse video.

1   Display the Bank Reconciliation screen.

2   Move the highlight to each listed transaction in turn and press **Enter** .

The transaction then becomes selected as indicated by the change in the colour or intensity of the highlight.

---

3   Select every transaction description except:

PP Supplier Payment to SLEEP of value 2223.67
SR Customer Deposit with Ref 20 and value 1777.77

These two transactions do not appear on the bank statement but all the remaining selected transactions do. The totals should now read:

Statement Balance recording -12552.50
Uncleared Items recording   -445.90

All the items on the bank statement are now matched by selected items from the nominal list of transactions on your screen and the **Statement Balance** total is the same as the final balance on the bank statement as issued by the bank. Reconciliation has been achieved.

4   When all the appropriate transactions have been selected press `Esc`.

The request to mark the selected transactions as reconciled appears again.

5   Press **Y** and then press `Enter`.

The reconciliation is then automatically effected by the system and you are returned to the Nominal Ledger screen.

Complete this activity with the Financial Controller screen on display.

11.6   Backing up data to a floppy diskette

You have now completed Chapter Eleven and have entered data into the Sage Sterling Financial Controller accounting system which has been stored on your computer's hard disk. While the hard disk is a very reliable medium it is worthwhile reminding yourself that it is storing your only copy of the data and that the disk itself is not infallible. Data can be irretrievably lost if your hard disk fails. Therefore, it is advised that you back up your data onto a floppy diskette (refer to page xvi of *Getting started*).

 A word of caution. When backing up data to a floppy diskette from your hard disk, all the current information in the data files on your hard disk is copied to the floppy diskette. As a consequence, it is always best to back up using the Backup/Restore facility available within the Sage Sterling Financial Controller accounting system which backs up and restores *all* the data files. If you use any other method which enables you to select which data files to back up or restore you may be tempted not to back up or restore all of your data files. In such an event your data could very easily become corrupted and, therefore, worthless.

Remember to take the diskette out of the floppy drive and to store it in a safe place.

Month end routine

At the end of each month a number of housekeeping tasks need to be performed to ensure that the accounts are fully up to date. Because many of these tasks are sensitive to the system date in relation to the dates of entered transaction it is essential that the correct system date be in force. Make sure that the system date is 31 January 1994.

- All the recurring entries, prepayments, accruals and depreciations for the past month need to be posted to the ledgers.

- The monthly financial statements and analysis that describe the financial state of the company and its profit or loss for the period need to be produced.

In addition to these procedures, every third month:

- The quarterly VAT analysis needs to be performed to enable the assessment of Total Bedrooms' current VAT liability to HM Customs and Excise.

To assist in this process the Sage Sterling +2 accounting system provides a Month End function which is accessed from the **Utilities** screen accessed via the Financial Controller screen.

When the Month End process is activated it is capable of automatically:

- Posting the Recurring Entries for that month
- Posting the Prepayments and Accruals for that month
- Posting the Depreciation for that month
- Clearing the Audit Trail of any allocated, paid and reconciled transactions up to a specified date
- Clearing the customer, supplier and stock files of any historical data that refers to that month to enable the new month's data to be recorded.

Each of these capabilities are activated by selection as we shall see, but once they have been so selected and activated their effect is irreversible - any information deleted cannot be recovered. Because the Month End function has such an irreversible effect we need to to be sure that we have all the relevant information relating to the financial affairs of the company before we activate the process and thereby destroy valuable information. *Printouts and backups are essential.*

Stock reports

By accessing the Stock Control screen, print a copy of each of the stock reports:

Stock History
Stock Valuation
Profit Report

Sales ledger reports

By accessing the Sales Ledger screen, print a copy of each of the sales ledger reports:

Account Balances (Aged)
Transaction History

Customer Statements

The end of the month is the time when you should be sending each customer with an outstanding debt a statement of their account. These account reports can be accessed via the Sales Ledger screen by selecting the **Statement** option. The Statement screen opens to display a collection of defaults:

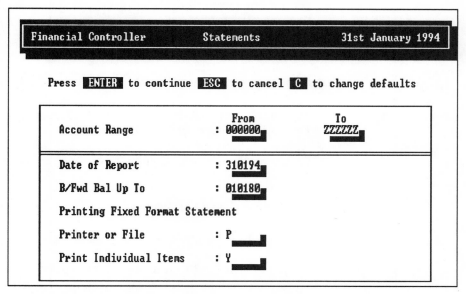

```
Financial Controller          Statements          31st January 1994


        Press  ENTER  to continue  ESC  to cancel  C  to change defaults

                                    From                To
        Account Range          : 000000            ZZZZZZ


        Date of Report         : 310194

        B/Fwd Bal Up To        : 010180

        Printing Fixed Format Statement

        Printer or File        : P

        Print Individual Items : Y
```

Accept all the defaults and produce statements for all the customers.

Purchase ledger reports

By accessing the Purchase Ledger screen, print a copy of each of the purchase ledger reports:

Account Balances (Aged)
Transaction History

Nominal ledger reports

By accessing the Nominal Ledger screen, print a copy of each of the nominal ledger reports:

Trial Balance
Transaction History

Financial reports

By accessing the Nominal Ledger accessible from the Financial Controller screen, print a copy of the report:

Asset Valuation

The three reports:

Profit and Loss (P & L)
Balance Sheet
Audit Trail

will be produced after activating the Month End function.

This will ensure that you have a hard copy of all the relevant information necessary for a proper evaluation of the company's financial state of affairs.

12.2 Closing stock

An adjustment needs to be included for stock remaining at the end of the month. This will be done by means of a journal entry.

Ensure that the Financial Controller screen is on display and the system date is 31 January 1994.

1   Display the Nominal Ledger screen and select the **Journal Entries** option.

2   Make the following journal entry against Department 3 and with **Ref 007**:

Debit the account **1001 Stock** with **110,804.00**, the value of the closing stock at the end of the month, noting that the **Tc** entry is **T9**. This figure for the closing stock is obtained from the stock valuation report at 31/01/94.

Credit the account **5201 Closing Stock** with the same figure.

The result of this entry is to reduce the month's opening stock and purchases by stock remaining at the month end and to include the stock as a current asset on the balance sheet.

You have now completed this month's trading and have entered data into the Sage Sterling Financial Controller accounting system which has been stored on your computer's hard disk. While the hard disk is a very reliable medium it is worthwhile reminding yourself that it is storing your only copy of the data and that the disk itself is not infallible. Data can be irretrievably lost if your hard disk fails. Therefore, it is advised that you back up your data onto a floppy diskette (refer to p[age xvi of *Getting started*).

A word of caution. When backing up data to a floppy diskette from your hard disk, all the current information in the data files on your disk is copied to the floppy diskette. As a consequence, it is always best to back up using the Backup/Restore facility available within the Sage Sterling Financial Controller accounting system which backs up and restores *all* the data files. If you use any other method which enables you to select which data files to back up or restore you may be tempted not to back up or restore all of your data files. In such an event your data could very easily become corrupted and, therefore, worthless.

When you have backed up your data files label the diskette:

BACKUP: 31/01/94
Before VAT Analysis and Month End

The next VAT Analysis is not due until the end of March.

Everything has now been prepared for the activation of the Month End function. Ensure that the Financial Controller screen is on display.

1   Select the **Utilities** option to reveal the Utilities screen.

2   Select the **Month End** option to reveal the Month End Routines screen:

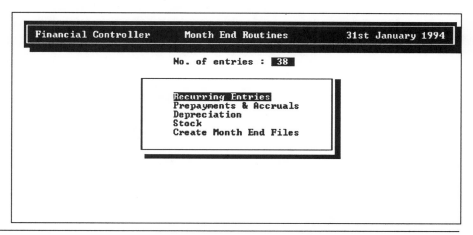

```
 Financial Controller      Month End Routines        31st January 1994


                        No. of entries :  38


                    ┌──────────────────────────────┐
                    │ Recurring Entries            │
                    │ Prepayments & Accruals       │
                    │ Depreciation                 │
                    │ Stock                        │
                    │ Create Month End Files       │
                    │                              │
                    └──────────────────────────────┘
```

3   Select the **Recurring Entries** option to reveal the Recurring Entries screen:

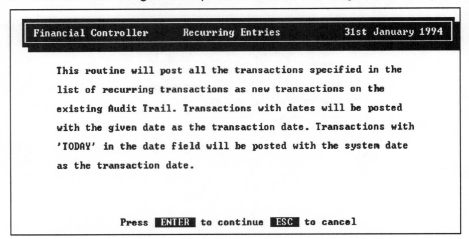

4   Read the contents of this screen to ensure that you are aware of the message.

5   Press Enter to activate the posting of the recurring entries to the ledgers.

A report will be issued and you are asked whether you wish it to be sent directly to the printer or to a file for access at a later date.

6   Accept the default **P** and press Enter.

The recurring entries are posted to the ledgers and a report is sent to the printer. When this is complete you are returned to the Month End Routines screen.

7   Select the **Prepayments & Accruals** option to reveal the Prepayments & Accruals screen:

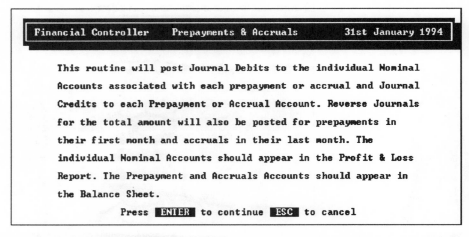

8   Read the contents of this screen to ensure that you are aware of the message.

9   Press Enter to activate the posting of the recurring entries to the ledgers.

A report will be issued and you are asked whether you wish it to be sent directly to the printer or to a file for access at a later date.

10   Accept the default **P** and press Enter .

The recurring entries are posted to the ledgers and a report is sent to the printer. When this is complete you are returned to the Month End Routines screen.

11   Select the **Depreciation** option to reveal the Depreciation screen:

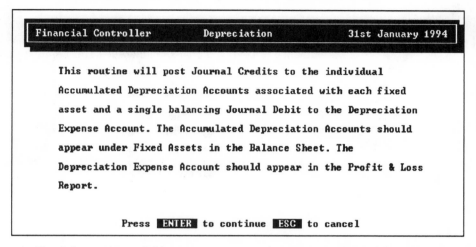

```
Financial Controller        Depreciation         31st January 1994


    This routine will post Journal Credits to the individual
    Accumulated Depreciation Accounts associated with each fixed
    asset and a single balancing Journal Debit to the Depreciation
    Expense Account. The Accumulated Depreciation Accounts should
    appear under Fixed Assets in the Balance Sheet. The
    Depreciation Expense Account should appear in the Profit & Loss
    Report.


              Press  ENTER  to continue  ESC  to cancel
```

12   Read the contents of this screen to ensure that you are aware of the message.

13   Press Enter to activate the posting of the recurring entries to the ledgers.

A report will be issued and you are asked whether you wish it to be sent directly to the printer or to a file for access at a later date.

14   Accept the default **P** and press Enter .

The recurring entries are posted to the ledgers and a report is sent to the printer. When this is complete you are returned to the Month End Routines screen.

15   Select the **Stock** option to reveal the Stock screen:

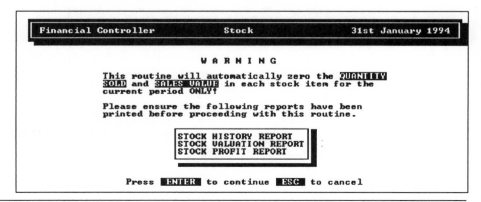

```
Financial Controller           Stock             31st January 1994
                           W A R N I N G
     This routine will automatically zero the QUANTITY
     SOLD and SALES VALUE in each stock item for the
     current period ONLY!

     Please ensure the following reports have been
     printed before proceeding with this routine.

             STOCK HISTORY REPORT
             STOCK VALUATION REPORT
             STOCK PROFIT REPORT


              Press  ENTER  to continue  ESC  to cancel
```

16   Read the contents of this screen to ensure that you are aware of the message.

17   Press ⌈Enter⌋ to activate the posting of the recurring entries to the ledgers.

A report is not issued during this procedure as it is assumed that all three reports referred to in the message have been acquired.

The stock adjustments are posted to the ledgers and when this is complete you are returned to the Month End Routines screen.

The final option that we have yet to select is **Create Month End Files** but we do not select this option just yet. We have to produce the Profit and Loss report, the Balance Sheet and a printout of the Audit Trail before we complete the month end procedures by creating the month end files.

12.5   Financial statements

There are three final reports to produce before we complete the month end procedures. These are the:

    Audit Trail
    Profit and Loss Account
    Balance sheet

If a business is a registered as a limited company it is required by company law to produce further statements such as a Director's Report and a Cash Flow statement at the end of each financial year. Using the Sage Sterling Financial Controller it is only possible to produce the Profit and Loss Account and the Balance Sheet.

Audit Trail
The Audit Trail is accessed via the **Utilities** option in the Financial Controller screen.

1   Produce a printed copy of the **Audit Trail** report and ensure that when the report is complete the Financial Controller screen is on display.

You will notice that there are some three pages of this report listing all of the 122 transactions that have been entered into the system.

Transactions	Details
1 to 13	Customer opening balances registered as sales invoices (**SI**). Those that have been paid are annotated with a **Y** and the date of payment.
14 to 32	Supplier opening balances registered as purchase invoices (**PI**). Those that have been paid are annotated with a **Y** and the date of payment.

33 to 52	Journal entries. The journal debits to the various accounts listed were entries made via the keyboard and the corresponding journal debits to the Suspense account 9998 were made automatically by the Sage Sterling Financial Conbtroller accounting system. Here we see double-entry book-keeping being maintained by the system. We shall say more about the Suspense account in Part III of this book.
53 to 82	Various sales and purchase invoices and credits. Notice the **N** in the column headed **VAT**. This means that these invoices have not yet been reconciled against a VAT Return.
83 to 94	Various bank payments to suppliers and bank receipts from customers. Notice the **R** and **N** in the column headed **Bank**. The **R** refers to the fact that the particular payment or receipt has been reconciled with a bank statement. The **N** refers to the fact that the particular payment or receipt has not yet been reconciled with a bank statement.
95	Payment of VAT at the end of January.
96 to 98	The direct journal entry of the van purchase entered from the keyboard.
99 to 102	Journal entries made in respect of prepayments.
103	The additional bank charge entered when reconciling the bank statement.
104 to 105	The closing stock entries.
106 to 107	Bank payments in respect of recurring entries.
108 to 122	Prepayment, accrual and depreciation postings made automatically during the execution of the Month End function.

Notice that the accrual transactions record the monthly accruals as a debit to the appropriate account and a credit to the Accruals account 2109. The prepayment transactions, on the other hand, not only record the monthly amounts credited to the appropriate accounts and debited to the Prepayment account 1103 but they also record the total amount of each set of prepayments debited and credited to the appropriate accounts.

The depreciation transactions are recorded in the appropriate accounts, each as a credit. The total of these three depreciations is recorded in transaction 122 as a debit in the Depreciation account 8000 thereby maintaining the balance of the accounts.

1   Ensure that the Nominal Ledger screen is on display.

2   Select the **P&L and Balance Sheet** option to reveal the P&L and Balance Sheet screen.

3   Change the default **D** for Display to **P** for Printer and send the two reports to the printer.

The profit and loss report lists sales, purchases and overheads for both this month and the year to date. Negative amounts are shown in brackets. The profit and loss account shows the profit or loss the company has made during a given period. The trading account describes the gross profit generated by the company. This is done by comparing the sales with the cost of sales. In the profit and loss account the expenses of the company are deducted from the gross profit to give the net profit for the period.

The balance sheet, listing information under the headings Fixed Assets, Current Assets, Current Liabilities and Financed by for this month and the year to date, is said to be a snapshot of the financial state of a business at one moment in time.

Assets
These are resources owned or controlled by the company. There are two classes of asset:

Fixed assets
Assets used within the company with a view to earning profits. They are not for resale. Examples are land, buildings, motor vehicles.

Current assets
Assets acquired for conversion into cash in the ordinary course of business. Examples are stock and debtors.

Liabilities
Liabilities are obligations owed by the company. These can be either short term such as bank overdraft and trade creditors, or long term such as loans.

Complete this activity with the Financial Controller screen on display.

You have now completed Chapter Twelve and have entered data into the Sage Sterling Financial Controller accounting system which has been stored on your computer's hard disk. While the hard disk is a very reliable medium it is worthwhile reminding yourself that it is storing your only copy of the data and that the disk itself is not infallible. Data can be irretrievably lost if your hard disk fails. Therefore, it is advised that you back up your data onto a floppy diskette (refer to page xvi of *Getting started*).

A word of caution. When backing up data to a floppy diskette from your hard disk, all the current information in the data files on your hard disk is copied to the floppy diskette. As a consequence, it is always best to back up using the Backup/Restore facility available within the Sage Sterling Financial Controller accounting system which backs up and restores *all* the data files. If you use any other method which enables you to select which data files to back up or restore you may be tempted not to back up or restore all of your data files. In such an event your data could very easily become corrupted and, therefore, worthless.

Remember to take the diskette out of the floppy drive and to store it in a safe place.

13 Sales order processing

13.1 The aim of sales orders

When making sales of stock it is necessary at all times to have a correct record of the stock levels. If you do not then you may find yourself selling stock that you do not have, which can cause problems with customers. To avoid problems such as these the Sage Sterling Financial Controller accounting system permits the processing of sales orders.

The processing of a sales order enables all stock sold to a customer to be allocated to an order prior to the stock being despatched and invoiced to the customer. This means that the stock records maintain a distinction between allocated and non-allocated stock, thereby making it impossible to complete an invoice from stock if there is insufficient non-allocated stock available.

We start this chapter in month 2 of Total Bedrooms' use of this accounting package so make sure that the system date is 28 February 1994 (see *Getting started*).

13.2 Creating a sales order

An order has arrived in the post from Main Line Hotels:

Order From: Main Line Hotels Plc
Date: 5 February 94
Order: 30 single beds
            40 double wardrobes
            10 table lamps
            40 sets of single bedding

With delivery to be made to their store at:

Main Line Hotel (Store)
103 Brook St
London SW11 4RT

Previously this order would have been immediately typed on an invoice from stock as and when the order had been fulfilled and despatched by stores. To maintain a closer control of the documentation relating to sales the Sales Order Processing facility is to be used. Using this facility the documentation for the entire process of invoicing, fulfilling an order and despatching the order will be maintained within the Sage Sterling Financial Controller accounting system.

Ensure that the Financial Controller screen is on display.

1   Select the **Sales Order Processing** option to reveal the Sales Orders screen:

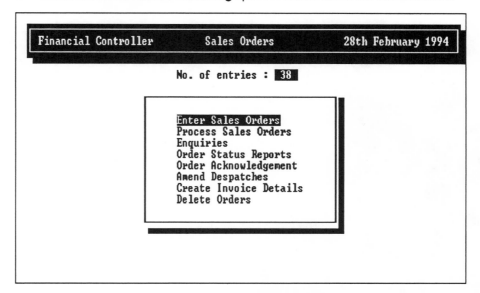

```
┌─────────────────────────────────────────────────────────────┐
│  Financial Controller      Sales Orders      28th February 1994 │
└─────────────────────────────────────────────────────────────┘

                    No. of entries :  38

                    ┌──────────────────────────────┐
                    │ Enter Sales Orders           │
                    │ Process Sales Orders         │
                    │ Enquiries                    │
                    │ Order Status Reports         │
                    │ Order Acknowledgement        │
                    │ Amend Despatches             │
                    │ Create Invoice Details       │
                    │ Delete Orders                │
                    └──────────────────────────────┘
```

2   Select the **Enter Sales Orders** option to reveal the Enter Sales Orders screen:

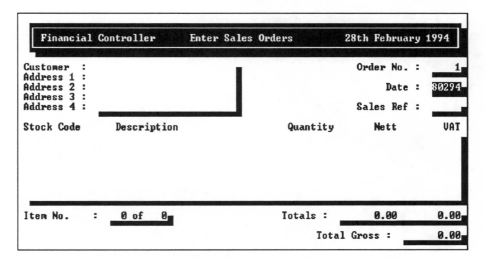

```
┌─────────────────────────────────────────────────────────────┐
│  Financial Controller     Enter Sales Orders   28th February 1994 │
└─────────────────────────────────────────────────────────────┘

Customer  :                              Order No. :        1
Address 1 :
Address 2 :                                   Date : 80294
Address 3 :
Address 4 :                              Sales Ref :

Stock Code    Description        Quantity      Nett       VAT




Item No.   :    0 of    0        Totals :      0.00      0.00

                              Total Gross :               0.00
```

The **Order No.** entry is automatically entered as the number **1**.

3   Amend the **Order No.** entry to:

1348

This is the same as the next invoice number in the sequence of invoices produced
so far.

4   Change the displayed system date to the date of the order, namely:

050294

5   Use `F4` to enter **Sales Ref** as:

M001

The name and address of Main Line Hotels Plc is then automatically entered by the system.

6   Press `Enter` until the highlight to the box beneath the heading **Stock Code** to place the cursor there and use `F4` to enter the stock code:

101 for Single bed

The Stock Item window appears.

7   Enter the **Quantity** as:

30

8   Press `Esc` to close the Stock Item window and to return to the Enter Sales Orders screen containing all the details of this first item of the order.

9   Enter the other three items of the order:

40 double wardrobes
10 table lamps
40 sets of single bedding

The details of the order are now complete and show a total gross value of £16920.00. Next we shall amend the default items that appear on the order.

10   Press `F3`, the **Order** key, to reveal the Order Details window:

```
Invoice No.          :        0
Customer Order No. :
Customer Phone No. : 071 334 1234
Order Taken By       :
Deliver To           : ------- AS INVOICED -------
Address 1            :
Address 2            :
Address 3            :
Address 4            :
Due Delivery         :
Notes 1              :
  ..    2            :
  ..    3            :

Allocation Status    :
Despatch  Status     :
```

Amongst other items this window enables Total Bedrooms to have the order delivered to an address that is different from the address on the invoice.

11   Enter the **Customer Order No** as:

1348

Notice that you cannot change the invoice number which is currently reading **1348**. Invoice numbers are generated automatically when processing orders.

12   Enter **Order taken by** as:

Received mail

13   Enter **Deliver To: , Address 1:** and **Address 2:** as:

Main Line Hotel (Store)
103 Brook St
London SW11 4RT

14   Enter the due **Delivery** as two weeks after the order has been received:

190294

15   In **Notes 1** and **2** enter:

For attention of store manager
Bill Sykes

Notice that you cannot enter anything into **Allocation Status** or **Despatch Status**. These entries are inserted automatically by the system when stock is allocated to the order and when the order is despatched.

16   Having completed the **Order Details** press Enter to close this window and to return to the Enter Sales Orders screen.

To complete the entry of this order we must now pay attention to the Footer.

17   Press F9, the **Footer** key, to reveal the Footer Details window.

There are three boxes in this window:

Carriage Values
Settlement Values
Global values

The fields in the **Carriage** box permit any costs to be charged for delivery to be entered here along with the appropriate tax. Such costs can also be set against both a nominal account and a Department for future analysis.

The **Settlement** box permits a discount to be applied for early settlement. However, applying a discount at this stage will automatically adjust the VAT without affecting the net amount. Because of the VAT complications of such a manoeuvre we shall defer the application of a discount until later.

The fields in the **Global** box permit changes to the entire invoice. As the order stands at the moment different items on the order are linked to different nominal codes. Consequently the later analysis of this order can be done over different nominal accounts. If a nominal code is entered into the **Global** box then this later entry would override all the other codes on the order and enable the entire order to be analysed to a single nominal account.

The same is true of the **Tax Code** and **Department**. Anything entered into the **Global** box will override its equivalent on the order.

We do not wish to override anything on the order so nothing will be entered into the **Global** box.

18 Press Esc to close the Footer Details window and to return to the Enter Sales Orders screen.

We have now completed the entry of the sales order details. The next step to be taken is one of a choice of two. We can either defer any further processing of this order by batching it - storing it to disk for further processing at a later date - or we can proceed to process it now. We choose the latter.

19 Press Esc to reveal the legend:

```
Do you want to : Save  Edit Abandon Print Post
```

20 Select the **Post** option and press Enter .

The ledgers are then updated, the stock is allocated to the order and the invoice is created. When this process is complete you are returned to the Enter Sales Order screen with an empty order form displayed. The order number is displayed as **1349**.

21 Change the **Order No.** entry to:

1348

The order form then fills with the details of the order whose details you have just posted to the ledgers.

22 Press Esc to reveal the same legend as before.

23 Select **Print** and send the Order Acknowledgement to the printer.

When the printing is complete you are again returned to the Enter Sales Orders screen displaying an empty sales order form.

24 Press Esc to close this screen and return to the Sales Order Processing screen.

Having received the order by mail it is decided to acknowledge the order by the same means.

25 Select the **Order Acknowledgement** option to reveal the Order Acknowledgement screen:

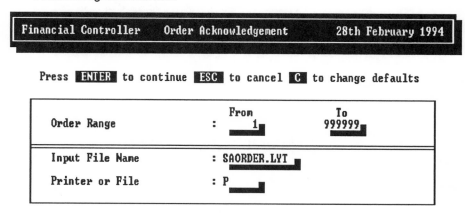

26 Accept all the defaults and print an order acknowledgement letter for onward transmission to Main Line Hotels.

The order that you have just entered into the Sage Sterling Financial Controller accounting system has now been saved to disk, a copy printed and stock has been allocated to the order in readiness for despatch. This completes the first stage in the processing of the sales order. We do not wish to enter another order just yet.

27 Ensure that the Sales Order Processing screen is on display and select the **Process Sales Orders** option to display the Process Sales Orders screen:

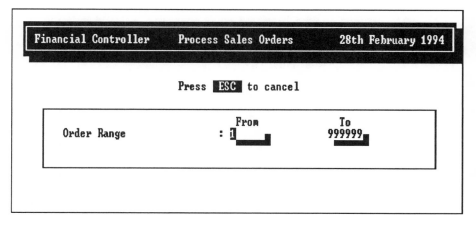

28 Accept the defaults by pressing Enter twice to reveal the following screen:

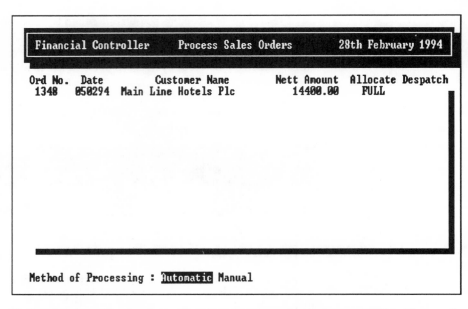

```
┌─────────────────────────────────────────────────────────────────┐
│  Financial Controller    Process Sales Orders    28th February 1994 │
│                                                                     │
│   Ord No.  Date        Customer Name      Nett Amount  Allocate Despatch │
│   1348    050294  Main Line Hotels Plc      14400.00    FULL        │
│                                                                     │
│                                                                     │
│                                                                     │
│                                                                     │
│                                                                     │
│                                                                     │
│                                                                     │
│                                                                     │
│   Method of Processing : Automatic Manual                           │
└─────────────────────────────────────────────────────────────────┘
```

Notice that the order details are listed and annotated with the word FULL. The word FULL describes the Status of the order and indicates that the order has been fully allocated - there is enough stock in store to enable the order to be immediately despatched.

You will remember that the delivery date was set at two weeks after the date of the order. This date is the latest date for delivery and is used as a safeguard in the event of there being insufficient stock to fulfil the order. It does not mean that we have to wait until two weeks have elapsed before we can despatch the order. On the contrary we are going to despatch the order as soon as we have seen the effect of this allocation of stock on our stock records.

29 Press **Esc** twice to return to the Financial Controller screen.

13.3 Allocated stock

We have just allocated stock to an order and this fact is recorded in the stock records. Ensure that the Financial Controller screen is on display.

1 Select the **Stock Control** option to reveal the Stock Control screen.

2 Select the **Stock Details** option and use the **F10** and **F9** keys to view the details of each item of stock. Pay particular attention to the items:

101 Single bed
204 Wardrobe - double
401 Table lamp
603 Bedding - single

3   Reveal the stock details of the first stock item **101 Single bed**.

Notice in the **Stock Levels** box there is an entry of **30** against **Allocated**. This means that despite the **In Stock** reading of **123** there are in fact only 93 single beds in stock that are available for sale because 30 of them have already been set aside to fulfil the Main Line Hotel order.

4   View the allocation of 40 double wardrobes.

5   View the further allocation of 10 table lamps and 40 sets of single bedding.

6   Press Esc twice to return to the Financial Controller screen.

We are now ready to despatch the sales order.

13.4   Despatching a sales order

Ensure that the Process Sales Orders screen is on display containing the description of the sales order number 1348, dated 050294, to Main Line Hotels Plc.

At the bottom of the screen is an annotation concerning the mode of processing:

```
Method of Processing : Automatic Manual
```

1   Select the default:

   Automatic

The order details are now highlighted and the annotation at the bottom of the screen has changed to:

```
Do you want to : Allocate Despatch
```

The order has already been allocated stock: it is now ready for despatch.

2   Select the **Despatch** option and the annotation at the bottom of the screen changes to:

```
Press ENTER to continue ESC to cancel PGDN next page PGUP previous
```

3   Press Enter to continue.

Notice the word COMPLETE beneath the heading Despatch which indicates that the order has been despatched and that the allocated stock has been recorded as having been removed from stock. The legend at the bottom of the screen now reads:

> Do you want to : **Allocate** Unallocate Cancel Hold-Credit Despatch

4   Select **Despatch** and a message appears to tell you that the order has been fully despatched.

5   Press $\boxed{\text{Esc}}$ to return to the Sales Order Processing screen.

We must now physically despatch the goods and record this by abstracting them from the stock records. At the same time we must produce an invoice. Fortunately, all this accounting is performed automatically by the Sage Sterling Financial Controller accounting system.

6   Press $\boxed{\text{Esc}}$ to return to the Financial Controller screen.

13.5   Stock records

Ensure that the Financial Controller screen is on display.

1   Display the **Stock Control** screen and select the **Stock Details** option.

2   Use the $\boxed{\text{F10}}$ and $\boxed{\text{F9}}$ keys to view the stock item details, paying particular attention to the following items:

101 Single bed
204 Wardrobe - double
401 Table lamp
603 Bedding - single

3   View the stock record of the first stock item **101 Single bed**.

Notice in the stock levels box that there is now no entry against **Allocated** and the **In Stock** box now reads **93** showing that the previously allocated 30 beds have been abstracted from the original stock of 123.

4   View the reduction in stock to 45 double wardrobes.

5   View the further reduction in stock to 176 table lamps and 117 sets of single bedding.

6   Press $\boxed{\text{Esc}}$ twice to return to the Financial Controller screen.

We are now ready to produce the invoice.

Having created, allocated stock to and despatched a sales order we now need to produce the invoice. The invoice was created at the time we selected to post the details of the sales order to the ledgers. All we need to do now is to send the invoice to the printer but before we do that we shall view the details of the invoice just to make sure that they are correct.

Ensure that the Financial Controller screen is on display.

1   Select the **Sales Ledger** option and then select the **Invoice Production** option from the Sales Ledger screen.

2   Select the **Display Index** option in the Invoice Production screen to reveal the Display Index screen. Accept the three default ranges of:

> Invoice Range
> Accounts Range
> Date Range

to display the list of invoices.

Notice that in this screen is displayed a collection of printed and posted invoices and one credit note dating back to January. At the bottom of this list is the invoice to Main Line Hotels that the Sage Sterling Financial Controller accounting system has produced automatically as a result of processing the sales order to which it corresponds.

3   Press ⌐Esc⌐ to return to the Invoice Production screen and print a copy of this invoice.

When this has been done you will be returned to the Invoice Production screen.

4   Select the **Update Ledgers** option to reveal the Update Ledgers screen:

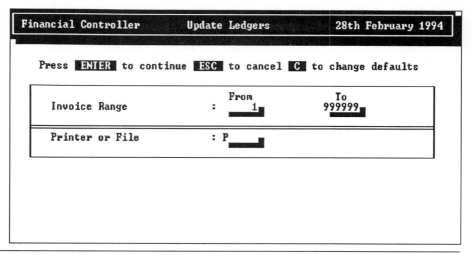

5   Accept each of the defaults and the details of the invoice are posted to the ledgers and a report of the posting is sent to the printer.

When this process is completed you are returned to the Invoice Production screen.

6   Select **Display Index** and display the list of invoices again.

Notice that Main Line Hotels' invoice now has the annotation **Yes** beneath both **Print** and **Post** to indicate that each of these processes has been performed and that the processing of the sales order is now completed.

13.7   Creating and despatching further sales orders

Process each of the following sales orders, printing and posting them for further processing at a later date. When they have all acquired COMPLETE status print the invoices and update the ledgers with the information that they contain.

Note: A number of these orders will cause the customers to exceed their credit limits. This had been foreseen before the orders were despatched and outstanding amounts due were requested by Total Bedrooms. All those settlements requested arrived within the two weeks delay between receiving an order and despatching it.

Order From: George Hotel
Date: 8 February 94
Order: 50 double beds
             30 table lamps
             40 decor packs

Order From: Budget Hostelry
Date: 13 February 94
Order: 35 single beds
             35 pairs of linen curtains
             35 sets of single bedding

Order From: Innkeepers
Date: 15 February 94
Order: 15 single beds
             40 single wardrobes
             25 sets of single bedding

Order From: Main Line Hotels
Date: 18 February 94
Order: 40 double beds
             40 decor packs

1   When you have printed and posted this last order, press $\boxed{\text{Esc}}$ twice to return to the Financial Controller screen.

2   Select the **Sales Ledger** option and produce the invoices via the **Invoice Production** option in the Sales Ledger screen.

3   When the invoices have all been printed select the **Update Ledgers** option in the Invoice Production screen and complete the processing of these sales orders.

Complete this activity with the Financial Controller screen on display.

13.8   Receipts

 During the month a number of customer receipts were received. Record the following customer receipts as Bank receipts against the appropriate accounts:

Receipt From: Main Line Hotels
Against Invoice: 1307 and 1321 (enter Ref as 07/21)
Amount: 13121.92
Date Received: 03/02/94

Receipt From: Budget Hostelry
Against Invoice: 1319
Amount: 6754.11
Date Received: 10/02/94

Receipt From: Innkeepers
Against Invoice: 1327
Amount: 4306.82
Date Received: 12/02/94

Receipt From: Queens Hotel
Against Invoice: 1333
Amount: 6887.01
Date Received: 14/02/94

Complete this part of the activity with the Financial Controller screen on display.

13.9   Insufficient stock

The following sales order was received from Budget Hostelry on the 21st February and when the order was processed it was found that there was insufficient stock to fulfil the order. Entering the order entails a partial allocation of stock. This partial allocation must be topped up to fully allocate as and when new stock arrives.

Order From: Budget Hostelry Plc
Date: 21 February
Order: 30 double beds
             10 decor packs

Ensure that the Financial Controller screen is on display.

 1 Display the Sales Order Processing screen.

2 Select the **Enter Sales Orders** option to reveal the Enter Sales Order screen.

 When you come to enter the **Quantity** in the Stock Item window you will be warned that there is insufficient stock to completely fulfil the order. This message is for information only and does not prevent you from continuing to complete the entry of the details of the order.

3 Complete the entry of the details of the order as listed above and when they are fully entered post the details of the order to the ledgers and stock files and send a copy of the order to the printer.

4 Press Esc to return to the **Sales Orders** screen and select the **Process Sales Orders** option to reveal the Processing Sales Orders screen in which you will see a list of all the sales orders.

Against the details of this order is the word PART to indicate that there is insufficient stock to fully allocate stock to it.

5 Allocate stock to this order and when this process is complete return to the Financial Controller screen.

6 Select the **Stock Control** option to reveal the Stock Control screen.

7 Select the **Stock Details** option and view the details of the stock items **102 Double bed, 704 Decor pack**

From the Decor pack stock record you will see that there are 9 units in stock and all 9 of them have been allocated to Budget's order in partial fulfilment of an order for 10 Decor packs. A similar situation exists with respect to the double beds.

8 Return to the Financial Controller screen and continue processing the following orders through to the partial allocation of stock and the despatch of the orders:

Order From: Innkeepers Plc
Date: 21 February 94
Order: 20 single beds
            20 table lamps
            60 sets of single bedding

Order From: Main Line Hotels Plc
Date: 22 February 94
Order: 20 single wardrobes
            20 pairs of linen curtains
            20 decor packs

Complete this activity with the Financial Controller screen on display.

Having despatched the last three orders we shall now batch print the invoices.

1   Ensure that the Sales Ledger screen is on display and select the **Invoice Production** option to reveal the Invoice Production screen.

2   Select the **Display Index** and display all the invoices contained within the system.

3   Make a note of the invoice numbers of the last three invoices that have yet to be printed and posted and then press Esc to return to the Invoice Production screen.

5   Select the **Print Invoices** option and amend the defaults to ensure that the batch printing of the last three invoices is completed.

6   When the printing is complete update the ledgers with the details of these three invoices.

Complete this activity with the Financial Controller screen on display.

13.11   Backing up data to a floppy diskette

You have now completed Chapter Thirteen and have entered data into the Sage Sterling Financial Controller accounting system which has been stored on your computer's hard disk. While the hard disk is a very reliable medium it is worthwhile reminding yourself that it is storing your only copy of the data and that the disk itself is not infallible. Data can be irretrievably lost if your hard disk fails. Therefore, it is advised that you back up your data onto a floppy diskette (refer to page xvi of *Getting started*).

A word of caution. When backing up data to a floppy diskette from your hard disk, all the current information in the data files on your hard disk is copied to the floppy diskette. As a consequence, it is always best to back up using the Backup/Restore facility available within the Sage Sterling Financial Controller accounting system which backs up and restores *all* the data files. If you use any other method which enables you to select which data files to back up or restore you may be tempted not to back up or restore all of your data files. In such an event your data could very easily become corrupted and, therefore, worthless.

Remember to take the diskette out of the floppy drive and to store it in a safe place.

Purchase order processing

14.1 The purpose of purchase order processing

When making purchases of stock it is necessary at all times to have a correct record of the stock levels. If you do not then you may find yourself re-purchasing stock that is already on order. To avoid problems such as these the Sage Sterling Financial Controller accounting system permits the processing of purchase orders.

The processing of purchase orders enables stock ordered on a purchase order to be recorded in the stock as being On Order thereby providing a warning against excessive ordering. It also provides a record which can be consulted when the stock arrives to check that the quantities and prices are correct.

Make sure that the system date is 28 February 1994 (see *Getting started*).

14.2 Creating a purchase order

It had been recognised that the number of double beds in stock was becoming too low to satisfy demand. If you look at the stock record you will see that there are only 29 in stock (and all of these are spoken for) which is substantially below the reorder level of 50. Consequently, it was decided to place an order for 60 with EEZEE Beds to replenish the stock. The order is:

Order To: EEZEE BEDS
Date: 10/02/94
Order: 60 double beds

with delivery to be made as soon as possible.

Ensure that the Financial Controller screen is on display.

   1   Select the **Purchase Order Processing** option to reveal the Purchase Orders screen:

```
Enter Purchase Orders
Process Purchase Orders
Enquiries
Orders Status Reports
Order Document
Amend Deliveries
Delete Orders
```

2   Select the **Enter Purchase Orders** option to reveal the Enter Purchase Orders screen:

```
┌──────────────────────────────────────────────────────────────────────┐
│ ┌──────────────────────────────────────────────────────────────────┐ │
│ │ Financial Controller    Enter Purchase Orders    28th February 1994│ │
│ └──────────────────────────────────────────────────────────────────┘ │
│                                                                        │
│  Supplier  :                              Order No. :          1       │
│  Address 1 :                                                           │
│  Address 2 :                                 Date : 280294             │
│  Address 3 :                                                           │
│  Address 4 :                              Purchase Ref :               │
│                                                                        │
│  Stock Code     Description          Quantity      Nett      VAT       │
│                                                                        │
│                                                                        │
│                                                                        │
│                                                                        │
│                                                                        │
│  Item No.   :    0 of   0           Totals :       0.00     0.00       │
│                                              Total Gross :   0.00       │
└──────────────────────────────────────────────────────────────────────┘
```

The screen displays an empty purchase order form with number **1** and the default system date.

3   Amend the **Order No.** entry to **5087** and change the **Date** to the date of the order, namely:

100294

4   Use $\boxed{\text{F4}}$ to enter the **Purchase Ref** as:

EEZEE

All the relevant details of the EZEE Beds account are then entered into the purchase order form automatically.

5   Move the highlight to the space below the heading **Stock Code** to place the cursor there and use $\boxed{\text{F4}}$ to enter the stock code:

102 for Double bed

The Stock Item window appears.

6   Enter the quantity as **60**.

7   Press $\boxed{\text{Esc}}$ to close the Stock Item window and to return to the Enter Purchase Orders screen containing all the details of this item on the order form.

The details of the order are now complete and show a total gross value of £4230.00. Next we shall amend the default items that appear on the order.

8   Press the **Order** key $\boxed{\text{F3}}$ to reveal the Order Details window.

9   Enter the **Supplier Reference** number as **EEZEE**.

10   Enter **Deliver To, Address 1** and **Address 2** as:

Total Bedrooms
As per order

11   Having completed the **Order Details** press $\boxed{\text{Esc}}$ to return to the Enter Sales Orders screen.

To complete the entry of this order we must now pay attention to the Footer.

12   Press the **Footer** key $\boxed{\text{F9}}$ to reveal the Footer Details window.

There are two boxes in this window:

Carriage
Settlement

The fields in the **Carriage** box permit any costs to be charged for delivery to be entered here along with the appropriate tax. Such costs can also be set against both a nominal account and a Department for future analysis.

The **Settlement** box permits a discount to be applied for early settlement. EEZEE Beds do not charge carriage and do not give any discount for early settlement of the order. As a consequence there is nothing to enter in the Footer.

13   Press $\boxed{\text{Esc}}$ to return to the Enter Purchase Orders screen.

We have now completed the entry of the purchase order details. The next step to be taken is one of a choice of two. We can either defer any further processing of this order by batching it - storing it to disk for further processing at a later date - or we can proceed to process it now. We choose the latter.

14   Press $\boxed{\text{Esc}}$ and select the **Print** option to send the order to your printer.

A message appears warning you to ensure that your printer is switched on and on-line

15   Ensure that your printer is ready and then press $\boxed{\text{Enter}}$.

The Purchase Order is then sent to the printer.

16   Press $\boxed{\text{Esc}}$ to return to the Purchase Orders screen and select **Process Purchase Orders** to reveal the Process Purchase Orders screen containing

the details of the purchase order that you have just entered:

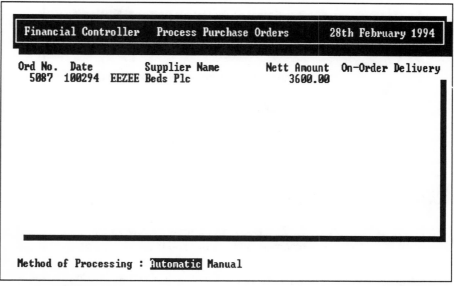

```
┌─────────────────────────────────────────────────────────────────────┐
│ ┌─────────────────────────────────────────────────────────────────┐ │
│ │ Financial Controller   Process Purchase Orders   28th February 1994│ │
│ └─────────────────────────────────────────────────────────────────┘ │
│                                                                       │
│ Ord No.  Date            Supplier Name       Nett Amount  On-Order Delivery │
│   5087  100294  EEZEE  Beds Plc                 3600.00                │
│                                                                       │
│                                                                       │
│                                                                       │
│                                                                       │
│                                                                       │
│                                                                       │
│                                                                       │
│                                                                       │
│ Method of Processing : Automatic Manual                               │
└─────────────────────────────────────────────────────────────────────┘
```

The legend at the bottom of the screen is asking if you want the system to process this order automatically or whether you wish to do it manually.

17 Select **Manual**.

The order is highlighted and the legend at the bottom of the screen changes to:

```
┌─────────────────────────────────────────────────────────────────────┐
│ Press ENTER to continue ESC to cancel PGDN next page PGUP previous    │
└─────────────────────────────────────────────────────────────────────┘
```

18 Press Enter to continue.

The legend changes to:

```
┌─────────────────────────────────────────────────┐
│ Do you want to : Order Cancel Delivery           │
└─────────────────────────────────────────────────┘
```

19 Select **Order**.

The details of the order are then annotated with ON-ORDER to indicate that the order has been placed with EEZEE Beds Plc but not yet delivered.

20 Press Esc twice to return to the Financial Controller screen.

14.3 Ordered stock

We have just placed an order for stock and this fact is recorded in the stock records. Ensure that the Financial Controller screen is on display.

1 Select the **Stock Control** option to reveal the Stock Control screen.

2 Select Stock Details and use F10 to view the details of the stock item:

102 Double bed

Notice in the **Stock Levels** box there is an entry of **60** against **On Order**.

3 Press Esc twice to return to the Financial Controller screen.

We are now ready to take delivery of the purchase order.

14.4   Taking delivery of a purchase order

EEZEE Beds rang through to say that they were consigning 35 double beds in part
fulfilment of the order and that the other 25 beds would follow in two or three days.

Ensure that the Processing Purchase Orders screen is on display containing the
description of the purchase order number 5087, dated 10/02/94 from EEZEE Beds
Plc.

1 Select the **Amend Deliveries** option to display the Amend Deliveries screen:

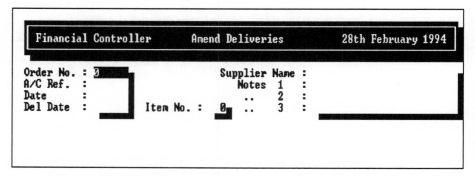

2 Enter the **Order No.** as 5087 and immediately all the details of the EEZEE
order are displayed.

3 Presss Enter to reveal the legend:

```
Quantity Delivered : 60.00
```

4 Amend the **Quantity Delivered** to:

35 and press Enter

The order details now change to display the delivered quantity as 35.

We now need to record the fact that we have taken delivery of this part order.

5   Press ⌷Esc⌷ to display the Process Purchase Orders screen.

6   Select **Process Purchase Orders** to reveal the Purchase Orders screen with
     the details of the EEZEE order on display.

At the bottom of the screen is the legend:

```
Method of Processing : Automatic Manual
```

7   Select **Manual** and the legend changes to:

```
Press ENTER to continue ESC to cancel PGDN next page PGUP previous
```

8   Press ⌷Enter⌷ to reveal the question:

```
Do you want to : Order Cancel Delivery
```

9   Select **Delivery** and the details of the order are annotated with PART to
     indicate that only part of the complete order has been delivered.

10   Complete this activity with the Financial Controller screen on display.

14.5   Stock records

Ensure that the Financial Controller screen is on display.

1   Select the Stock Control screen.

2   Select the **Stock Details** option and view the stock item:

     102 Double bed

Notice in the **Stock Levels** box the entry against **On Order** now reads **25** showing
that the previously ordered 60 beds has been reduced by the part delivery. Also the
In Stock entry which was **29** now reads **64** which accounts for the 35 beds that
have been delivered.

3   Press ⌷Esc⌷ twice to return to the Financial Controller screen.

We are now ready to record the completion of the order.

Eventually the final part of the purchase order arrives and is entered into stock.

Ensure that the Financial Controller screen is on display.

1   Select the **Purchase Order Processing** option to reveal the Purchase Orders screen with the EEZEE order on display.

2   Press ⌷Esc⌷ and then select the method of processing as **Manual.**

3   In response to the question that appears at the bottom of the screen select **Deliveries.**

The annotation then changes from PART to COMPLETE to indicate that the original order has been fully delivered.

4   Press ⌷Esc⌷ to return to the Financial Controller screen.

5   Check the Double bed stock record to see that this further part delivery has been added to the stock and abstracted from the **On Order** box to put **89 In Stock.**

Complete this activity with the Financial Controller screen on display.

14.7 Creating and taking delivery of further purchase orders

During February a number of purchases were made to replenish the stock which was being depleted due to the sales.

1   Enter each of the following purchase orders, batching them for processing at a future time:

Order To: Commercial Carpenters Ltd
Date: 12 February 94
Order: 10 small vanity units
            10 double wardrobes

Order To: Fabrico
Date: 15 February 94
Order: 75 sets of single bedding
            10 sets of linen curtains

Order To: Artwork
Date: 20 February 94
Order: 100 decor packs

Due Delivery: As soon as possible

Change the Tax Code in the Stock Item window to **T0** because Artwork are not registered for VAT.

Order To: Sleepwell Ltd
Date: 24 February 94
Order: 20 sets of double bedding
               20 sets of single bedding

Complete this activity with the Purchase Orders screen on display.

2   Press ⌈**Esc**⌉ and select **Automatically** to process these orders automatically.

3   Complete the processing with a printout of each order where each order is first recorded as having ON-ORDER status and then COMPLETE status as the deliveries are recorded as being made in full.

Complete this activity with the Financial Controller screen on display.

14.8   Entering purchase invoices

Unlike the sales order processing facility where invoices are created automatically during the completion of the sales orders, purchase invoices have to be entered into the system as a separate procedure. Remember that purchases are Department 2.

1   Enter the following purchase invoices that arrived in the post after each of the previous five stock deliveries. Follow the procedure laid down in Chapter 6, taking note that the stock does not need to be adjusted. The stock adjustment was done automatically when the purchase orders were completed.

A/C: EEZEE
Ref: 5087
Date: 15/02/94
N/C: 5001
Purchase of: 60 double beds   3600.00

               VAT   630.00
               Total   4230.00

A/C:	COMM	
Ref:	5088	
Date:	17/02/94	
N/C:	5002	
Purchase of:	10 small vanity units	500.00
	10 double wardrobes	1800.00
	VAT	402.50
	Total	2702.50

A/C:	FABRIC	
Ref:	5089	
Date:	20/02/94	
N/C:	5006	
Purchase of:	75 sets of single bedding	1500.00
	10 sets of linen curtains	400.00
	VAT	332.50
	Total	2232.50

A/C:	ART	
Ref:	5090	
Date:	25/02/94	
N/C:	5007	
Purchase of:	100 decor packs	2000.00
	Total	2000.00

A/C:	SLEEP	
Ref:	5091	
Date:	28/02/94	
N/C:	5006	
Purchase of:	20 sets of double bedding	600.00
	20 sets of single bedding	400.00
	VAT	175.00
	Total	1175.00

14.9   Payments

During the month a number of payments were made. Record the following payments as Bank payments against the appropriate accounts:

Payment To:	Commercial Carpenters
Against Invoice:	5021
Amount	3421.67

Date Paid: 10 February 1994
Cheque Number: 100

Payment To: Artwork
Against Invoice: 5044
Amount   226.66
Date Paid: 15 February 1994
Cheque Number: 101

Payment To: EEZEE Beds
Against Invoice: 5035 and 5060
Amount   3601.78
Date Paid: 18 February 1994
Cheque Number: 102

Payment To: Seats and Things
Against Invoice: 5061
Amount   719.55
Date Paid: 18 February 1994
Cheque Number: 103

Payment To: Sleepwell
Against Invoice: 5040
Amount   3998.67
Date Paid: 18 February 1994
Cheque Number: 104

Payment To: Forward Bedding
Against Invoice: 5050
Amount   998.49
Date Paid: 22 February 1994
Cheque Number: 105

Payment To: Hand Craft Ltd
Against Invoice: 5027
Amount   5934.34
Date Paid: 22 February 1994
Cheque Number: 106

Complete this activity with the Financial Controller screen on display.

We still have a number of orders that we have entered into the system but there was insufficient stock to fulfil them.

Ensure that the Financial Controller screen is on display.

1   Display the Processing Sales Orders screen.

2   Select **Processing Sales Orders** to reveal the Sales Orders screen with a number of orders on display.

We can see that there is a part fulfilled order to Budget Hostlery. This order was for 30 double beds and 10 decor packs but only 29 double beds and 9 decor packs have been allocated. This is because there was insufficient stock available at the time the allocation was performed. Since that time we have taken delivery of more double beds and more decor packs so there should be sufficient stock available to complete the order. First we check the stock levels.

3   Press $\boxed{\text{Esc}}$ twice to return to the Financial Controller screen.

4   Display the Stock Control screen and select the **Stock Details** option.

5   View the stock items:

   102 - Double bed
   704 - Decor pack

We can see that there are 89 double beds with 29 allocated leaving 60 available for sale and 109 decor packs with 9 allocated leaving 100 for sale. This is more than enough to fulfil the order.

6   Return to the Process Sales Orders screen with the Budget Hostelry PART order on display.

7   Press $\boxed{\text{Esc}}$ to activate the processing and select **Manual**.

8   Move the highlight to the Budget Hostelry order number 1353 that has status PART and press $\boxed{\text{Enter}}$.

9   From the legend that appears at the bottom of the screen select **Allocate**.

The annotation changes from PART to FULL. We have now fully allocated stock to this order and we have despatched and invoiced the earlier part delivery to Budget. We now need to raise a further invoice for the balance of the order.

10   Press $\boxed{\text{Esc}}$ and from the Process Sales Orders screen select the **Create Invoice Details** to reveal the Create Invoice Details screen.

11   Send the details to the printer and return to the Process Sales Orders screen.

The invoice details have now been created automatically by the system. All we need do now to complete this order is to print the invoice and then record the despatch as having been made.

12   Ensure that the Sales Orders screen is on display and select **Process Sales Orders**.

13   Press $\boxed{\text{Esc}}$ and, to activate the processing, select **Manual.**

14   At the question that appears select **Deliveries** and the annotation on the order changes to COMPLETE.

The despatch has now been recorded and the appropriate stock reduction will be automatically reflected in the stock records. All that remains to be done is to print the invoice and post the invoice details to the ledgers.

15   Return to the Financial Controller screen and select the **Sales Ledger** option.

16   Select the **Print Invoice** option and print the invoice.

When the invoice has been printed select **Update Ledgers** from the Sales Ledger screen and complete this transaction.

17   Repeat this procedure for order number 7 to Innkeepers.

Complete this activity with the Financial Controller screen on display.

14.11   Cancelling or deleting orders

Main Line Hotels have just rung through to say that they wish to cancel the order as something has happened to delay their requirements for further stock.

Ensure that the Financial Controller screen is on display.

1   Display the Sales Order Processing screen.

2   Select the **Enquiries** option to reveal a list of sales orders.

3   Move the highlight to Main Line Hotel's order number 1355 and press $\boxed{\text{Enter}}$.

The details of this order are then displayed in the Enquiries screen.

We can see that the order consists of:

20 single wardrobes
20 sets of linen curtains
20 decor packs

of which all but the decor packs have been allocated to the order.

4   Press $\boxed{\text{Esc}}$ three times to return to the Financial Controller screen.

5   Display the Stock Details screen and view the details of the stock items:

203   Wardrobe - single
601   Curtains - linen
704   Decor pack

We can see that item with code:

203 has 50 In Stock
         0 On-Order
         20 Allocated

601 has 141 In Stock
         0 On-Order
         20 Allocated

704 has 99 In Stock
         0 On-Order
         0 Allocated

6   Press $\boxed{\text{Esc}}$ twice to return to the Financial Controller screen.

7   Display the Sales Orders screen.

8   Select the **Delete Order** option to reveal a Delete Orders screen.

9   Enter the numbers of the sales orders to delete as:

From: 1355
To: 1355

10   Press $\boxed{\text{Enter}}$ and the sales order is deleted.

11   Press $\boxed{\text{Esc}}$ to return to the Financial Controller screen.

12   Display the Stock Details screen and view the details of the stock items:

203   Wardrobe - single
601   Curtains - linen
704   Decor pack

We can see that the **In Stock** quantities are unaltered but now all the **Allocated** quantities have been amended to zero. Complete this activity with the Financial Controller screen on display.

14.12 Backing up data to a floppy diskette

You have now completed Chapter Fourteen and have entered data into the Sage Sterling Financial Controller accounting system which has been stored on your computer's hard disk. While the hard disk is a very reliable medium it is worthwhile reminding yourself that it is storing your only copy of the data and that the disk itself is not infallible. Data can be irretrievably lost if your hard disk fails. Therefore, it is advised that you back up your data onto a floppy diskette (refer to page xvi of *Getting started*).

A word of caution. When backing up data to a floppy diskette from your hard disk, all the current information in the data files on your hard disk is copied to the floppy diskette. As a consequence, it is always best to back up using the Backup/Restore facility available within the Sage Sterling Financial Controller accounting system which backs up and restores *all* the data files. If you use any other method which enables you to select which data files to back up or restore you may be tempted not to back up or restore all of your data files. In such an event your data could very easily become corrupted and, therefore, worthless.

Remember to take the diskette out of the floppy drive and to store it in a safe place.

15 Further ledger processing

15.1 Contra entries

A contra entry is a ledger entry where a number of sales invoices are matched with a number of purchase invoices to the same total value thereby cutting out the necessity for a number of cash transactions in settlement of each of the respective sales and purchase invoices. This particular type of ledger entry is particularly useful when the same company is both a supplier and a customer.

David Peterson of Seats and Things, one of Total Bedrooms' suppliers, has been dealing successfully with the hotel trade for a number of years and recently Seats and Things have decided to purchase a small hotel in the country with a view to managing the hotel remotely. One of Peterson's acquaintances of many years standing was the Sales Director of Total Bedrooms and he approached him for advice on methods of remote stock control. Realising that he was asking for professional assistance he offered to pay for consultancy services and it was agreed to offset the first consultation against an item on Seats and Things' outstanding invoice to Total Bedrooms of £540.50. The accounts department accordingly entered a contra entry.

15.2 Creating a sales account

Before the contra entry can be entered the existing supplier, Seats and Things, must first be registered as a customer as well.

Ensure that the Financial Controller screen is on display and that the system date is 28 February 1994.

 1   Display the Sales Ledger screen.

2   Select the **Customer details** option and display an empty customer record.

3   Create a new customer record for:

Account Reference	S001
Acount Name	Seats and Things
Address	112 Batley Road
..	Huddersfield
..	West Yorkshire
..	HD5 7TC
Credit Limit	1000

Telephone No	0484 673298
Contact Name	David Peterson
Analysis Code	Sales - Sundries
VAT Reg Number	012 4455 66
VAT Country Code	GB
Default VAT Code	T1

In the **Defaults** box, enter:

Nominal	7602 for Consultancy Fees
Tax Code	T1 17.50%

4   Save this new customer record to disk and return to the Financial Controller screen.

Complete this activity with the Financial Controller screen on display.

Having created this new customer record we are now in a position to create an invoice for the consultancy services rendered. This procedure will be quite different from either invoicing from stock or invoicing via the Customers screen because both these methods have a standard entry format based on the company's stockholding. The invoice to be issued for consultancy services will need to contain the details of the service given and these do not follow any standard format. Fortunately, the Sage Sterling Financial Controller accounting system can cater for this situation by permitting a free text invoice to be created.

1   Select the **Invoice Production** option in the Sales Ledger screen to reveal the Invoice Production screen.

2   Select the **Free Text Invoice** option to reveal the Free Text Invoice screen:

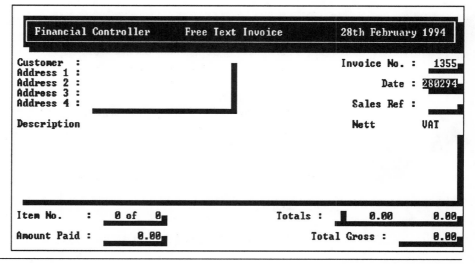

The invoice number and the system date are automatically entered.

3   Enter the **Date** as:

150294

4   Use F4 to select the **Sales Ref** entry as **S001**.

5   Place the highlight on the first line under the heading **Description** to locate the text cursor there.

In the body of the invoice there are seven lines available for entering invoiced items and for each item line there are nine lines of free text entry available.

6   Press F4 to open the Details window:

```
Line 1 :
Line 2 :
Line 3 :
Line 4 :
Line 5 :
Line 6 :
Line 7 :
Line 8 :
Line 9 :
Price   :        0.00
Tax Code    :           Tax %  :          0.00
Nominal Code:
Department  :    0
```

Each of the lines in the Free Text Invoice screen is capable of accounting for a specific item on the invoice and there are nine lines available for free text entry via the Details window for each item line in the Free Text Invoice screen.

7   Enter the following:

Line 1:   Account for:
Line 2:
Line 3:   Consultancy services re:
Line 4:   stock control procedures

Price : 460.00
Tax Code: T1   Tax % :   17.50%
Nominal   7602
Department 1 Sales

8   In the Details window the **Price** is shown as:

460.00

With VAT added the gross amount will then be 540.50.

9   Press **Esc** and the Details window closes to reveal the Free Text Invoice screen displaying the completed invoice.

Notice that only the first line of the description per item is visible. When the invoice is printed, however, the entire text will be output.

As with any other type of invoice it can have an order and a footer associated with it.

10   Press **F3** to view the Order window and press **Esc** to close it.

11   Press **F9** to view the Footer window and press **Esc** to close it.

12   Press **Esc** and send the invoice to the printer.

13   When the printing is done re-display the invoice and post it to the ledgers.

Complete this activity with the Financial Controller screen on display.

15.4   **Making the contra entry**

Ensure that the Financial Controller screen is on display.

1   Display the Sales Ledger screen.

2   Select the **Contra Entries** option to display the Contra Entries screen.
Note: This option is not available via the Purchase Ledger screen.

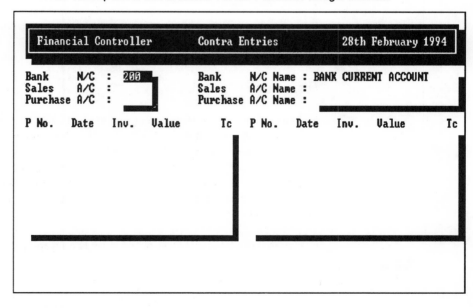

```
 Financial Controller        Contra Entries        28th February 1994

Bank      N/C  : 200          Bank      N/C Name : BANK CURRENT ACCOUNT
Sales     A/C  :              Sales     A/C Name :
Purchase  A/C  :              Purchase  A/C Name :

P No.   Date   Inv.   Value      Tc   P No.   Date   Inv.   Value      Tc
```

3   Use **F4** to enter the:

Sales A/C as   S001
Purchase A/C as   SEATS

The two panels on either side of this screen now display all invoices that remain unpaid - the left-hand panel displaying the one sales invoice and the right-hand panel displaying the two items on the one purchase invoice numbered 5084. The **Total** boxes below each of the panels are both recording **0.00** because no invoices have yet been selected.

4   With the highlight over the sales invoice in the left-hand panel press **Enter** and the **Total** box below now reads **540.50**.

The sales invoice has been selected.

5   Use the cursor control keys to place the highlight over the purchase invoice number 5084 in the right-hand panel. Press **Enter** and the **Total** box below now reads **540.50**.

6   Press **Esc** and post the details to the ledgers. The details in the Contra Entries screen clear. Press **Esc** again to return to the Sales Ledger screen.

7   Select the **Transaction History** option and view the transaction history of the account **S001** where you will see the posting of the contra entry as a Sales Receipt (**SR**) with reference CONTRA leaving a **0.00** balance.

8   View the equivalent record from the suppliers side where you will see the posting of the contra entry as a Purchase Payment (**PP**), again with reference CONTRA.

Complete this activity with the Financial Controller screen on display.

15.5   Refunds

In January the George Hotel took delivery and paid for 100 metres of carpeting. Some time later their fitters arrived to find that the carpeting was defective and unfit for the purposes required. The carpeting was, accordingly, returned to Total Bedrooms on the 5th February who returned it to their suppliers. In the meantime the George Hotel required a refund of the £2115.00 that they had already paid. They were duly refunded using cheque number 107 and the fact must now be recorded in the company's accounts.

Ensure that the Financial Controller screen is on display.

1   Display the Sales Ledger screen.

2   Select the **Refunds** option to reveal the Sales Refunds screen:

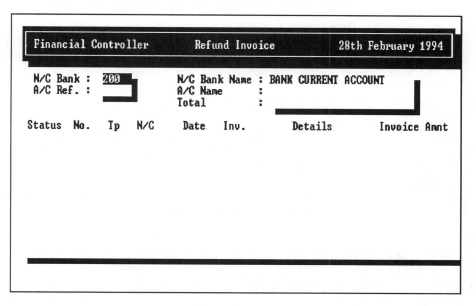

Cancel Cheque
Refund Invoice

3   Select **Refund Invoice** to reveal the Refund Invoice screen:

| Financial Controller | Refund Invoice | 28th February 1994 |

N/C Bank : 200   N/C Bank Name : BANK CURRENT ACCOUNT
A/C Ref. :   A/C Name   :
                         Total   :

Status No.   Tp   N/C   Date   Inv.   Details   Invoice Amnt

4   Use F4 to enter the customer code **G001** in the **A/C Ref.** box.

The name of the account is then automatically entered into the **A/C Name** box as
are all the paid invoices that still exist on the audit trail. In this case there is only
one.

5   Ensure that the description of this invoice is highlighted and press Enter.

The description is then annotated under **Status** as REFUNDED.

6   Press Esc and post the details to the ledgers.

The refund is then automatically entered into the accounts and the details cleared
from the screen in readiness for another refund to be entered.

7   Press Esc twice to return to the Sales Ledger screen.

8   View the transaction history of the George Hotel account.

You will see that the sales ledger account has been credited with a sales credit (**SC**)
referenced as **Refund** and debited with a sales invoice (**SI**) referenced as
Allocation - Refund.

9   Press Esc three times to return to the Financial Controller screen.

In the nominal ledger the account **4005 Sales - Carpeting** has been debited by the refund and the **Bank Current Account**, code **1200**, has been credited by the refund.

10   Display the Nominal Ledger screen and select the **Transaction History** option.

11   View the transaction histories of the nominal accounts **1200, 2200** and **4005**.

You will see that in account **1200 Bank Current Account** the gross value of the refund has been entered as a journal credit (**JC**) with reference REFUND. Notice the description:

Refunds <S> - G001

This indicates that the refund was a sales refund to a customer with code **G001**. In account **4005 Sales - Carpeting** the net value of the refund has been debited as a sales credit (**SC**).

In addition to this posting you will see that in account **2200 Tax Control Account** the refunded tax has been recorded as a debit of **315.00**.

15.6   Refunds and the control accounts

We have seen that the net value of the refund was recorded as a debit to the nominal sales account 4005 and the tax as a debit to the tax control account 2200. These debits were equal to the gross value of the refund which was posted as a credit to the bank account 1200. However, it is also necessary to record the refund in the Debtors control account as a sales credit (SC) . To effect all these postings it is necessary to pass through a number of control accounts first.

The total debit to the value of the gross refund record is first counterbalanced by a sales credit (SC) to account 1100, the Debtors Control Account. In addition a dummy sales invoice is posted as a debit to account 1100 to balance that account and then posted as a credit to the account 9999, the Mispostings account. Finally a journal debit (JD) is posted as debit to the account 9999 to balance that account and a corresponding journal credit posted to account 1200, the Bank Current Account. The eventual outcome is as follows:

Account	Type	Posting	Amount
4005 Sales -Carpeting	Sales credit	Debit	Net amount
2200 Tax Control	Sales credit	Debit	Tax amount
1100 Debtors Control	Sales credit	Credit	Gross
1100 Debtors Control	Sales invoice	Debit	Gross
9999 Mispostings	Sales invoice	Credit	Gross

9999 Mispostings	Journal debit	Debit	Gross
1200 Bank Current	Journal credit	Credit	Gross

Ensure that the Nominal Ledger screen is on display.

1   View the transaction histories of the accounts:

1100 Debtors Control Account
1200 Bank Current Account
2200 Tax Control Account
4005 Sales - Carpeting
9999 Mispostings Account

and verify that the appropriate postings have been made.

Complete this activity with the Financial Controller screen on display.

15.7   Returned cheques

A bounced cheque is bad news for anyone and Total Bedrooms were disconcerted to discover that the payment made by The Swallows Nest of £1616.13 in settlement of a December 93 invoice had resulted in the bank returning the cheque marked 'Returned to Drawer'.

The outcome of a returned cheque which has been entered into the accounts as a bank receipt has to be reversed. This is achieved within the Sage Sterling Financial Controller accounting system by using the **Cancel Cheque** option from the **Refunds** option on either the Sales or Purchase Ledger screen.

It is also very important that no more goods be despatched to The Swallows Nest until the matter is satisfactorily cleared up.

Ensure that the Financial Controller screen is on display.

1   Display the Sales Ledger screen.

2   Select the **Refunds** option and from the Sales Refunds screen select **Cancel Cheque** to reveal the Cancel Cheque screen:

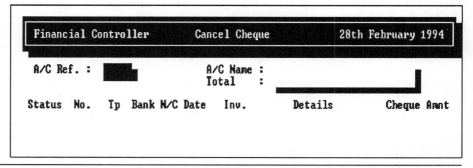

3   Enter the A/C Ref as:

T002 and press Enter

and the **A/C Name** and the details of the account are automatically entered into the screen by the system. The details of the cheque are already highlighted indicating that this cheque has been selected.

4   Press Enter and the details are annotated under **Status** as CANCEL'D.

5   Press Esc and post the details to the ledgers.

6   Press Esc twice to return to the Sales Ledger screen.

7   Select the **Transaction History** option and view the transaction history of the T002, The Swallows Nest account.

You will see that the sales receipt dated 31/01/94 has has its description amended from **Customer cheque** to read **Cancelled Cheque** and a further posting has been made - a sales debit to the account to the value **1616.13** annotated as **CancelledCheque**. This is really reinstating the original sales invoice.

A counterbalancing credit is made to the nominal ledger **Bank Current Account 1200** via the two control accounts **1100 Debtors Control** and **9999 Mispostings**.

8   Press Esc twice to return to the Financial Controller screen.

9   Display the Nominal Ledger screen and view the transaction histories of the accounts **1100 Debtors Control Account**, **1200 Bank Current Account** and **9999 Mispostings Account**.

In the Debtors Control Account the void cheque is debited as a sales invoice (*make a note of its transaction number in the audit trail you will need it later*), in the Mispostings Account the value of the returned cheque has been posted as a sales invoice, credited to the account to counterbalance the debit in the Debtors Control Account. In addition a journal debit referenced as CANCEL has also been posted to this account to balance the Mispostings account. In the Bank Current Account a journal credit referenced as CANCEL has been posted to counterbalance the overall debit created by balancing the Mispostings Account.

Complete this activity with the Financial Controller screen on display.

15.8   Write off transaction

After many phone calls between Total Bedrooms and The Swallows Nest it has been ascertained that there is little possibility of them paying for this sale in the near future as they are in financial trouble, having called in the receivers. Accordingly, Total Bedrooms, have been forced to accept this state of affairs and must now write the transaction off their books.

Ensure that the Financial Controller screen is on display.

 1   Display the Sales Ledger screen.

2   Select the **Bad Debt Write Off** option to reveal the Bad Debt Write Off screen:

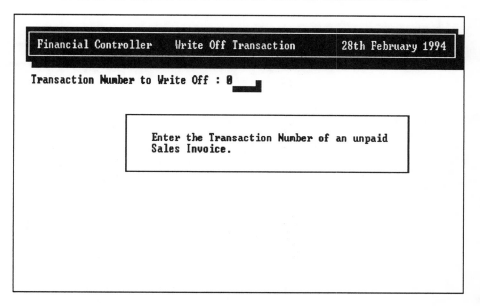

```
Write Off Account
Write Off Small Values
Write Off Transaction
```

3   Select **Write Off Transaction** to reveal the Write Off Transaction screen:

```
Financial Controller    Write Off Transaction    28th February 1994

Transaction Number to Write Off : 0

                Enter the Transaction Number of an unpaid
                Sales Invoice.
```

The transaction number of the audit trail is the number that you made a note of earlier. The reason you were asked to do this was because it is quite possible that you have made an error by now and your audit trail may not exactly match the audit trail presented in this book. If you do not know the transaction number view the Debtors Control Account and find it.

4   Enter the **Transaction Number** and press Enter .

The screen then displays the appropriate transaction and at the bottom of the screen you are asked if you wish to proceed:

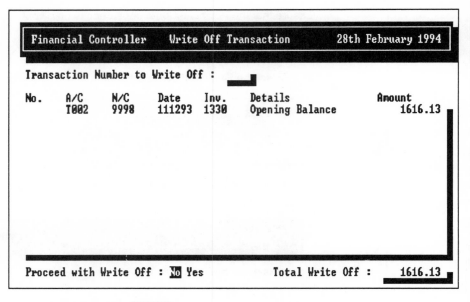

```
┌─────────────────────────────────────────────────────────────────┐
│  Financial Controller    Write Off Transaction    28th February 1994  │
│                                                                   │
│  Transaction Number to Write Off :      ▄▄▄                        │
│                                                                   │
│  No.   A/C    N/C    Date    Inv.   Details           Amount      │
│        T002   9998   111293  1330   Opening Balance    1616.13     │
│                                                                   │
│                                                                   │
│                                                                   │
│                                                                   │
│                                                                   │
│                                                                   │
│                                                                   │
│                                                                   │
│  Proceed with Write Off : No Yes         Total Write Off :  1616.13 │
└─────────────────────────────────────────────────────────────────┘
```

5   Enter **Y** and press **Enter**.

The transaction is then written off and you are returned to the Write Off Transaction screen in readiness to enter another transaction number.

6   Press **Esc** and you are returned to the Sales Ledger screen.

The effect of writing off a transaction is to credit the Debtors Control account with the gross amount and to debit the Bad Debt Write Off account with the same amount.

7   Press **Esc** twice to return to the Financial Controller screen.

8   Display the Nominal Ledger screen and view the transaction histories of the accounts **1100 Debtors Control Account** and **8100 Bad Debt Write Off**.

The transaction is recorded as a sales credit credited to the Debtors Control Account and a sales credit debited to the Bad Debt Write Off account.

Complete this activity with the Financial Controller screen on display.

15.9   Write off account

Total Bedrooms have learned that The Swallows Nest has gone into liquidation with virtually no assets. This means that Total Bedrooms are never going to recover their debts from this company and as a consequence have decided to write off the entire account from their books.

Ensure that the Financial Controller screen is on display.

 1   Display the Sales Ledger screen and select the **Bad Debt Write Off** option to reveal the Bad Debt Write Off screen.

2   Select **Write Off Account** to reveal the Write Off Account screen:

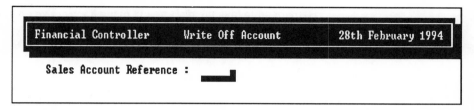

```
┌──────────────────────────────────────────────────────────────────────┐
│ Financial Controller      Write Off Account      28th February 1994   │
│                                                                        │
│   Sales Account Reference :    ▁▁▁                                     │
│                                                                        │
└──────────────────────────────────────────────────────────────────────┘
```

3   Use F4 to enter the account code **T002** in the **Sales Account Reference** box and press Enter.

The account is instantly written off and you are returned to the Write Off Account screen in readiness to enter another account reference.

4   Press Esc three times to return to the Financial Controller screen.

The account does not disappear from the books but remains with a balance of zero.

5   Display the Nominal Ledger screen and view the transaction histories of the accounts **1100 Debtors Control Account** and **8100 Bad Debt Write Off**.

You will see that in writing off the account the total amount written off is recorded as a credit of 3823.45 to the Debtors Control Account and as an appropriate debit to the Bad Debt Write Off account.

When you write off either a collection of transactions or an entire account there are going to be problems accounting for any VAT that is involved as the VAT paid on bad debts can be reclaimed. We shall consider such problems with VAT in Part III of this book. Complete this activity with the Financial Controller screen on display.

15.10   Backing up data to a floppy diskette

You have now completed Chapter Fifteen and have entered data into the Sage Sterling Financial Controller accounting system which has been stored on your computer's hard disk. While the hard disk is a very reliable medium it is worthwhile reminding yourself that it is storing your only copy of the data and that the disk itself is not infallible. Data can be irretrievably lost if your hard disk fails. Therefore, it is advised that you back up your data onto a floppy diskette (refer to page xvi of *Getting started*).

 A word of caution. When backing up data to a floppy diskette from your hard disk, all the current information in the data files on your hard disk is copied to the floppy diskette. As a consequence, it is always best to back up using the Backup/Restore facility available within the Sage Sterling Financial Controller accounting system which backs up and restores *all* the data files. If you use any other method which enables you to select which data files to back up or restore you may be tempted not to back up or restore all of your data files. In such an event your data could very easily become corrupted and, therefore, worthless.

Remember to take the diskette out of the floppy drive and to store it in a safe place.

16   Enquiries

Within the Sage Sterling Financial Controller accounting system various on-screen enquiries are available to enable you to view the current status of an account or product. For instance, a customer may ring up asking for a certain quantity of a certain product. By using the on-screen enquiry facilities you would be able to find out if enough of the item was in stock and if the customer had prearranged credit whilst speaking to the potential customer on the phone.

Account enquiries can be accessed via the **Transaction History** options that are present in the Sales Ledger, Purchase Ledger, Nominal Ledger and Stock Control screens. Many enquiries are sensitive to the system date in relation to an entered transaction date. As a consequence, it is essential that the system date for this chapter be 28 February 1994.

16.1   Customer and supplier record enquiries

Ensure that the Financial Controller screen is on display.

1   Display the Sales Ledger screen and select **Customer Details** to reveal an empty Customer Details screen.

2   Enter the code **M001** in the **Account Reference** box and press Enter.

Immediately the screen fills with the details of the Main Line Hotels Plc account which displays details in the form of:

● The sales ledger account code, the customer's name and address and the contact name.

● Three lines of information about the customer that can be used for analysis by means of the Report Generator - Credit Limit, Analysis Code and Turnover. A careful use of this facility can provide a wide range of analysis options for the company's sales. We shall be considering the Report Generator in detail in Part III of this book.

3   Press Esc and select **Abandon** to clear the details of this account from the screen.

4   Press Esc again to return to the Sales Ledger.

We have already accessed the **Transaction History** option. Instead, we shall access the Day Book reports.

5   Select the **Day Book** option in the Sales Ledger screen to reveal the Day Books screen:

```
Sales Invoices
Sales Credit Notes
Sales Receipts
Sales Discounts
```

6   Select the **Sales Invoices** option to reveal the Sales Invoices screen:

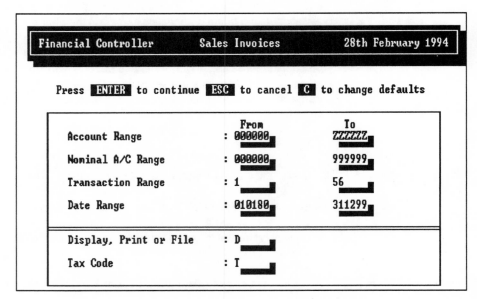

The Sales Invoices Day Book is a listing of sales invoices selected according to a variety of criteria. They can be listed according to:

Sales Ledger account range
Nominal Ledger account range
Transaction number range
Date range

In addition they can be restricted to a specific tax code. The report can be displayed on the computer monitor screen, sent to a printer or stored in a file for access at a later date.

7   Leave the default settings as they are and display the day book listing of all the sales invoices issued so far.

8   To quit the report press Esc.

The same set of Day Book reports are available in both the Purchase Ledger and the Nominal Ledger.

9 Access the Day Books in both the Purchase and Nominal Ledgers and produce a printed copy of each. When you have done this ensure that the Financial Controller screen is on display.

Within both the Sales and Purchase Order Processing screens there is an **Enquiries** option. This option can provide a report on all the orders issued to date.

A wider range of reports are available via the predefined reports in the Report Generator. Ensure that the Financial Controller screen is on display.

10 Select the **Report Generator** option to reveal the Report Generator screen which displays a selection of categories of report. Produce a printout of each report in turn to see exactly what information each one gives you:

Sales Ledger

```
NAME     TITLE
AGED     Sales Ledger Aged Debtors Analysis

AGED     Sales Ledger Aged Debtors Analysis
DEBT     Sales Accounts 30 Day Debt exceeding 1000 pounds
DEPT     Sales Ledger Departmental Analysis
ESL1     EC Sales List (ESL)
LEDG     Sales Ledger CSV File - SALES.CSV
LIMIT    Sales Accounts Credit Limit Exceeded
SELL     Top Customer List
TURN     Sales Ledger Nett Turnover Month & Year to date
VRN      List of VAT Registration Numbers
```

Purchase Ledger

```
NAME     TITLE
AGED     Purchase Ledger Aged Creditors

AGED     Purchase Ledger Aged Creditors
LEDG     Purchase Ledger CSV File - PURCHASE.CSV
```

Nominal Ledger

```
NAME     TITLE
DEPT     Nominal Ledger Departmental Analysis

DEPT     Nominal Ledger Departmental Analysis
LEDG     Nominal Ledger CSV File - NOMINAL.CSV
TRIAL    Nominal Ledger Trial Balance
```

Management Reports

```
NAME     TITLE
DEPT     Departmental Analysis (Totals)

DEPT     Departmental Analysis (Totals)
TAXAI    Tax Analysis (by Invoice)
TAXAP    Tax Analysis (by Payment)
TRANS    Audit Trail CSV File - TRANS.CSV
VATBC    Tax Analysis - Bank and Cash Accounts
VATIC    Tax Analysis - Invoices and Credits
VATPR    Tax Analysis - Payments and Receipts
```

Invoice Production

```
NAME     TITLE
FREE     Free Text Invoices

FREE     Free Text Invoices
LIST     Outstanding Invoices
```

Stock Control

```
NAME     TITLE
PRICE    Stock Price List

PRICE    Stock Price List
PROFW    Stock Period Profit
RECS     Stock Records CSV File - STOCK.CSV
REORD    Purchase ReOrder List
SALES    Full Stock Price List
SUPLY    Supplier List
TRANS    Stock Transactions CSV File - STKTRANS.CSV
VALUE    Stock Valuation
```

Sales Order Processing

```
NAME     TITLE
HOLD     Sales Order Hold List

HOLD     Sales Order Hold List
LIST     Sales Order List
PICK     Sales Order Picking List
```

Purchase Order Processing

```
NAME     TITLE
LIST     Purchase Order List

LIST     Purchase Order List
```

16.2 Nominal ledger budget report

Ensure that the Nominal Ledger screen is on display.

1   Select the **Budget Report** option to reveal the Budget Report screen:

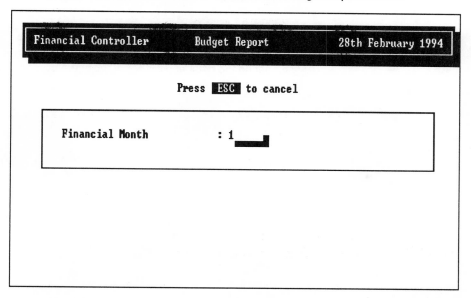

```
┌─────────────────────────────────────────────────────────────────┐
│ Financial Controller      Budget Report      28th February 1994 │
└─────────────────────────────────────────────────────────────────┘

                    Press  ESC  to cancel

   ┌─────────────────────────────────────────────────────┐
   │   Financial Month           : 1___                  │
   │                                                     │
   └─────────────────────────────────────────────────────┘
```

2   Enter the **Financial Month** as:

    1

3   Select the report to be sent to the printer.

This report lists the totals of all sales and purchases for the selected month and the year to date. By subtracting expenses that are related specifically to sales and purchases the report also gives the gross profit. In addition, the report lists the totals of all expenses incurred in the running of the company and finally produces the nett profit.

16.3 The Quick Ratio report

The quick ratio report gives a display of the current liquidity of the company. The default accounts set up to do this are:

1100 Debtors Control
The amount of money owed to the Company by its customers

1200 Bank Current Account
The amount of money in the bank account

1230 Petty Cash account
The amount of cash in petty cash

2100 Creditors Control
The Company's liabilities to its suppliers

2200 VAT control
The Company's liability to HM Customs and Excise

By comparing the debit and credit balances the quick ratio report displays the net balance.

EXERCISE

1   Display the Nominal Ledger screen and select the **Quick Report** option to reveal the Quick Ratio screen.

2   Select to print the report and obtain a hard copy of the quick ratio report.

Complete this activity with the Financial Controller screen on display.

16.4   Product record enquiries

Ensure that the Financial Controller screen is on display.

1   Display the Stock Control screen and select the **Stock Details** option to reveal the Stock Details screen displaying the first item of stock - **101 Single bed.** Press `F10` to reveal the Product Record screen with the record of stock item **102 Double bed** on display.

This record displays static details described as:

Product Details
The product details display everything that is required to be known about a particular item of stock. The assigned **Code**, **Category**, **Category Name** and **Department** identify the item of stock. The **Sales Price**, **Cost Price**, **Unit of Sale**, **Discount** and **Tax Code** describe the monetary aspects of he stock item. The **Re-order level** and **Re-order quantity** describe the means whereby the stock is to be replenished. The reorder level refers to the quantity of stock at, or below, which fresh stock should be ordered. The quantity here appears on the reorder report available via the **Reports** button on the Products screen. The **Nominal Code** describes the account in which sales of this item of stock will be accounted for.

Stock Levels
The three entries of **In Stock, On Order** and **Allocated** are not static but are updated by the Sage Sterling accounting system automatically whenever stock movements are generated via adjustments, invoicing from stock, crediting or creating orders.

In Stock

This entry reflects the quantity of this item that is currently held in stock.

On Order

This entry reflects the quantity of this item that remains to be delivered against a purchase order.

Allocated

This entry reflects the quantity of this item that has been allocated to sales orders. Because it is allocated but not yet delivered to a customer it remains in stock and as such is included in the **In Stock** total.

Make-Up

The last box to consider on this screen is labelled **Make-Up** and provides access to a facility within the Sage Sterling accounting system to enable products to be defined in terms of component items drawn from stock. For example, using this facility it would be possible to define a new item of stock called Single Suite which consisted of a single bed, two sets of single bedding, a small wardrobe, a small vanity unit and a chair. We shall deal with this aspect of product record keeping in Chapter 20.

Sales Information

The values of the stock sales are recorded in the **Value Sold Mth** and **YTD** and the movements of stock are recorded in the **Quantity Sold Mth**, **YTD** and the dates of the last sale and purchase. These last two entries, **Last Purchase Date** and **Last Purchase Quantity**, are updated automatically in the same manner as the **Cost Price** entry.

Supplier Information

The supplier information includes the account code of the supplier already defined in the supplier records. If more than one supplier is used for this particular item of stock then this entry can be left blank. Also included in the supplier information box are the part reference (such as the one used by the supplier).

Complete this activity with the Financial Controller screen on display.

16.5   Customer and supplier activity enquiries

In addition to the static details relating to customers and suppliers that we have already seen there is a collection of dynamic details available. These are automatically updated by the Sage Sterling Financial Controller accounting system as and when it is appropriate to do so.

Ensure that the Financial Controller screen is on display.

 1   Display the Purchase Ledger screen and select the **Account Balances (Aged)** option to reveal the Account Balances (Aged) screen.

2   Accept all the defaults and produce a display of the the aged balance of each of Total Bedrooms' suppliers. By using the cursor keys an **Aged Analysis** can be viewed.

To view a more detailed analysis of the Company's debt to each supplier you will have to view the transaction history of each supplier in turn where you see the details of the amounts that are owed by Total Bedrooms to its suppliers.

As you will see the transaction history lists the details of every transaction entered into the Sage Sterling accounting system that has affected this account. These transactions are of various types and the type of any particular transaction is coded beneath the heading **Tp**. The different types of transaction that can be listed here are coded as follows:

Code	Transaction
PI	purchase invoice
PR	purchase receipt
PC	purchase credit note
PD	discount on a purchase payment
PA	purchase payment on account

The equivalent coding for the Customer Transaction History screen accessible via the Customers screen is:

Code	Transaction
SI	sales invoice
SR	sales receipt
SC	sales credit note
SD	discount on a sales receipt
SA	sales receipt on account

If there are more transactions than can be fitted into the information panel as it is displayed then pressing **PgDn** will enable you to scroll through all the transactions.

Every transaction has a value associated with it and these values are listed under the heading **Value**. Also indicated here is the status of the transaction:

An asterisk (*) indicates that a transaction is unpaid.

A letter P to the right of the value indicates that the transaction has been part paid and the remaining amount due is displayed beneath the value of the part paid transaction.

No marker at all indicates that the transaction has been paid in full, or, in the case of a credit note, has been fully allocated.

In the top right hand corner of the screen are three further figures that display the amount outstanding on this account, the amount paid this month and the turnover for the year to date. The credit limit with the account reference and account name are shown in the top left hand corner of the screen. In addition the age of the debt is shown under a number of columns where the columns all relate to an amount that is due to be paid to a supplier and the length of time that it has been due.

Future
Any transaction dated later than the system date.

Current
This column totals the supplier invoices that have been entered into the Sage Sterling accounting system whose date is the current month.

30 days
This column totals the supplier invoices that have been entered into the Sage Sterling accounting system whose date is the previous month.

60 days
This column totals the supplier invoices that have been entered into the Sage Sterling accounting system whose date contains a month that is two months prior to the current month.

90 days
This column totals the supplier invoices that have been entered into the Sage Sterling accounting system whose date contains a month that is three months prior to the current month.

Older
This column totals the supplier invoices that have been entered into the Sage Sterling accounting system whose date contains a month that is more than three months prior to the current month.

Note: If an account balance exceeds the credit limit then an asterisk is displayed after the account code.

Complete this activity with the Financial Controller screen on display.

16.6 Nominal ledger activity enquiries

In addition to the static details relating to the nominal ledger that we have already seen there is a collection of dynamic details available. These are automatically updated by the Sage Sterling accounting system as and when it is appropriate to do so.

Ensure that the Financial Controller screen is on display.

 1 Display the Nominal Ledger screen and select the **Transaction History** option.

2   Select the account **1200 Bank Current Account** and the contents of the
     Nominal Ledger Transaction History screen change to display the transaction
     history of the chosen account.

As you will see the transaction history lists the details of every transaction entered
into the Sage Sterling accounting system that has affected this account. These
transactions are of various types and the type of any particular transaction is coded
beneath the heading **Tp**. We have already seen some of the different types of
transaction that can be listed here; others are coded as follows:

Code	Transaction
BP	bank payment
BR	bank receipt
PP	purchase payment
SR	sales receipt
JC	journal credit
JD	journal debit

If there are more transactions than can be fitted into the central box as it is displayed then pressing ‎ **PgDn** ‎ will enable you to scroll through all the transactions.

Every transaction has a value associated with it and these values are listed under
the heading **Value**. Also indicated is whether the value of the transaction has been
debited or credited to the account.

Beneath the central box are three further figures that display the total debits and
credits of this account and the balance on the account, which will either be a debit or
a credit. Complete this activity with the Financial Controller on display.

17 Credit control

It is common practice for a company to separate the physical process of delivering its goods and services to a customer from the need for the customer to pay for them. To enable this to happen the company must give the customer a credit rating - a fixed amount up to which the customer can purchase without paying immediately on delivery. The effect of this is that goods pass from the company's possession to the customer's possession without any immediate money passing in the other direction to compensate. This places the customer in debt to the company and the more time that passes between the debt being incurred and the debt being settled by payment the more problems the company can experience in paying its own suppliers. All this requires a properly maintained credit control system and the Sage Sterling Financial Controller accounting system provides a number of features to enable this.

Before doing any business with a customer it is essential that all trading conditions are explicitly explained and agreed. These conditions will include, amongst other things, the amount of credit the customer will be permitted and the maximum length of time that a particular bill will be allowed to be outstanding. To ascertain the credit level of a potential customer Total Bedrooms must do a credit check on the customer using the various sources of information that are available. For example, a customer's creditworthiness can be ascertained from a credit reference agency, from a bank reference and from other references provided by the customer's other suppliers.

The maximum amount of time that a bill will be allowed to be outstanding will vary from customer to customer but the usual trading standard is the 30 day account. This formally means that all bills will be settled 30 days after the goods were delivered.

The amount of credit given to a customer in the first instance depends upon a number of factors, not least external credit references. Once a credit level is established then it must be agreed by the customer that trading will be maintained within the prescribed limits.

Having agreed with all the customers their respective settlement terms and credit limits it is then incumbent on the company to maintain a proper system of credit control to ensure that the customers do indeed keep to their side of the bargain.

17.1　　Aged debt analysis

Within the Sage Sterling Financial controller accounting system an immediate record is available that will give the company all the necessary information relating to the historical debt record of any customer.

Ensure that the Financial Controller screen is on display and that the system date is 28 February 1994.

1　　Display the Sales Ledger screen and select the **Transaction History** option.

2　　Accept the defaults in this screen and display the transaction history of every customer account on the computer monitor, one account at a time.

We can see from the various transaction histories that:

B001 has a 60 days overdue amount of £5196.86 and G002, I001, M001 and T001 are all due to pay amounts this month because they all have entries in the 30 days column.

This view has given us an immediate sight of which customers are due to pay this month and which customers are overdue on their payments. Also we can see which customers have been allowed to exceed their credit limits - these are G001 and I001 as indicated by the word **Exceeded** alongside their credit limits.

Complete this activity with the Financial Controller screen on display.

17.2　　Statements

From the printed Aged Debtors Analysis it is evident that a number of customers are due to pay their outstanding accounts in the near future. It is felt that it is time to give those customers a gentle reminder of their obligations by sending each one of them a statement of account. Indeed, as a matter of course, every customer will be sent a statement at the beginning or end of every month.

Ensure that the Financial Controller screen is on display.

EXERCISE　1　　Display the Sales Ledger screen and select the **Statements** option.

2　　Produce a printed a statement for every customer listing their debts between 01/01/94 and 28/02/94.

After some time all the statements will have been sent to the printer and you will be returned to the Sales Ledger screen.

From the printed Aged Debtors Analysis you will see that there is one customer with an outstanding account beyond the normal settlement terms. A reminder letter must now be sent to this customer indicating that Total Bedrooms are aware of the fact that their account is substantially outstanding and requires immediate attention.

Ensure that the Customers screen is on display and that the system date is 28 February 1994.

1   Display the Sales Ledger screen and select the **Letters** option to reveal the Letters screen:

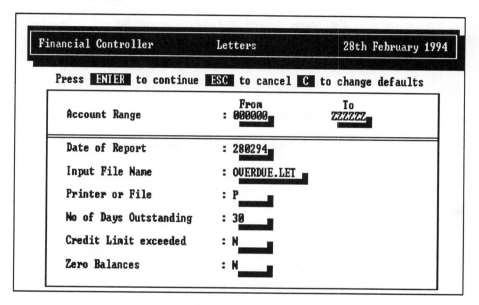

2   Accept all the defaults in this screen and generate letters to all those customers whose accounts are 30 days or more outstanding.

It is possible to amend the contents and layout of this letter and it is also possible to create more letters from scratch. We shall see how to do this later in the *Guide*.

Complete this activity with the Financial Controller screen on display.

A year's trading

In order to complete Part II of this book we need to consider the year end procedures that complete a full year's accounting. Before we can do this, however, we need to have covered a full year's accounting and this is what this chapter is about. We shall first complete the accounting for the month of February 1994 and then continue entering transactions until we have completed December's transactions. The year end procedures will then be considered in the following chapter.

Complete February's accounting by:

1   Enter the following customer receipts:

Code	Name	Date	Invoice	Amount
B001	Budget Hostelry Plc	15/02/94	1329	5196.86
I001	Innkeepers Plc	15/02/94	1342	1122.13
M001	Main Line Hotels Plc	16/02/94	1340 & 1347	2397.00

This latter receipt settles the account amount of £2420.50 against invoices 1340 and 1347 after the credit note of £23.50 for a returned table lamp has been paid in full.

T001	The Regency	17/02/94	1346	293.75

2   Enter the following supplier payments:

Code	Name	Date	Cheque	Invoice	Amount
COMM	Commercial Carpenters	15/02/94	108	5030	4571.56
FLASH	Flash Lighting	17/02/94	109	5047	4931.33
HAND	Hand Craft Ltd	20/02/94	110	5073	3953.25
SLEEP	Sleepwell	21/02/94	111	5048	1268.66
SYKES	Sykes Mills Ltd	22/02/94	112	5025	539.41

3   Process the Recurring entries for February.

4   Complete the month by:

Printing any reports necessary and transferring the closing stock value of £90,204.00 with a journal entry with Ref. 008 and date 28/02/94. This is achieved by first reversing the stock journal entry performed at the end of January and then entering the closing stock value of £90,204.00 in the usual manner. The completed journal entry should then look as follows:

		Debit	Credit
1001	Reverse January		110804.00
5201	Reverse January	110804.00	
1001	February	90204.00	
5201	February		90204.00

Running the Month End function and:
    posting accruals and prepayments
    posting depreciation
    clearing the stock files
Printing the audit trail.

18.2   March

1   Before you enter the following transactions for March change the system date to 31 March 94.

2   Enter the following sales orders, batching each of them for further processing:

Order To	Number	Date	Order
Budget Hostelry Plc	9	10/03/94	75 chairs
			50 decor packs
			20 large vanity units
			40 table lamps
Gibbert Arms	10	10/03/94	10 double beds
			40 sets of double bedding
Main Line Hotels	11	22/03/94	1500 metres carpeting

3   Process the sales orders, printing them and allocating stock as you do so.

4   Complete their despatch, printing the delivery notes and updating the stock and invoice records as you do so.

5   When the sales orders have the status of COMPLETE print the sales invoices, posting the details to the ledgers as you do so.

From the overdrawn state of their bank account, Total Bedrooms could see that their cash flow was in a precarious position. If they continued to trade at their present level with such a high level of stockholding then they may have to approach the bank for an increase in the overdraft facility. At the same time, a great part of their trade was the result of their ability to deliver immediately from stock. Because the stockholding was rather large and a lot of money was being tied up in stock Total Bedrooms have decided to gradually reduce their stockholding until the amount of each item held is only slightly above the reorder level. They therefore made no stock purchases during March.

6   Enter the following customer receipts:

Code	Name	Date	Invoice	Amount
B001	Budget Hostelry Plc	15/03/94	1350	6168.75
G001	George Hotel	18/03/94	1349	7402.50
G002	Gibbert Arms	22/03/94	1345	799.00
I001	Innkeepers	25/03/94	1351	11338.75
M001	Main Line Hotels	31/03/94	1348/52	22560.00

7   Enter the following supplier payments:

Code	Name	Date	Cheque	Invoice	Amount
COMM	Commercial Carpenters	26/03/94	113	5065	1974.28
WILM	Wilminster Carpets	26/03/94	114	5055	8232.80
HAND	Hand Craft	26/03/94	115	5082	10046.25

As sales and purchase orders are completed they do nothing other than take up space. It is a good idea to delete all the previous month's sales and purchase orders that have the status COMPLETE.

Ensure that the Financial Controller screen is on display.

8   Display the Sales Orders screen and select the **Delete Orders** option to delete every sales order that has status COMPLETE.

9   Repeat the above procedure to delete all purchase orders with the status of COMPLETE.

18.3   Recurring entries

EXERCISE   Post all the recurring entries for March.

18.4   Quarterly bills

EXERCISE   The following quarterly bills arrived during March:

Telephone £385.63 + VAT (£67.49) dated 05/03/94
Electricity £510.37 + VAT (£89.31) dated 09/03/94

These bills are for services received and are due. Prior to the Spring of 1994 the VAT rate for fuel was zero. However, in the Spring of 1994 the VAT rate became 8%, rising to 17.5% in the Spring of 1995. For simplicity the rate has been kept at 17.5% in line with all other items.

1 Enter the telephone payment as a **Bank Payment** using cheque number **116**, date **15/03/94** and nominal code **7502**.

2 Enter the electricity payment as a **Bank Payment** using cheque number **117**, date **15/03/94** and nominal code **7200**.

Complete this activity with the Financial Controller screen on display.

18.5 Month end procedures

EXERCISE Complete the month by:

Printing any reports necessary and transferring the closing stock value of £62,904.00 with a journal entry, Ref. 009 and dated 31/03/94 (see Section 18.1)
Running the Month End function and:
   posting accruals and prepayments
   posting depreciation
   clearing the stock files
Printing the audit trail.

Notice that the Bank Current Account now stands at £14,327.32 - a healthier cash flow but care still needs to be maintained to avoid overstocking.

18.6 The VAT Return

At the end of every quarter it is necessary to file a VAT Return with HM Customs and Excise. The facility to create the VAT Return is available using the **VAT Return Analysis** in the Nominal Ledger screen.

Ensure that the Financial Controller screen is on display and that the system date is 31 March 1994.

 1 Display the Nominal Ledger screen and select the **VAT Return Analysis** option to reveal the VAT Return Analysis screen:

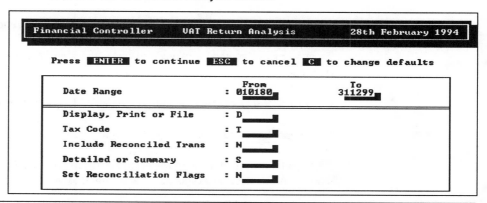

```
┌──────────────────────────────────────────────────────────────────────┐
│ Financial Controller    UAT Return Analysis      28th February 1994  │
└──────────────────────────────────────────────────────────────────────┘

    Press  ENTER  to continue  ESC  to cancel  C  to change defaults

   ┌──────────────────────────────────────────────────────────────────┐
   │                                 From              To               │
   │   Date Range                 : 010180         311299              │
   │                                                                    │
   │   Display, Print or File     : D                                   │
   │   Tax Code                   : T                                   │
   │   Include Reconciled Trans   : N                                   │
   │   Detailed or Summary        : S                                   │
   │   Set Reconciliation Flags   : N                                   │
   └──────────────────────────────────────────────────────────────────┘
```

2   Accept the defaults in this screen ensuring that the default for:

Set Reconciliation Flags is **N** for No.

3   Press $\boxed{\textbf{Enter}}$ and the VAT analysis is performed:

```
┌─────────────────────────────────────────────┐
│                                             │
│  Finding Outstanding Transactions           │
│                                             │
│     Transaction No. :      47▮              │
│                                             │
└─────────────────────────────────────────────┘
```

When the analysis is complete a message appears telling you how many transactions have been found. The message also tells you to press any key to continue.

4   Press any key and the VAT Return Analysis appears on your computer monitor screen.

The tax return is listed against a number of specific entries, the only ones being shown to have an amount against them being:

VAT due this period on Sales
Total VAT due

VAT reclaimed in this period on Purchases
Net VAT paid or reclaimed by you

Total value of sales excluding VAT
Total value of purchases excluding VAT

5   Place the highlight on each item in turn and press $\boxed{\textbf{Enter}}$.

A detailed breakdown of each amount is then given in the form of a matrix listing of:

Invoices and credits
Payments or Receipts
Journal entries

against each individual tax codes.

6   Place the highlight against any amount in this matrix listing and press $\boxed{\textbf{Enter}}$.

An even more detailed breakdown of where the amount has come from is then displayed.

7   Press $\boxed{\textbf{Esc}}$ and you are returned to the VAT Return Analysis.

8   Press $\boxed{\textbf{Esc}}$ again and you are returned to the Nominal Ledger screen.

What you have just done is to review the detailed analysis that is available whenever a VAT analysis is executed. Now we need to produce a VAT Return Analysis and account for the fact that we have done so within the accounting system. In other words we need to produce a VAT Return Analysis that is reconciled against the accounts.

The details on this displayed VAT Return need to be copied onto the VAT Return form that is provided by HM Customs and Excise. However, before this is done the Sage Sterling Financial Controller VAT Return has to be reconciled with the accounts to ensure that when you produce a VAT Return next quarter you will not include any VAT from this quarter.

To effect this the Sage Sterling Financial Controller accounting system has a facility for marking those VAT amounts that have already been accounted for in a previous month. This is done by flagging each transaction that is included in the analysis.

1   With the Nominal Ledger screen on display select the **VAT Return Analysis** option once more.

2   Set the options in the VAT Return Analysis screen to be:

Date Range:
From: **010194** To: **310394**. This covers the appropriate accounting period.

Tax Code:
The default is **T**, or any other code the user has set up.

Output:
P for Print. We shall need a hard copy of the analysis to transfer the details to the HM Customs and Excise form.

Include reconciled transactions:
N for No. This is not a problem here as we have not run a VAT analysis before so there are no such reconciled transactions.

Type of report:
D for Detailed. This will produce a listing of every transaction that has been included in the analysis.

Set Reconciliation Flags:
Y for Yes. It is important that we do this otherwise the transactions used this quarter will re-appear in next quarter's analysis.

3   When you are satisfied that all the options are correctly assigned, check that your printer is switched on and on-line and press $\boxed{\text{Enter}}$.

The reconciliation is effected returning you to the display of the Nominal Ledger screen. The VAT to be paid to HM Customs and Excise is given as £12,051.03. The search of all the sales and purchase transactions that include a VAT component missed out the journal entry of the van purchase. Consequently, the £1,400.00 VAT paid when the van was purchased can also be claimed back thereby reducing the VAT liability to £10,651.03. It is necessary to transfer this liability from the Tax Control Account 2200 to the VAT Liability Account 2201. Debit account 2200 with 10,651.03 and credit account 2201 with the same amount.

18.8 April

 1   Before you enter the following transactions for April change the system date to 30 April 1994.

2   Enter and process the following sales orders through to completion, producing all the appropriate invoices, updating stock records and posting the details to the ledgers:

Order To	Number	Date	Order
Budget Hostelry Plc	12	05/04/94	40 small vanity units
			40 large vanity units
			10 single wardrobes
			25 double wardrobes
Innkeeper	13	12/04/94	60 stools
			25 table lamps
			40 standard lamps
Main Line Hotels	14	18/04/94	200 metres carpeting
			80 sets of linen curtains
			100 sets of lace curtains
			50 sets of single bedding
			100 sets of double bedding
Queens Hotel	15	24/04/94	80 pictures
			150 ashtrays
The Regency	16	28/04/94	40 waste bins
			30 decor packs

3   Enter the following purchase order:

Order From	Number	Date	Order
Seats and Things	6	02/04/94	30 Chairs @ £100.00

4   Print the purchase order to ensure that it attains ON-ORDER status as recorded in the Sales Order Processing screen information panel.

5   Complete the despatch and update the stock.

6   Enter and post the purchase invoice received against this delivered purchase order:

A/C: Seats and Things
Invoice Number: 5092
Date: 10/04/94
N/C: 5003
Purchase of: 30 Chairs @ £100.00   3000.00

                   VAT   525.00
                   Total   3525.00

7   Enter the following customer receipts:

Code	Name	Date	Invoice	Amount
B001	Budget Hostelry Plc	02/04/94	1353/56	21596.50
M001	Main Line Hotels Plc	02/04/94	1358	31725.00
I001	Innkeepers Plc	15/04/94	1354	3995.00
G002	Gibbert Arms	22/04/94	1357	2937.50

8   Enter the following supplier payments:

Code	Name	Date	Cheque	Invoice	Amount
ART	ArtWork	16/04/94	118	5083	420.00
EEZEE	EEZEE Beds	16/04/94	119	5080	3055.00
FLASH	Flash Lighting	18/04/94	120	5081	587.50
FOR	Forward Bedding	18/04/94	121	5086	1351.25
SEAT	Seats and Things	18/04/94	122	5084	2937.50
WILM	Wilminster Carpets	18/04/94	123	5085	5875.00

9   Delete all sales orders with the status of COMPLETE.

10   Delete all purchase orders with the status of COMPLETE.

EXERCISE   From the VAT Return it is evident that Total Bedrooms owe HM Customs & Excise £10,651.03 for the first quarter.

1   Enter the payment of £10,651.03 to HM Customs & Excise as a Bank Payment using code 2201 for VAT Liability, date 30/04/94, cheque 124 and tax code T9.

18.9   Month end procedures

EXERCISE   Complete the month by:

Processing all the recurring entries
Printing any reports necessary and transferring the closing stock of £40,454.00 with a journal entry with Ref. 010 and date 30/04/94 (see Section 18.1)

Running the Month End function and:
    posting accruals and prepayments
    posting depreciation
    clearing the stock files
Printing the audit trail.

 1   Before you enter the following transactions for May change the system date to 31 May 94.

2   Enter and process the following sales orders:

Order For	Number	Date	Order
George Hotel	17	05/05/94	25 single beds
			30 double beds

When you allocate stock to this order you will find that you are 2 single beds short. You decide not to despatch the order. You decide to wait until you have replenished your stock before you completely fulfil the order.

Order For	Number	Date	Order
Main Line Hotels Plc	18	12/05/94	30 large vanity units
			30 single wardrobes
			35 double wardrobes

When you allocate stock to this order you will find that you are 5 double wardrobes short. You decide not to despatch the order. You decide to wait until you have replenished your stock before you completely fulfil the order.

Order For	Number	Date	Order
The Regency	19	14/05/94	50 stools
			15 chairs
			40 standard lamps
Innkeepers	20	22/05/94	250 metres of carpet
Gibbert Arms	21	29/05/94	40 sets of lace curtains

When you complete the processing of the last three orders display the Invoice Production screen in the Sales Ledger and select the option **Display Index**. You will notice that there are no invoices yet for the two incomplete orders.

3   Enter and process the following purchase orders:

Order To	Number	Date	Order
EEZEE Beds Plc	7	03/05/94	30 single beds @ £40.00
			40 double beds @ £60.00

Commercial Carpenters	8	10/5/94	20 double wardrobes @ £180.00
Artwork	9	15/05/94	25 pictures @ £15.00

4 Enter the following invoices that accompanied deliveries against the purchase orders:

A/C:	EEZEE	
Ref:	5093	
Date:	12/05/94	
N/C:	5001	
Purchase of:	30 single beds	1200.00
	40 double beds	2400.00
	VAT	630.00
	Total	4230.00

A/C:	COMM	
Ref:	5094	
Date:	15/05/94	
N/C:	5002	
Purchase of:	20 double wardrobes	3600.00
	VAT	630.00
	Total	4230.00

A/C:	ART	
Ref:	5095	
Date:	22/05/94	
N/C:	5007	
Purchase of:	25 pictures	375.00
	Total	375.00

5 Return to the Sales Order Processing facility and complete the processing of the two sales orders that could not be fully allocated stock.

6 Enter the following customer receipts:

Code	Name	Date	Invoice	Amount
B001	Budget Hostelry Plc	05/05/94	1359	19928.00
Q001	Queens Hotel	07/05/94	1362	3231.25
M001	Main Line Hotels Plc	15/05/94	1361	17507.50
T001	The Regency	18/05/94	1363	1762.50

7 Enter the following supplier payments:

Code	Name	Date	Cheque	Invoice	Amount
ART	Artwork	15/05/94	125	5090	2000.00

COMM	Commercial Carpenters	15/05/94	126	5088	2702.50
EEZEE	EEZEE Beds Plc	15/05/94	127	5087	4230.00
FABRIC	Fabrico	15/05/94	128	5089	2232.50
SEATS	Seats and Things	15/05/94	129	5092	3525.00
SLEEP	Sleepwell	15/05/94	130	5091	1175.00

8   Delete all sales orders with the status of COMPLETE.

9   Delete all purchase orders with the status of COMPLETE.

18.11   Month end procedures

EXERCISE   Complete the month by:

Processing all the recurring entries
Printing any reports necessary and transferring the closing stock of £26,129.00 with a journal entry with Ref. 011 and date 31/05/94 (See Section 18.1)
Running the Month End function and:
   posting accruals and prepayments
   posting depreciation
   clearing the stock files
Printing the audit trail.

18.12   June

1   Before you enter the following transactions for June change the system date to 30 June 94.

2   Enter the following sales:

Order To	Number	Date	Order
Budget Hostelry Plc	22	06/06/94	35 single beds
			35 double beds
			50 large vanity units
			30 stools
Queens Hotel	23	15/06/94	1500 metres of carpeting
Gibbert Arms	24	29/06/94	150 ashtrays
			45 waste bins
			25 decor packs

When you attempt to process each of these sales orders you will find that there is insufficient stock available to complete the allocation. Here Total Bedrooms are finding problems keeping a balance between maintaining a healthy cash flow and a viable stockholding.

To avoid disappointing customers by delaying delivery Total Bedrooms decided to deliver what they could against each of these three orders and to forward the balance as and when it arrived in stock.

3   Display the Process Sales Orders screen.

You will see displayed in the information panel three sales orders each with PART status to indicate that they have only been partially allocated stock.

4   Obtain an Order Status Report of the Budget Hostelry order via the Sales Orders screen.

You will note that the order has been allocated 7 single beds and 38 large vanity units short. You are going to deliver what you have.

5   Display the Process Sales Orders screen and select **Manual** processing.

6   Highlight the Budget Hostelry order and press $\boxed{\text{Enter}}$.

7   Select **Despatch** and the order is partially fulfilled with available stock.

The order is annotated as PART delivered.

8   Print the delivery note and update the stock and invoice details.

9   Despatch all available stock that has been allocated on the other two orders.

10   Display the list of customer invoices via the **Display Index** option in the Invoice Production screen of the Sales Ledger.

You will see that there are three invoices listed against the three partially fulfilled orders that you have just despatched.

11   Print the three invoices and post their details to the ledgers.

When the invoices are printed you will notice that they only invoice for the items delivered and not for the items ordered. When the balance of an order is despatched then a new invoice will be issued for the balance of the order.

12   Enter the following purchases and process through to delivery:

Order From	Number	Date	Order
EEZEE Beds Plc	10	07/06/94	30 single beds
Commercial Carpenters	11	09/06/94	45 large vanity units 15 single wardrobes 20 double wardrobes
Seats and Things	12	19/06/94	10 chairs

Wilminster Carpets Ltd	13	25/06/94	1150 metres of carpeting
Hand Craft Ltd	14	15/06/94	55 ashtrays
			20 waste bins
			25 decor packs

13 Enter the following invoices that accompanied deliveries against the purchase orders:

A/C: EEZEE
Ref: 5096
Date: 14/06/94
N/C: 5001
Purchase of: 30 single beds   1200.00

            VAT   210.00
            Total   1410.00

A/C: COMM
Ref: 5097
Date: 15/06/94
N/C: 5002
Purchase of: 45 large vanity units   3600.00
             15 single wardrobes   2250.00
             20 double wardrobes   3600.00

            VAT   1653.75
            Total   11103.75

A/C: SEATS
Ref: 5098
Date: 25/06/94
N/C: 5003
Purchase of: 10 chairs   1000.00

            VAT   175.00
            Total   1175.00

A/C: WILM
Ref: 5099
Date: 26/06/94
N/C: 5005
Purchase of: 1150 metres of carpeting   11500.00

            VAT   2012.50
            Total   13512.50

```
A/C:       HAND
Ref:       5100
Date:      20/06/94
N/C:       5007
Purchase of: 55 ashtrays                110.00
             20 waste bins              200.00
             25 decor packs            500.00

             VAT                        141.75
             Total                      951.75
```

18.13   Completing back sales orders

There are a number of back sales orders that need to be completed now that sufficient stock has been delivered.

Ensure that the Financial Controller screen is on display.

1   Display the Process Sales Orders screen with PART fulfilled orders on display.

2   Select the **Manual** processing option.

3   Place the highlight on the Budget Hostelry order and press Enter.

4   Select **Allocate**, press Enter and then select **Despatch**.

5   Print a new delivery note and update the stock records.

6   Return to the Process Sales Orders screen where you will find that the order is now COMPLETE.

7   Display the list of customer invoices where you will see that a second invoice to the value of £6253.35 has been created to cover the balance of the order just despatched.

8   Print this invoice and post the details to the ledgers.

9   Repeat this procedure to complete the Queens Hotel sales order.

You will find that there is still insufficient carpeting to complete the order; it will still be 111 metres short.

10 Despatch the short order and make a note that this outstanding sales order will still be on the books next month.

11 Complete the processing of the Gibbert Arms sales order.

12 Enter the following customer receipts:

Code	Name	Date	Invoice	Amount
G001	George Hotel	12/06/94	1367	4935.00
G002	Gibbert Arms	16/06/94	1366	470.00
I001	Innkeepers Plc	20/06/94	1360	4206.50
M001	Main Line Hotels Plc	22/06/94	1368	23112.25
T001	The Regency	28/06/94	1364	5875.00

13 Enter the following supplier payment

Code	Name	Date	Cheque	Invoice	Amount
EEZEE	EEZEE Beds Plc	15/06/94	131	5093	4230.00

14 Delete all sales orders with the status of COMPLETE.

15 Delete all purchase orders with the status of COMPLETE.

18.14 Quarterly bills

EXERCISE The following quarterly bills arrived during June:

Telephone £476.45 + VAT (83.38) dated 05/06/94
Electricity £493.66 + VAT (86.39) dated 09/06/94

These bills are for services received and are due.

1 Enter the telephone payment as a **Bank Payment** using cheque number **132**, date **15/06/94** and nominal code **7502**.

2 Enter the electricity payment as a **Bank Payment** using cheque number **133**, date **15/06/94** and nominal code **7200**.

18.15 Month end procedures

EXERCISE Complete the month by:

Processing all the recurring entries
Printing any reports necessary and transferring the closing stock of £27,149.00 with a journal entry with Ref. 012 and date 30/06/94 (see Section 18.1)
Running the Month End function and:
    posting accruals and prepayments
    posting depreciation
    clearing the stock files
Printing the audit trail.

EXERCISE   **1**   Calculate and reconcile the VAT Return for the period 01/04/94 to 30/06/94.

From the VAT Return it is evident that Total Bedrooms owe HM Customs & Excise £13,605.71 for the second quarter. This amount must be paid by the end of July. It is necessary to transfer this liability from the Tax Control Account 2200 to the VAT Liability Account 2201. Debit account 2200 with 13,605.71 and credit account 2201 with the same amount.

18.17   July

1   Before you enter the following transactions for July change the system date to 31 July 94.

2   Enter the following sales:

Order From	Number	Date	Order
Main Line Hotels Plc	25	03/07/94	40 single beds
			40 double beds
			25 small vanity units
			30 large vanity units
			20 single wardrobes
			40 double wardrobes
Budget Hostelry Plc	26	06/07/94	53 stools
			17 chairs
			30 table lamps
			43 standard lamps
The Regency	27	14/07/94	1250 metres of carpeting
George Hotel	28	23/07/94	45 sets of lace curtains
			21 sets of single bedding
			20 sets of double bedding
Innkeepers Plc	29	28/07/94	250 ashtrays
			43 waste bins

None of these sales orders can be fully allocated. Indeed, the Regency order cannot even be partially allocated.

3   Enter the VAT payment to HM Customs and Excise for the second quarter of £13,605.71 as a Bank Payment analysed against account 2201 VAT Liability, dated 31/07/94 using cheque 134 and tax code T9.

4   Enter the following purchases:

Order To	Number	Date	Order
EEZEE Beds Plc	15	03/07/94	30 single beds 60 double beds
Commercial Carpenters	16	03/07/94	60 large vanity units 10 double wardrobes
Seats and Things	17	21/07/94	25 stools
Wilminster Carpets	18	14/07/94	2500 metres of carpeting
ABC Fabrics	19	23/07/94	10 sets of lace curtains
Hand Crafts	20	28/07/94	200 ashtrays 50 waste bins

5   Enter the following invoices issued against the delivered purchase orders:

A/C:	EEZEE	
Ref:	5101	
Date:	07/07/94	
N/C:	5001	
Purchase of:	30 single beds	1200.00
	60 double beds	3600.00
	VAT	840.00
	Total	5640.00

A/C:	COMM	
Ref:	5102	
Date:	08/07/94	
N/C:	5002	
Purchase of:	60 large vanity units	4800.00
	10 double wardrobes	1800.00
	VAT	1155.00
	Total	7755.00

A/C:	SEATS	
Ref:	5103	
Date:	12/07/94	
N/C:	5003	
Purchase of:	25 stools	250.00
	VAT	43.75
	Total	293.75

```
A/C:        WILM
Ref:        5104
Date:       21/07/94
N/C:        5005
Purchase of: 2500 metres of carpeting        25000.00

            VAT                               4375.00
            Total                            29375.00


A/C:        ABC
Ref:        5105
Date:       25/07/94
N/C:        5006
Purchase of: 10 sets of lace curtains           50.00

            VAT                                  8.75
            Total                               58.75


A/C:        HAND
Ref:        5106
Date:       29/07/94
N/C:        5007
Purchase of: 200 ashtrays                      400.00
            50 waste bins                      500.00

            VAT                               157.50
            Total                            1057.50
```

6   Return to the Sales Order Processing screen and complete the processing of all the outstanding sales orders. The Budget Hostelry order is still 16 stools short but despatch the order anyway.

7   Enter the following customer receipts:

Code	Name	Date	Invoice	Amount
B001	Budget Hostelry	10/07/94	1369/72	14382.00
G002	Gibbert Arms	12/07/94	1371/74	2555.63
I001	Innkeepers Plc	15/07/94	1365	5287.50
Q001	Queens Hotel	18/07/94	1370/73	29377.35

8   Enter the following supplier payments:

Code	Name	Date	Cheque	Invoice	Amount
ART	Artwork	15/07/94	135	5095	375.00
COMM	Commercial Carpenters	15/07/94	136	5094	4230.00
EEZEE	EEZEE Beds	15/07/94	137	5096	1410.00
WILM	Wilminster Carpets	15/07/94	138	5099	13512.50

9   Delete all sales orders with the status of COMPLETE.

10   Delete all purchase orders with the status of COMPLETE.

Month end procedures

EXERCISE   Complete the month by:

Processing all the recurring entries
Printing any reports necessary and transferring the closing stock of £27,454.00
with a journal entry with Ref. 013 and date 31/07/94 (see Section 18.1)
Running the Month End function and:
    posting accruals and prepayments
    posting depreciation
    clearing the stock files
Printing the audit trail.

August

 1   Before you enter the following transactions for August change the system date
to 31 August 94.

Total Bedrooms have reduced their stock levels to the extent that last month they
were needing to order from their suppliers a significant number of items that had
already been placed on order by their customers. Their cash flow is good but their
reputation as a fast deliverer is starting to suffer. This month they have decided to
concentrate on purchasing stock so that they can minimise the delay in fulfilling a
customer's order and at the same time keep their stockholding costs to a minimum.
They have decided to purchase early to permit the stock level of each item to stand
at one and a half times the reorder level.

2   Process the following purchases orders:

Order To	Number	Date	Order
EEZEE Beds	21	02/08/94	35 single beds
			30 double beds
Commercial Carpenters	22	02/08/94	30 small vanity units
			10 large vanity units
			40 single wardrobes
			40 double wardrobes
Seats and Things	23	02/08/94	50 stools
			20 chairs

| Flash Lighting | 24 | 02/08/94 | 40 table lamps |
| | | | 35 standard lamps |

Fabrico	25	02/08/94	30 sets of linen curtains
			45 sets of lace curtains
			50 sets of single bedding
			40 sets of double bedding

Artwork	26	02/08/94	15 pictures
			80 ashtrays
			20 waste bins
			25 decor packs

3   Enter the following supplier invoices that arrived with the delivery of the purchase orders:

A/C:	EEZEE	
Ref:	5107	
Date:	05/08/94	
N/C:	5001	
Purchase of:	35 single beds	1400.00
	30 double beds	1800.00
	VAT	560.00
	Total	3760.00

A/C:	COMM	
Ref:	5108	
Date:	04/08/94	
N/C:	5002	
Purchase of:	30 small vanity units	1500.00
	10 large vanity units	800.00
	40 single wardrobes	6000.00
	40 double wardrobes	7200.00
	VAT	2712.50
	Total	18212.50

A/C:	SEATS	
Ref:	5109	
Date:	10/08/94	
N/C:	5003	
Purchase of:	50 stools	500.00
	20 chairs	2000.00
	VAT	437.50
	Total	2937.50

A/C:	FLASH	
Ref:	5110	
Date:	07/08/94	
N/C:	5004	
Purchase of:	40 table lamps	400.00
	35 standard lamps	1050.00
	VAT	253.75
	Total	1703.75

A/C:	FABRIC	
Ref:	5111	
Date:	09/08/94	
N/C:	5006	
Purchase of:	30 sets of linen curtains	1200.00
	45 sets of lace curtains	225.00
	50 sets of single bedding	1000.00
	40 sets of double bedding	1200.00
	VAT	634.38
	Total	4259.38

A/C:	ART	
Ref:	5112	
Date:	12/08/94	
N/C:	5007	
Purchase of:	15 pictures	225.00
	80 ashtrays	160.00
	20 waste bins	200.00
	25 decor packs	500.00
	Total	1085.00

4   Process the following sales orders through to sales invoices, starting with the final part of the Budget Hostelry order from the last month:

Order From	Number	Date	Order
Queens hotel	30	03/08/94	40 single beds
			30 double beds
			40 small vanity units
			30 large vanity units
			20 single wardrobes
			35 double wardrobes
Gibbert Arms	31	08/08/94	25 stools
			10 chairs
			30 table lamps
			40 standard lamps

Innkeepers Plc	32	15/08/94	1000 metres of carpeting
George Hotel	33	22/08/94	32 sets of linen curtains 25 sets of lace curtains 15 sets of single bedding 25 sets of double bedding
Budget Hostelry Plc	34	25/08/94	24 pictures 100 ashtrays 24 waste bins 35 decor packs

5   Enter the following customer receipts:

Code	Name	Date	Invoice	Amount
B001	Budget Hostelry	15/08/94	1377	6810.30
G001	George hotel	15/08/94	1379	2209.00
I001	Innkeepers	16/08/94	1380	2226.63
M001	Main Line Hotels	21/08/94	1376	31513.50
Q001	Queens Hotel	22/08/94	1375	2347.65
T001	The Regency	23/08/94	1378	26437.50

6   Enter the following supplier payments:

Code	Name	Date	Cheque	Invoice	Amount
COMM	Commercial Carpenters	15/08/94	139	5097	11103.75
HAND	Hand Craft	15/08/94	140	5100	951.75
SEATS	Seats and Things	15/08/94	141	5098	1175.00

7   Delete all sales orders with the status of COMPLETE.

8   Delete all purchase orders with the status of COMPLETE.

18.20   Month end procedures

EXERCISE   Complete the month by:

Processing all the recurring entries
Printing any reports necessary and transferring the closing stock of £20,849.00 with a journal entry with Ref. 014 and date 31/08/94 (see Section 18.1)
Running the Month End function and:
    posting accruals and prepayments
    posting depreciation
    clearing the stock files
Printing the audit trail.

It would appear that Total Bedrooms' strategy of the early ordering of stock items to maintain a stock level of one and a half times the reorder level is paying dividends. There were no delivery hitches during August and the cash flow is maintaining a healthy position. It was decided to continue with the policy.

 1   Before you enter the following transactions for September change the system date to 30 September 94.

2   Process the following purchase orders:

Order To	Number	Date	Order
EEZEE Beds	27	02/09/94	40 single beds 30 double beds
Commercial Carpenters	28	02/09/94	40 small vanity units 30 large vanity units 20 single wardrobes 35 double wardrobes
Seats and Things	29	02/09/94	25 stools 10 chairs
Flash Lighting	30	02/09/94	35 table lamps 45 standard lamps
Wilminster Carpets	31	02/09/94	1200 metres of carpeting
Fabrico	32	02/09/94	30 sets of linen curtains 25 sets of lace curtains 20 sets of single bedding 25 sets of double bedding
Artwork	33	02/09/94	100 ashtrays 15 waste bins 30 decor packs

3   Enter the following supplier invoices that arrived with the delivery of the purchase orders:

A/C:	EEZEE	
Ref:	5113	
Date:	05/09/94	
N/C:	5001	
Purchase of:	40 single beds	1600.00
	30 double beds	1800.00
	VAT	595.00
	Total	3995.00

A/C:	COMM	
Ref:	5114	
Date:	04/09/94	
N/C:	5002	
Purchase of:	40 small vanity units	2000.00
	30 large vanity units	2400.00
	20 single wardrobes	3000.00
	35 double wardrobes	6300.00
	VAT	2397.50
	Total	16097.50

A/C:	SEATS	
Ref:	5115	
Date:	10/09/94	
N/C:	5003	
Purchase of:	25 stools	250.00
	10 chairs	1000.00
	VAT	218.75
	Total	1468.75

A/C:	FLASH	
Ref:	5116	
Date:	07/09/94	
N/C:	5004	
Purchase of:	35 table lamps	350.00
	45 standard lamps	1350.00
	VAT	297.50
	Total	1997.50

A/C:	WILM	
Ref:	5117	
Date:	07/09/94	
N/C:	5005	
Purchase of:	1200 metres of carpeting	12000.00
	VAT	2100.00
	Total	14100.00

A/C:	FABRIC	
Ref:	5118	
Date:	09/09/94	
N/C:	5006	

Purchase of:	30 sets of linen curtains	1200.00
	25 sets of lace curtains	125.00
	20 sets of single bedding	400.00
	25 sets of double bedding	750.00
	VAT	433.13
	Total	2908.13

A/C:	ART	
Ref:	5119	
Date:	12/09/94	
N/C:	5007	
Purchase of:	100 ashtrays	200.00
	15 waste bins	150.00
	30 decor packs	600.00
	Total	950.00

4 Process the following sales orders through to sales invoices:

Order From	Number	Date	Order
Budget Hostelry	35	03/09/94	45 single beds
			35 small vanity units
			30 single wardrobes
The Regency	36	08/09/94	30 stools
			20 chairs
Main Line Hotels	37	15/09/94	1200 metres of carpeting
George Hotel	38	22/09/94	60 sets of linen curtains
			40 sets of lace curtains
Queens Hotel	39	25/09/94	40 pictures
			20 waste bins
			35 decor packs

5 Enter the following customer receipts:

Code	Name	Date	Invoice	Amount
B001	Budget Hostelry	15/09/94	1381/86	3287.65
G001	George Hotel	15/09/94	1385	4253.50
G002	Gibbert Arms	16/09/94	1383	5228.75
I001	Innkeepers	16/09/94	1384	21150.00
Q001	Queens Hotel	22/09/94	1382	30044.75

6 Enter the following supplier payments:

Code	Name	Date	Cheque	Invoice	Amount
ABC	ABC Fabrics	15/09/94	142	5105	58.75
COMM	Commercial Carpenters	19/09/94	143	5102	7755.00
EEZEE	EEZEE Beds	15/09/94	144	5101	5640.00
HAND	Hand Craft	15/09/94	145	5106	1057.50
SEATS	Seats and Things	15/09/94	146	5103	293.75
WILM	Wilminster Carpets	15/09/94	147	5104	29375.00

7   Delete all sales orders with the status of COMPLETE.

8   Delete all purchase orders with the status of COMPLETE.

18.22   Quarterly bills

EXERCISE   The following quarterly bills arrived during September:

Telephone £396.77 + VAT (£69.43) dated 05/09/94
Electricity £515.78 + VAT (£90.26) dated 09/09/94

These bills are for services received and are due.

1   Enter the telephone payment as a **Bank Payment** using cheque number **148**, date **15/09/94** and nominal code **7502**.

2   Enter the electricity payment as a **Bank Payment** using cheque number **149**, date **15/09/94** and nominal code **7200**.

Complete this activity with the Financial Controller screen on display.

18.23   Month end procedures

EXERCISE   Complete the month by:

Processing all the recurring entries
Printing any reports necessary and transferring the closing stock of £29,874.00 with a journal entry with Ref. 015 and date 30/09/94 (see Section 18.1)
Running the Month End function and:
    posting accruals and prepayments
    posting depreciation
    clearing the stock files
Printing the audit trail.

18.24   The VAT Return

EXERCISE   1   Calculate and reconcile the VAT Return for the period 01/07/94 to 30/09/94.

From the VAT Return it is evident that Total Bedrooms owe HM Customs & Excise £10,229.53 for the third quarter. It is necessary to transfer this liability from the Tax Control Account 2200 to the VAT Liability Account 2201. Debit account 2200 with 10,229.53 and credit account 2201 with the same amount.

18.25 October

 1 Before you enter the following transactions for October change the system date to 31 October 94.

2 Process the following purchase orders:

Order From	Number	Date	Order
EEZEE Beds	34	02/10/94	40 single beds
Commercial Carpenters	35	02/10/94	35 small vanity units 30 single wardrobes
Seats and Things	36	02/10/94	35 stools 25 chairs
Wilminster Carpets	37	02/10/94	1500 metres of carpeting
Fabrico	38	02/10/94	60 sets of linen curtains 40 sets of lace curtains
Artwork	39	02/10/94	40 pictures 20 waste bins 35 decor packs

3 Enter the following supplier invoices that arrived with the delivery of the purchase orders:

A/C:	EEZEE	
Ref:	5120	
Date:	05/10/94	
N/C:	5001	
Purchase of: 40 single beds		1600.00
	VAT	280.00
	Total	1880.00

A/C:	COMM	
Ref:	5121	
Date:	04/10/94	
N/C:	5002	
Purchase of: 35 small vanity units		1750.00

30 single wardrobes		4500.00
	VAT	1093.75
	Total	7343.75

A/C:	SEATS	
Ref:	5122	
Date:	10/10/94	
N/C:	5003	
Purchase of:	35 stools	350.00
	25 chairs	2500.00
	VAT	498.75
	Total	3348.75

A/C:	WILM	
Ref:	5123	
Date:	07/10/94	
N/C:	5005	
Purchase of:	1500 metres of carpeting	15000.00
	VAT	2625.00
	Total	17625.00

A/C:	FABRIC	
Ref:	5124	
Date:	09/10/94	
N/C:	5006	
Purchase of:	60 sets of linen curtains	2400.00
	40 sets of lace curtains	200.00
	VAT	455.00
	Total	3055.00

A/C:	ART	
Ref:	5125	
Date:	12/10/94	
N/C:	5007	
Purchase of:	40 pictures	600.00
	20 waste bins	200.00
	35 decor packs	700.00
	Total	1500.00

4 Process the following sales orders through to sales invoices:

Order To	Number	Date	Order
Gibbert Arms	40	03/10/94	50 double beds
			35 large vanity units
			40 double wardrobes
Innkeepers	41	08/10/94	40 chairs
Budget Hostelry	42	15/10/94	50 table lamps
			30 standard lamps
Main Line Hotels	43	22/10/94	40 sets of lace curtains
			50 sets of single bedding
The Regency	44	25/10/94	35 decor packs

5 Enter the VAT payment to HM Customs & Excise for the months of July to September of £10,229.53 as a Bank Payment analysed against account 2201 VAT Liability, dated 31/10/94, cheque 150 and tax code T9.

6 Enter the following customer receipts:

Code	Name	Date	Invoice	Amount
B001	Budget Hostelry	15/10/94	1387	13101.25
G001	George Hotel	15/10/94	1390	4700.00
M001	Main Line Hotels	16/10/94	1389	25380.00
T001	The Regency	17/10/94	1388	3924.50
Q001	Queens Hotel	22/10/94	1391	2761.25

7 Enter the following supplier payments:

Code	Name	Date	Cheque	Invoice	Amount
ART	Artwork	15/10/94	151	5112	1085.00
COMM	Commercial Carpenters	15/10/94	152	5108	18212.50
EEZEE	EEZEE Beds	15/10/94	153	5107	3760.00
FABRIC	Fabrico	15/10/94	154	5111	4259.38
FLASH	Flash Lighting	15/10/94	155	5110	1703.75
SEATS	Seats and Things	15/10/94	156	5109	2937.50

8 Delete all sales orders with the status of COMPLETE.

9 Delete all purchase orders with the status of COMPLETE.

18.26   Month end procedures

EXERCISE   Complete the month by:

Processing all the recurring entries
Printing any reports necessary and transferring the closing stock of £40,934.00

with a journal entry with Ref. 016 and date 31/10/94 (see Section 18.1)
Running the Month End function and:
    posting accruals and prepayments
    posting depreciation
    clearing the stock files
Printing the audit trail.

 1   Before you enter the following transactions for November change the system date to 30 November 94.

2   Process the following purchase orders:

Order From	Number	Date	Order
EEZEE Beds	40	02/11/94	50 double beds
Commercial Carpenters	41	02/11/94	35 large vanity units 35 double wardrobes
Seats and Things	42	02/11/94	35 chairs
Flash Lighting	43	02/11/94	50 table lamps 30 standard lamps
Fabrico	44	02/11/94	40 sets of lace curtains 50 sets of single bedding
Artwork	45	02/11/94	30 decor packs

3   Enter the following supplier invoices that arrived with the delivery of the purchase orders:

A/C: EEZEE
Ref: 5126
Date: 05/11/94
N/C: 5001
Purchase of: 50 double beds   3000.00

            VAT   525.00
            Total   3525.00

A/C: COMM
Ref: 5127
Date: 04/11/94
N/C: 5002
Purchase of: 35 large vanity units   2800.00
            35 double wardrobes   6300.00

VAT		1592.50
Total		10692.50

A/C:	SEATS	
Ref:	5128	
Date:	10/11/94	
N/C:	5003	
Purchase of: 35 chairs		3500.00
	VAT	612.50
	Total	4112.50

A/C:	FLASH	
Ref:	5129	
Date:	07/11/94	
N/C:	5004	
Purchase of: 50 table lamps		500.00
	30 standard lamps	900.00
	VAT	245.00
	Total	1645.00

A/C:	FABRIC	
Ref:	5130	
Date:	09/11/94	
N/C:	5006	
Purchase of: 40 sets of lace curtains		200.00
	50 sets of single bedding	1000.00
	VAT	210.00
	Total	1410.00

A/C:	ART	
Ref:	5131	
Date:	12/11/94	
N/C:	5007	
Purchase of: 30 decor packs		600.00
	Total	600.00

4   Process the following sales orders through to sales invoices:

Order To	Number	Date	Order
Main Line Hotels	45	03/11/94	35 double beds
			35 small vanity units

The Regency	46	08/11/94	35 stools
Budget Hostelry	47	15/11/94	1200 metres of carpeting
George Hotel	48	22/11/94	40 sets of lace curtains 35 sets of double bedding
Queens Hotel	49	25/11/94	40 pictures 20 waste bins 30 decor packs

5   Enter the following customer receipts:

Code	Name	Date	Invoice	Amount
B001	Budget Hostelry	15/11/94	1394	2937.50
G002	Gibbert Arms	15/11/94	1392	23752.63
I001	Innkeepers	16/11/94	1393	6580.00
T001	The Regency	22/11/94	1396	1233.75

Because Budget Hosteltry's purchase this month has put their balance over £7000.00 above their credit limit they have been requested to pay £7380.00 on account and they have agreed to do so. This must now be entered into their account.

6   Enter the following details:

A/C   **B001**

The form then displays the single outstanding invoice **1399** for the amount **25380.00**.

7   In the **Cheque Amount** box enter:

7380.00 and press Enter

8   Move the highlight to **Manual** and press Enter to highlight the first line of the account.

9   Press Enter.

10   Select the **Type of payment** as:

PART

11   Enter the **Amount** of the payment in the box that has just appeared as:

7380 and press Enter

The **Cheque Balance** now reads **0.00** and the 1399 invoice is annotated PART.

12   Press Esc and post the details to the ledgers.

13 Display Budget Hostelry's account via the **Account Balances (Aged)** option in the Sales Ledger screen and you will see that the outstanding amount has now been reduced to 18000.00.

Complete this activity with the Financial Controller screen on display.

14 Enter the following supplier payments:

Code	Name	Date	Cheque	Invoice	Amount
ART	Artwork	15/11/94	157	5119	950.00
COMM	Commercial Carpenters	15/11/94	158	5114	16097.50
EEZEE	EEZEE Beds	15/11/94	159	5113	3995.00
FABRIC	Fabrico	15/11/94	160	5118	2908.13
SEATS	Seats and Things	15/11/94	161	5115	1468.75
FLASH	Flash Lighting	15/11/94	162	5116	1997.50
WILM	Wilminster Carpets	15/11/94	163	5117	14100.00

Total Bedrooms have been requested by Commercial Carpenters and Fabrico to keep within their agreed credit limit. It has been agreed that Total Bedrooms will pay:

Commercial Carpenters	£3036.25
Fabrico	£1465.00

Both payments will be on account.

Ensure that the Payments screen is on display.

15 Display the **COMM** account and enter the cheque number **164**.

16 In the **Cheque Amount** box enter the amount to be paid as:

6000 and press Enter

17 Move the highlight to **Manual** and press Enter to highlight the first line of the account.

18 Press Enter.

19 Select the **Type of payment** as:

FULL

20 Press Esc and opt to post the details of the account and a message appears at the bottom of the screen asking if you want to **Post-Unallocated-Amount**. It is not desirable to overpay for any item on an invoice.

21 Select to **Abandon** the entry.

22 Re-enter the Payments screen and pay Commercial Carpenters the amount

3036.25 against the amount **5287.50** thereby bringing Total Bedrooms' overall debt to Commercial Carpenters to their credit limit.

23   Delete all sales orders with the status of COMPLETE.

24   Delete all purchase orders with the status of COMPLETE.

18.28   Credit notes

Main Line Hotels have returned 10 damaged double beds that were delivered against sales order 45. Total Bedrooms have issued a credit note in their favour and this now needs to be recorded. Before you do this, however, check the stockholding of double beds and you will find that there are 39 in stock.

Ensure that the Financial Controller screen is on display.

1   Display the Sales Ledger screen and select the **Invoice Production** option.

2   From the Invoice Production screen select the **Credit Note Production** option to reveal the Credit Note Production screen.

The credit note is filled by following the same procedures as those that are followed to fulfil an invoice.

3   Enter the following details:

A/C	M001
Credit Number	2
Date	05/11/94
Stock Code	102
Description	Double beds
Qty	10

4   Press Esc and post the details to the ledgers.

5   Re-display the credit note details and produce a printed copy.

Ensure that you complete this part of the activity with the Financial Controller screen on display.

If you now check the stockholding you will find that there are now 49 double beds in stock - the 10 returned have been added to stock.

When the 10 beds were returned to Total Bedrooms they were forwarded to Commercial Carpenters as the fault was one of theirs. Commercial Carpenters accordingly issued a credit note to Total Bedrooms to cover the payment for the 10 beds returned. This credit note must now be entered into the system and the 10 beds adjusted out of stock.

Ensure that the Financial Controller screen is on display.

6   Display the **Purchase Ledger** screen and select **Batched Data Entry** to reveal the Batched Data Entry screen.

7   Select the **Purchase Credit Notes** option to reveal the Purchase Credit Notes screen.

8   Enter the following details:

A/C	COMM
Credit Number	1
Date	16/11/94
N/C	5002
Description	Double beds
Amount	600.00
VAT	105.00
Total	705.00

9   Press Esc and post the details to the ledgers.

Complete this activity with the Financial Controller screen on display.

Next we must adjust the stock to remove the 10 double beds that were placed there when we created the customer credit note.

10   Select the **Stock Control** option followed by the **Adjustments Out** option.

11   Enter the following details into the Adjustments Out form:

Ref	1
Code	102
Description	Double beds
Qty	10

12   **Post** these details to the ledgers and complete this activity with the Financial Controller screen on display.

18.29   Month end procedures

EXERCISE   Complete the month by:

Processing all the recurring entries
Printing any reports necessary and transferring the closing stock of £39,324.00 with a journal entry with Ref. 017 and date 30/11/94 (see Section 18.1)
Running the Month End function and:
   posting accruals and prepayments
   posting depreciation

clearing the stock files
Printing the audit trail.

The month of December is usually a quiet month for trading and this December is no exception. The usual policy is to make only essential purchases to satisfy orders that cannot be completed from existing stock.

On the 2nd December Total Bedrooms received two orders which included requests for single beds where the quantity of single beds required on each order was in excess of the current stockholding of 43. The orders were:

Order To	Number	Date	Order
Innkeepers Plc	50	02/12/94	80 single beds
			40 sets of single bedding
Main Line Hotels Plc	51	02/12/94	60 single beds
			25 double beds

Here we see that the requirement is for 140 single beds where the current stock level is 43. By looking at the stock record you will see that this represents a shortfall of 97 beds. It was decided that they should place an order with a supplier for 110 single beds to enable them to satisfy both of the orders and to leave 13 beds in stock. To this end Total Bedrooms contacted EEZEE Beds to see if they could supply them with the necessary quantity of single beds only to be told that EEZEE could not deliver to Total Bedrooms before January. Total Bedrooms then contacted Sleepwell to see if they could supply them. They were loath to do this because Sleepwell had let them down in the past but they had been left with no alternative. Sleepwell claimed that they could meet Total Bedrooms' order and that they could deliver the 110 single beds by the 5th December. This agreed, Total Bedrooms decided that they would share out the current stock between the two customers and then forward the balance on the 5th December when their delivery from Sleepwell was expected.

 1   Before you enter the following transactions for December change the system date to 31 December 94.

2   Enter the details of the sales order placed by Innkeepers Plc and **Save** it for further processing. Do not post the details to the ledgers.

It had been decided to deliver the order short to Innkeepers by including just 20 single beds and to forward the balance of 60 single beds when the delivery from Sleepwell arrived at Total Bedrooms. Because it is not possible to partially allocate stock to an order if there is sufficient stock to completely fulfil the order we must delete the order and create a new one. The only way an order can be deleted is if it is either COMPLETE or it has been cancelled.

Ensure that the Process Sales Orders screen is on display.

3   Select the processing to be **Manual** and move the highlight over the Innkeepers sales order details.

4   At the prompt at the bottom of the screen select:

Cancel

5   Return to the Sales Orders screen and select **Delete Orders** and delete the sales order to Innkeepers.

6   Enter a new sales order for Innkeepers but this time make it out for:

20 single beds
40 sets of single bedding

7   Process this order through to completion and the issuing of an invoice.

8   Repeat this process by despatching the Main Line order, again with a part allocation of 20 single beds but a full allocation of 25 double beds.

9   Process the following purchase order:

Order From	Number	Date	Order
Sleepwell	46	02/12/94	110 single beds

Complete this activity with the Financial Controller screen on display.

On the 5th December Sleepwell delivered only 50 single beds against the order for 110.

10   Display the Purchase Orders screen and select **Amend Deliveries** to reveal the Amend Deliveries screen.

11   Enter the order number **5091** and the order details are displayed with a highlight.

Notice that the delivered quantity is shown as 110 despite the fact that this has not been recorded as received.

12   Press Enter and a **Quantity Delivered** box appears at the bottom of the screen.

13   Enter the amended **Quantity Delivered** as:

50

The order details are then altered to reflect this new quantity.

14   Press Esc and post these details to the ledgers.

15 Display the Purchase Orders screen and select **Manual** processing.

16 Place the highlight over the Sleepwell order and press Enter.

17 Select the **Delivered** option and the details of the order are annotated with the **Delivered** status of PART.

18 Return to the Financial Controller screen.

19 Enter the following supplier invoice for the 50 single beds delivered:

    A/C: SLEEP
    Ref: 5132
    Date: 05/12/94
    N/C: 5001
    Purchase of: 50 single beds   2000.00

                  VAT   350.00
                  Total   2350.00

Because Sleepwell had let Total Bedrooms down by not delivering the 110 as promised it was not possible to complete both orders simultaneously as a total of 100 single beds were still outstanding against the two orders. It was decided that it was better to complete one of the sales orders rather than leave both orders still only partly fulfilled. The only order that could be completed was the Main Line order that required a further 40 single beds delivered to them to complete their order.

20 Complete the allocation of the Main Line Hotels' sales order by creating a new order for the balance of the single beds.

You will recall that 40 single beds are required to complete the allocation.

21 Despatch these newly allocated single beds and complete the process of printing the delivery note, updating the stock and invoice records, printing the invoice and posting the details to the ledgers.

22 Repeat this process by despatching and invoicing Innkeepers with a further 10 single beds.

This will still leave them requiring 50 single beds to complete their original order.

The balance of 60 single beds arrived from Sleepwell on the 10th December, along with a supplier invoice:

    A/C: SLEEP
    Ref: 5133
    Date: 10/12/94
    N/C: 5001
    Purchase of: 60 single beds   2400.00

VAT	420.00
Total	2820.00

23 Complete the delivery of this purchase order and enter the supplier invoice.

24 Complete the allocation and despatch of single beds to the Innkeepers outstanding sales order and update the stock and invoice records.

25 Print a third invoice against this sales order and post the details to the ledgers.

Despite all the setbacks involved in trying to satisfy customers who are upset due to no fault of yours accounting life still goes on.

26 Enter the following customer receipts:

Code	Name	Date	Invoice	Amount
B001	Budget Hostelry	15/12/94	1399	18000.00
G001	George Hotel	15/12/94	1400	2115.00
M001	Main Line Hotels	16/12/94	1395	2232.50
Q001	Queens Hotel	16/12/94	1401	2585.00
T001	The Regency	21/12/94	1398	740.25

27 Enter the following supplier payments:

Code	Name	Date	Cheque	Invoice	Amount
ART	Artworks	15/12/94	166	5125	1500.00
COMM	Commercial Carpenters	15/12/94	167	5121	4307.50
EEZEE	EEZEE Beds	15/12/94	168	5120	1880.00
FABRIC	Fabrico	15/12/94	169	5124	1590.00
SEATS	Seats and Things	15/12/94	170	5122	3348.75
WILM	Wilminster Carpets	15/12/94	171	5123	17625.00

28 Delete all sales orders with the status of COMPLETE.

29 Delete all purchase orders with the status of COMPLETE.

18.31   Quarterly bills

EXERCISE   The following quarterly bills arrived during December:

Telephone £533.65 + VAT (£93.39) dated 05/12/94
Electricity £505.99 + VAT (£88.55) dated 09/12/94

These bills are for services received and are due.

1 Enter the telephone payment as a **Bank Payment** using cheque number **172**, date **15/12/94** and nominal code **7502**.

2 Amend the telephone **Accruals** so that the value of the December accrual ensures that all the accruals over the whole year add up to the total of the four quarterly bills.

3 Enter the electricity payment as a **Bank Payment** using cheque number **173**, date **15/12/94** and nominal code **7200**.

4 Amend the electricity **Accruals** so that the value of the December accrual ensures that all the accruals over the whole year add up to the total of the four quarterly bills.

Complete this activity with the Financial Controller screen on display.

18.32   Month end procedures

EXERCISE   Complete the month by:

Processing all the recurring entries
Printing all the necessary reports and transferring the closing stock of £35,824.00 with a journal entry, Ref. 018 and date 31/12/94 (see Section 18.1)
Running the Month End function and:
    posting accruals and prepayments
    posting depreciation
    clearing the stock files
Printing the audit trail.

18.33   The VAT Return

EXERCISE   **1** Calculate and reconcile the VAT Return for the period 01/10/94 to 31/12/94.

18.34   Backing up data to a floppy diskette

You have now completed Chapter Eighteen and have entered data into the Sage Sterling Financial Controller accounting system which has been stored on your computer's hard disk. While the hard disk is a very reliable medium it is worthwhile reminding yourself that it is storing your only copy of the data and that the disk itself is not infallible. Data can be irretrievably lost if your hard disk fails. Therefore, it is advised that you back up your data onto a floppy diskette (refer to page xvi of *Getting started*).

 A word of caution. When backing up data to a floppy diskette from your hard disk, all the current information in the data files on your hard disk is copied to the floppy diskette. As a consequence, it is always best to back up using the Backup/Restore facility available within the Sage Sterling Financial Controller accounting system which backs up and restores *all* the data files. If you use any other method which enables you to select which data files to back up or restore you may be tempted not to back up or restore all of your data files. In such an event your data could very easily become corrupted and, therefore, worthless.

19 Year end routines

Just as all accounts are subject to month end procedures at the end of every calendar month so the accounts are subject to year end procedures at the end of every financial year. The purpose of the year end procedures is to produce a picture of the company's performance during the course of the year and to clear any data files of unwanted information.

19.1 Year end procedures

Having carried out the normal month end activities for December we are now ready to run the Year End function for the end of the financial year which ran from 1st January to 31st December 1994.

Ensure that the Financial Controller screen is on display.

1   Before you attempt to run the Year End function it is necessary to ensure that the system date is later than 31 December 94. Change the system date to 1 January 95.

2   Display the **Utilities** screen.

3   Select the **Year End** option to reveal the Year End Routines screen:

```
Accounts
Stock
```

This screen informs us that there are two aspects to the year end routines. One that deals with the accounts and the other that deals with the stock records.

4   Select **Accounts** to display the Year End screen which describes exactly what will happen to the account records during the processing of the year end routine:

```
┌─────────────────────────────────────────────────────────────┐
│  ┌───────────────────────────────────────────────────────┐  │
│  │ Financial Controller        Year End      31st December 1994 │
│  └───────────────────────────────────────────────────────┘  │
│                                                               │
│      This routine will post Journal Debits and Journal Credits, as │
│                                                               │
│      appropriate, to all Nominal Ledger Accounts appearing in the │
│                                                               │
│      Profit & Loss Report to zero the balances in all these  │
│                                                               │
│      accounts. A final balancing Journal entry will be posted to the │
│                                                               │
│      Retained Profit & Loss Account. This account should appear │
│                                                               │
│      under the "Financed By" category in the Balance Sheet.  │
│                                                               │
│                                                               │
│              Press  ENTER  to continue  ESC  to cancel       │
└─────────────────────────────────────────────────────────────┘
```

5   Press **Enter** and select to send the report to the printer.

When the report has been printed you are returned to the Year End Routines screen.

6   Select **Stock** to reveal the Year End screen:

```
┌─────────────────────────────────────────────────────────────┐
│  ┌───────────────────────────────────────────────────────┐  │
│  │ Financial Controller        Stock        31st December 1994 │
│  └───────────────────────────────────────────────────────┘  │
│                                                               │
│                      W A R N I N G                           │
│                                                               │
│      This routine will automatically zero the QUANTITY       │
│      SOLD and SALES VALUE in each stock item for the         │
│      current period and Year-to-Date                         │
│                                                               │
│      Please ensure the following reports have been           │
│      printed before proceeding with this routine.            │
│                                                               │
│                 ┌─────────────────────────┐                  │
│                 │ STOCK HISTORY REPORT     │                  │
│                 │ STOCK VALUATION REPORT   │                  │
│                 │ STOCK PROFIT REPORTS     │                  │
│                 └─────────────────────────┘                  │
│                                                               │
│              Press  ENTER  to continue  ESC  to cancel       │
└─────────────────────────────────────────────────────────────┘
```

Again this display informs you of the action of the year end routine on the stock files. The three reports that are referred to have already been produced during the month end routine at the end of December's accounting.

7   Press **Enter** to set the routine into operation.

When the year end routine is complete you are returned to the Year End Routine screen.

8   Press Esc twice to return to the Financial Controller screen.

To complete the year end routines we need to reconfigure the accounts.

19.2   Audit considerations

Whenever the Sage Sterling Financial Controller is used for maintaining business records it is essential that before any records are input into the system the company's auditors are approached so they are fully aware of the change and can if necessary suggest amendments to the proposed scheme. Also before any year end reconfiguration occurs the auditors should be asked what records they will require for their audit. These should include the following printouts:

Audit trail
Sales and purchase ledger balances and history
Nominal ledger balances and history
Stock valuation and history
Trial balance
Balance sheet and profit and loss account.

It is also essential that backup diskettes are kept in case of problems.

19.3   Asset valuations

This report gives a summary of fixed assets that are being depreciated showing the value, monthly depreciation and the current value of the fixed asset.

19.4   Reconfiguration

Ensure that the Financial Controller screen is on display.

1   Select the **Utilities** option to display the Utilities screen.

2   Select the **Data File Changes** option in the Utilities screen and then select the **Reconfiguration** option to display the Reconfiguration screen:

```
┌─────────────────────────────────────────────────────────────┐
│ Financial Controller      Reconfiguration      31st December 1994 │
└─────────────────────────────────────────────────────────────┘

                          WARNING!!

      1.   Have you made at least TWO copies of your Data Files?

      2.   Have you taken the following printouts ? :-
           Audit Trail.
           Monthly Day Books.
           Sales/Purchase & Nominal Listings.
           VAT Return.


           Do you wish to take a backup of your data ?   Y

              Press  ENTER  to continue  ESC  to cancel
```

The Reconfiguration routine has three facets to its operation:

- it removes all the fully allocated and reconciled transactions from the audit trail so releasing disk space. This is why it is so important to have both produced all the relevant reports and to have backed up all the data files

- it rebuilds the data files, again releasing disk space

- it constructs a new set of stock, invoicing and order files, deleting records and reducing file sizes where possible. Again this has the effect of increasing the available disk space for next year's accounts.

3   Enter **N** and press ⌷Enter⌷ to initiate the reconfiguration routine:

```
┌─────────────────────────────────────────────────────────────┐
│ Financial Controller      Reconfiguration      31st December 1994 │
└─────────────────────────────────────────────────────────────┘

        Please Note that reconfiguration will NOT affect

        unreconciled taxable transactions or unreconciled

        bank transactions. These must have been entered in

        a VAT Return and flagged by that report and/or marked

        in a Bank Reconciliation before they can be cleared.


           Remove completed transactions up to 311294

              Press  ENTER  to continue  ESC  to cancel
```

4   Press Enter and the routine commences giving a display of its progress:

```
Resetting SALES.DTA
Resetting PURCHASE.DTA
Resetting NOMINAL.DTA
```

When the routine is complete you are returned to the Utilities screen.

5   Press Esc to return to the Financial Controller screen.

19.5   Backing up data to a floppy diskette

You have now completed Chapter Nineteen and have entered data into the Sage Sterling Financial Controller accounting system which has been stored on your computer's hard disk. While the hard disk is a very reliable medium it is worthwhile reminding yourself that it is storing your only copy of the data and that the disk itself is not infallible. Data can be irretrievably lost if your hard disk fails. Therefore, it is advised that you back up your data onto a floppy diskette (refer to page xvi of *Getting started*).

A word of caution. When backing up data to a floppy diskette from your hard disk, all the current information in the data files on your hard disk is copied to the floppy diskette. As a consequence, it is always best to back up using the Backup/Restore facility available within the Sage Sterling Financial Controller accounting system which backs up and restores *all* the data files. If you use any other method which enables you to select which data files to back up or restore you may be tempted not to back up or restore all of your data files. In such an event your data could very easily become corrupted and, therefore, worthless.

Remember to take the diskette out of the floppy drive and to store it in a safe place.

Part III

Advanced level

The Sage Sterling Financial Controller stock accounting system has the facility to create assemblies from existing stock. By using the Make-Up facility provided via a Product Record screen the component parts of an assembly can be associated with an assembly item so that whenever an assembly item is sold from stock then the abstraction of each component part from stock is recorded automatically. In addition, already defined assemblies can be grouped together as sub-assemblies of a larger assembly.

20.1   Stock assemblies

The first stock assembly we shall define is to have the name Bedset and it will consist of:

    1 single bed
    2 sets of single bedding

Before we can define the components of Bedset we must first define Bedset as a unit of stock.

Ensure that the Financial Controller screen is on display and that the system date is 31 January 1995.

1   Display the Stock Control screen.

2   Select the **Update Stock Details** option to reveal an empty stock record.

3   Enter the details of the unit of stock as:

Code	801	
Description	Bedset	
Category	8	No name will appear against this number
Sale Price	110	This price represents £10.00 less than purchasing the components separately
Unit of Sale	Set	
Nominal	4000 Suite Sales	
Rorder level	0	
Re-order qty	0	
Department	1 Sales	
Tax Code	T1	

4   With the highlight on **Make Up** press F4 to reveal the screen into which component details are to be entered:

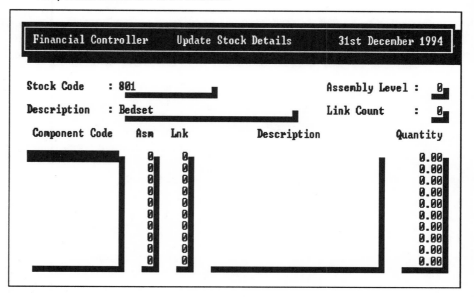

Notice that the Stock Code and the Description are already entered. We now need to enter the components.

5   Use F4 to enter the **Component Code** in the first line of the form as:

101

Automatically the system enters the description as **Single bed**.

Notice that the number **1** has appeared under **Assembly Level** in the top right-hand corner of the form. This refers to the fact that this is the assembly level 1 - it is the first level up from the component level.

6   Use the cursor control keys to move the highlight to the first **0.00** in the **Quantity** column and enter the **Quantity** as:

1

7   Use F4 to enter the next component as:

603

with description Bedding - single.

8   Amend the default **Quantity** from **0** to **2**.

This completes the specification of Bedset's components.

9   Press Esc to return you to the Update Stock Details of item 801.

10 Press $\boxed{\text{Esc}}$ and post these details to the ledgers and to clear the product record form in readiness for the entry of another stock item.

11 Repeat this procedure to define the two new assembled items of stock:

Code	Item	Components	Set Price
802	Furnset	1 double wardrobe 1 large vanity unit	395.00
803	Readset	1 table lamp 1 chair	145.00

Both of these items, sold by the set, are to have a nominal code of 4000 and a category of 8.

Complete this activity with the Stock Control screen on display.

The next task is to create a fourth assembly called SuiteS that consists of:

2 Bedsets
1 Furnset
1 Readset

12 Create the assembly 901 SuiteS with seliing price £600.00 whose components are:

2 Bedsets
1 Furnset
1 Readset

Notice that as you define the components of SuiteS the **Assembly Level** is now automatically entered as **2**.

Link Count (**Lnk**) is the number of different assemblies to which a particular sub-assembly belongs. Each sub-assembly only belongs to one assembly, namely SuiteS, and if you were to return to the Stock Details screen for each of the three sub-assemblies then you would find that the Link Count has changed to 1 in each case.

Complete this activity with the Financial Controller screen on display.

20.2 Stock explosion

1 Display the Stock Control screen and select the predefined report named **Stock Explosion**. As you will see, this report describes the construction of the assembly SuiteS and all its sub-assemblies.

Complete this activity with the Financial Controller screen on display.

Allocating stock to stock assemblies

Having entered the details of these four assemblies you will notice that their respective **In Stock** entries are all zero. This is because we have not yet assigned any components to the assemblies from our existing stock. This we do via the **Stock Transfers** option in the Stock Control screen.

Ensure that the Stock Control screen is on display.

 1   Select the **Stock Details** option and check the stock levels of the components of all the assemblies:

Assembly	Stock Item	In Stock
Bedset	101 Single bed	13
	603 Bedding - single	36
Furnset	202 Vanity unit - large	47
	204 Wardrobe - double	40
Readset	302 Chair	36
	401 Table lamp	76

When an item of stock is transferred as a component to an assembly it is no longer available for sale as an item in its own right. Indeed, when a quantity of one item is transferred to an assembly then the In-Stock level of the item is reduced accordingly. We do not wish to allocate all our stock so we shall assign sufficient stock to make:

5 Bedsets
25 Furnsets
20 Readsets

2   Return to the Stock Control screen and select the **Stock Transfers** option to reveal the Stock Transfers screen:

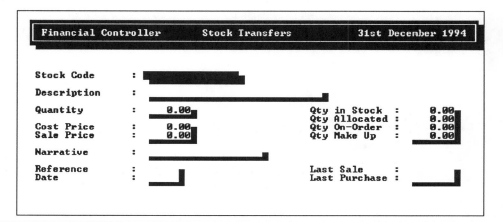

3   Use $\boxed{\text{F4}}$ to enter the first item to which stock will be automatically transferred as:

801

4   The **Description**:

Bedset is entered automatically.

5   Enter the **Quantity** of Bedsets as:

5

6   Use $\boxed{\text{F7}}$ to enter the **Narrative** as:

Stock Transfer

This transfer, when saved, will automatically reduce the item **101 Single bed In Stock** quantity by 5 - there is 1 single bed per Bedset - and reduce the **In Stock** quantity of stock item **603 Bedding - single** by 10 as there are 2 per Bedset. At the same time it will increase the **In Stock** quantity of the stock item **801 Bedset** by 5.

7   Press $\boxed{\text{Esc}}$ and post the details to the ledgers.

8   Transfer stock to furnish 25 Furnsets and 20 Readsets.

9   When you have completed the last transfer press $\boxed{\text{Esc}}$ to return to the Stock Control screen from which you can review the state of your stock.

You will find that the appropriate stock levels have been reduced to:

Stock Item	In Stock
101 Single bed	8
603 Bedding - single	26
202 Vanity unit - large	22
204 Wardrobe - double	15
302 Chair	16
401 Table lamp	56

and the assemblies now have **In Stock** quantities:

Assembly	In Stock
Bedset	5
Furnset	25
Readset	20
SuiteS	0

Notice that we do not yet have any of the assembly SuiteS. We have to transfer the sub-assemblies Bedset, Furnset and Readset to SuiteS.

10   Use the **Stock Transfers** option in the Stock Control screen to transfer sub-
      assemblies to ensure a stock holding of 2 SuiteS.

11   Review the state of your stock where you will see that the appropriate
      sub-assemblies have been assigned to SuiteS:

Assembly	In Stock
Bedset	1
Furnset	23
Readset	18
SuiteS	2

Having defined the assembly SuiteS and its sub-assemblies these items will behave
as normal items of stock and can be sold as such as well as being Adjusted In and
Adjusted Out.

20.4   Backing up data to a floppy diskette

You have now completed Chapter Twenty and have entered data into the Sage
Sterling Financial Controller accounting system which has been stored on your
computer's hard disk. While the hard disk is a very reliable medium it is worthwhile
reminding yourself that it is storing your only copy of the data and that the disk itself
is not infallible. Data can be irretrievably lost if your hard disk fails. Therefore, it is
advised that you back up your data onto a floppy diskette (refer to page xvi of
Getting started).

A word of caution. When backing up data to a floppy diskette from your hard disk, all
the current information in the data files on your hard disk is copied to the floppy
diskette. As a consequence, it is always best to back up using the Backup/Restore
facility available within the Sage Sterling Financial Controller accounting system
which backs up and restores *all* the data files. If you use any other method which
enables you to select which data files to back up or restore you may be tempted not
to back up or restore all of your data files. In such an event your data could very
easily become corrupted and, therefore, worthless.

Remember to take the diskette out of the floppy drive and to store it in a safe place.

21 Discounts

It is not unusual for a supplier to offer a customer a discount on part of an invoice or even on the total invoice. We shall consider two situations where discounts can apply. The first is where Total Bedrooms grant a 10% trade discount on all purchases to a particular customer and the second is where Total Bedrooms discount a specific item of stock by 15% when a customer purchases that particular item.

21.1 Customer discounts and stock discounts

If a particular customer is to be awarded a trade discount on all purchases then the percentage amount of that discount must be recorded on the customer's record. Tade discounts are awarded against the fulfilment of some condition like early payment and as such they are accepted at the customer's discretion. To set the discounts we need to make some global settings first.

Ensure that the Financial Controller screen is on display and that the system date is 31 January 1995.

 1   Select the **Utilities** option to display the Utilities screen.

2   Select the **Global Changes** option to display the Global Changes screen:

```
Ledger Files
Stock Files
```

3   Select **Stock Files** to reveal the Stock Files options:

```
Sales Price
Purchase Price
Re-Order Level
Re-Order Quantity
Discount A
Discount B
Discount C
```

4   Select **Discount A** to reveal the Global Changes screen:

```
┌─────────────────────────────┐
│  Add Amount                 │
│  Subtract Amount            │
│  Multiply By                │
│  Divide By                  │
│  Increase By %              │
│  Decrease By %              │
│  Give Figure                │
│                             │
└─────────────────────────────┘
```

5   Select **Give Figure** to reveal the **Amount** box:

```
┌──────────────────────────────────────────────┐
│  Amount to Change by :  0.00              ▄   │
└──────────────────────────────────────────────┘
```

6   Enter the **Amount to Change by** as:

10 for 10%

7   Press **Enter** to reveal the Discount A screen:

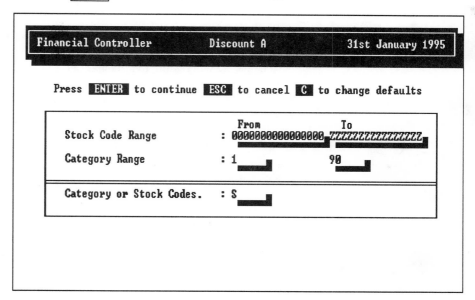

8   Accept all the defaults and press **Enter** to reveal a warning:

```
┌──────────────────────────────────────────────────────────────────┐
│ The program will now give the value 10.00 to the Discount A       │
│       WARNING!  The following changes are NOT Reversible.         │
└──────────────────────────────────────────────────────────────────┘
```

9   Select **Proceed** and the value of 10% will be associated with every occurrence
     of the Discount Code A.

10   Repeat this procedure to set the Discount Code B at 5%.

Complete the activity with the Financial Controller screen on display.

11 View all the stock details where you will find that on every stock record the Discount A is set at 10.00, Discount B is set at 5.00 and Discount C is set at 0.00.

This does not mean that these items of stock are automatically discounted whenever they are sold. What it does mean is that if a customer is awarded a 10% or 5% discount then that information is entered on the customer's record as a Discount Code of A or B. We shall see the effect of this now as we are ready to assign discount to customers and to stock.

12 Display the Main Line Hotels Plc customer record.

At the moment the **Discount Code** entry is blank.

13 Amend the **Discount Code** entry to read:

A

Main Line Hotels are being offered a 10% discount on all their purchases.

14 Post this record and return to the Financial Controller screen.

15 Display the Invoice Production screen and select the **Invoicing from Stock** option to reveal the Invoice screen.

We are going to create an invoice from stock to Main Line Hotels in this screen to demonstrate the effect of discounting. The same procedure will operate when processing a sales order.

16 Enter the **Date** as 100195, the customer code **M001** in the **Sales Ref** box and the name and address of Main Line Hotels appears on the invoice form.

17 Use F4 on the **Stock Code** column and when the Stock Codes screen appears select **102 Double bed**.

The Stock Item window appears, inside which you will notice that the **Discount** is set at **10.00**. This value has come from the customer record coupled with the global value of the discount code A.

18 Enter the Quantity as **10** and press Esc to close the Stock Item window.

The amount that appears under **Nett Amnt** for the double beds is:

£810.00

That is, 10 double beds @ £90.00 per bed less 10% discount at £9.00 per bed. The VAT is:

£141.75

Now, 17.5% of 900 is 157.50 so the VAT has not been charged on the full £900.00. Instead the 17.5% VAT has been charged on the discounted value of the goods using the customer's discount of 10%. At a 10% discount the discounted value of the double beds is:

£810.00 (10 double beds @ £90.00 less 10% per bed)

and the VAT at 17.5% on £810.00 is £141.75.

The outcome is that when an invoice is sent to a customer who is entitled to a discount the sale value displayed on the invoice is the discounted value with the VAT calculated on the discounted value.

19   Enter the **Quantity** as **5** and amend the **Discount** in this window from **10.00** to **15.00**.

To amend the discount on a particular item of stock, the amended discount must be applied at the time the invoice is created in the case of invoicing from stock or at the time a sales order is created in the case of sales order processing. Here we have decided to increase the discount on the single beds from 10% to 15%.

Consider now the sale value of the 5 single beds. Each bed, costing £60.00, has been discounted from stock by 15% so their discounted price is £51.00. When they are sold to Main Line Hotels who have a blanket 10% discount on all purchases the single beds are not discounted by a further 10% of their previously discounted price of £51.00 when the VAT is calculated. This means that:

10 single beds at £60.00 per bed are discounted by 15% to £51.00 per bed and this is the price that is used to work out the **Nett Amnt** for the invoice. That is 255.00 and the VAT of 17.5% is calculated on this 15% discounted price giving a total VAT amount of £44.63 for the 5 single beds.

Complete the processing of the invoice by printing it and updating the ledgers.

21.2   Paying a discounted invoice

When Main Line Hotels pay their invoice they do not have to remember that they are entitled to a 10% trade discount of the untaxed amount as the discount is already refelcted in the invoice. As a result they do not need to adjust their payment by calculating 10% of the net amount and then subtracting it from the net amount, assuming that the invoice is paid within the correct period to qualify for the discount.

   1   Display the **Receipts** screen.

2   Enter the Main Line Hotels code **M001** to display Main Line Hotels' outstanding invoices.

3   Press ⎡**F5**⎤ to enter the default system date in the **Date** box.

4   Enter the **Cheque Amount** as:

1351.38

5   Select **Manual** to process the receipt manually.

You will notice that the complete invoice consists of the two items single beds and double beds.

6   Place the highlight over the single beds portion of the invoice and press ⎡**Enter**⎤.

7   Select to pay in FULL.

Immediately the amount set against the single beds of 299.63 changes to 0.00 and the item is annotated with FULL.

8   Repeat this process for the double beds.

21.3   Supplier discounts

If a supplier offers Total Bedrooms a discount on all purchases then this must be recorded on the Supplier Record.

When a supplier invoice is entered into the account of a supplier who is giving a discount then, just as in the case with customer discounts, the net amount of the invoice will read as the discounted amount and the VAT will be calculated on the discounted value of the invoice.

Recording the Supplier Payment is executed in just the same manner as recording a Customer Receipt.

The Periscope program

There are occasions when, in the middle of entering data into the Sage Sterling accounting system, you find a need to access some information that is stored elsewhere within the system. Often, accessing that information will require you to abandon the current data entry causing you to lose all the data you have input so far. This can be annoying, especially if you know that you are going to have to re-enter it at some later time. For example, imagine that you are entering a sales order directly from a phone call and at the tenth item on the order you find that you do not have the required quantity in stock. How are you to find out if you have any on order? If they are on order how are you to find out when they were ordered to enable you to estimate their delivery date? The only way to do this is to abandon the sales order entry facility to enable you to access the stock control facility to find out. In the meantime, all the details of the sales order already entered into the system have to be abandoned.

To avoid problems such as these the Sage Sterling accounting system provides a facility called Periscope that enables you to make such on the spot enquiries of the system without leaving that part of the system within which you are currently operating. Periscope is a feature of the Sage Sterling system that permits enquiries to be made within a 'pop-up' window which can be invoked at any time, regardless of which routine is currently being operated.

22.1 Loading the Periscope program

The Periscope program is installed automatically when the Sage Sterling Financial Controller software was installed. However, its operability is not automatic. It has to be intentionally called into play. Periscope needs to be loaded into your computer's memory before you enter the Sage Sterling system.

 Ensure that your computer monitor is displaying the DOS prompt:

C:\SAGE>

1   At the DOS prompt type in:

VIEW and press Enter

This will cause the Periscope program to be loaded into memory. You will be prompted for your password and this refers to the password you use to access the Sage Sterling system. For the purposes of this *Guide* the password is LETMEIN.

Eventually a screen message tells you that Periscope has been successfully loaded and you are returned to the DOS prompt to enable you to access the Sage Sterling in the normal way.

It is possible to load Periscope and enter the password simultaneously. This is done by issuing the command:

```
VIEW -P LETMEIN
```

The disadvantage of this method of loading Periscope is, of course, that your password is visible on the monitor screen.

22.2   Accessing the Periscope program

The Periscope program, once loaded, can be accessed from within the Sage Sterling accounting system by issuing the command **Alt-Enter**.

1   Enter the Sage Sterling accounting system and ensure that the Financial Controller screen is on display.

2   Press the key combination **Alt-Enter** to reveal the Periscope window:

When the Periscope window is open in this way all interaction between the user and the system takes place within the Periscope window. To return to the accounting system:

3   Press **Esc** and the Periscope window closes.

Whenever the Periscope window is open pressing **Esc** closes it. This does not, however, release it from memory. It is still resident and can be invoked at any time. Indeed, the only way that it can be released from memory is by either re-setting or switching your computer off and then on again.

4   Re-display the Periscope window.

5   In the Periscope window highlight the **Sales Ledger** option and press Enter to reveal the Periscope Sales Ledger enquiry screen:

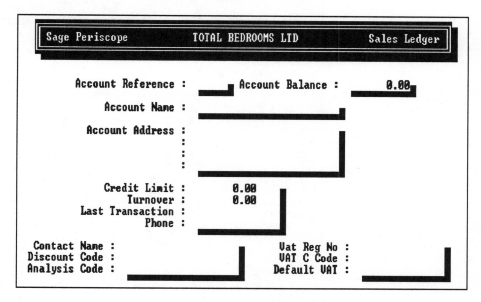

6   Here you see a form that is very similar to the customer record form that is used within the Sage Sterling accounting system to record a customer's details.

7   Enter the customer code:

M001 and press Enter

Immediately the screen fills with the customer details of Main Line Hotels.

8   Press F2 and a box opens in which are displayed all those transactions on the audit trail that are associated with this particular company.

This is typical of enquiries using Periscope. A record is displayed containing information pertinent to an aspect of the Sage Sterling system and by pressing F2 a box opens up listing all those transactions on the audit trail associated with that aspect.

9   Press Esc and the box closes.

10   Press Esc and you are returned to the Periscope main menu screen.

11   Close the Periscope window.

12   From the Financial Controller screen select **Sales Order Processing** and display an empty sales order in readiness to enter a sales order.

13   Open the Periscope window and select the **Stock Control** option to display the Periscope Stock Control window:

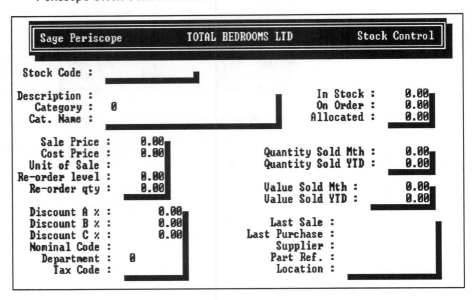

```
┌─────────────────────────────────────────────────────────────────────┐
│ ╔═══════════════════════════════════════════════════════════════╗   │
│ ║  Sage Periscope          TOTAL BEDROOMS LTD        Stock Control ║  │
│ ╚═══════════════════════════════════════════════════════════════╝   │
│                                                                       │
│  Stock Code :                                                         │
│                                                                       │
│  Description :                               In Stock :      0.00     │
│     Category :    0                          On Order :      0.00     │
│    Cat. Name :                               Allocated :     0.00     │
│                                                                       │
│     Sale Price :    0.00                                              │
│     Cost Price :    0.00          Quantity Sold Mth :       0.00      │
│   Unit of Sale :                  Quantity Sold YTD :       0.00      │
│ Re-order level :    0.00                                              │
│   Re-order qty :    0.00             Value Sold Mth :       0.00      │
│                                      Value Sold YTD :       0.00      │
│   Discount A % :      0.00                                            │
│   Discount B % :      0.00              Last Sale :                   │
│   Discount C % :      0.00          Last Purchase :                   │
│   Nominal Code :                         Supplier :                   │
│     Department :    0                    Part Ref. :                  │
│       Tax Code :                          Location :                  │
└─────────────────────────────────────────────────────────────────────┘
```

Here you will see that all the information relating to a stock item can be displayed whilst you are entering a sales order.

Complete this activity with the Periscope window closed and the Sage Sterling Financial Controller screen on display.

22.3   Changing the hotkey

The key combination Alt-Enter that is used to access the Periscope program is called a *hotkey*. On my keyboard the Alt key is on the opposite side of the keyboard to the Enter key. This means that I must use two hands to enter the hotkey. A more convenient hotkey combination is Alt-a because these two keys are almost adjacent to each other and can be activated with one hand. There is a facility within Sage Sterling to change the default hotkey that is available via the Utilities screen.

Ensure that the Financial Controller screen is on display.

1   Select the **Utilities** option to display the Utilities screen.

2   Select the **Defaults** option to display the Defaults screen.

3   Select the **Periscope Setup** option to reveal the Periscope Program control screen.

On this screen you will see that the **Hotkey scan code** is given as **28** and the **Interrupt vector** is given as **98,** the number 28 is hotkey scan code for the key combination Alt-Enter. The hotkey scan code for the key combination Alt-a is 30. There is a cursor flashing over the number 28.

4 Type in the number:

30 and press Enter

5 Press Esc and save the change to disk.

This change in the hotkey scan code will only become effective after you have turned your computer off and then rebooted it.

For a fuller description of all the available hotkey scan codes refer to page 4.42 of the *User Manual* that accompanies the software.

23 Document design

Within the Sage Sterling Financial Controller accounting system a number of predefined documents are available to assist in the smooth running of your accounting system. These documents include standard invoice and credit note formats as well as letters for onward transmission to customers and suppliers.

Each of these documents has been designed using variables to enable them to automatically include information that is specific to their production. For example, the invoice document is used to produce an invoice for onward transmission to any customer that will include the customer's name and address as well as the details relating to their specific purchase.

Because every company has its own preferences with regards to the format of such documents the Sage Sterling Financial Controller accounting system has created these documents in such a way that they can be readily amended or created.

23.1 Accessing the stationery layouts

All the documents stored within the Sage Sterling Financial Controller accounting system can be accessed via the **Stationery Layouts** option in the Utilities screen.

Ensure that the Financial Controller screen is on display.

1   Select the **Utilities** option to reveal the Utilities screen.

2   Select the **Stationery Layouts** option to reveal the Stationery Layouts screen which lists the documents according to type:

   Account Letters
   Statements
   Remittance Notes
   Invoices (Stock)
   Invoices (Free Text)
   Sales Orders
   Purchase Orders

3   Select the **Account Letters** option to reveal the Text Editor screen.

The Text Editor is a program that permits documents to be created and amended by typing directly into the Text Editor screen. At the top of this screen is a line that contains the word **Filename** with a box alongside in which you will see the name OVERDUE.LET.

This is the name of a document created by Sage that accompanies the Sage Sterling system.

4   Press ⌈Enter⌉ to load this docment into the Text Editor screen.

You will be able to see only the first few lines of this letter:

```
Account Name
Address Line 1
Address Line 2
Address Line 3
Address Line 4                                          Date3

Dear Sirs
            OVERDUE  ACCOUNT   $   Balance
            ---------------------------
```

This letter consists of text and variables where the variables are highlighted.

5   Press ⌈PgDn⌉ twice to view the rest of the document:

```
With reference to the above balance which is still
outstanding on your account. May I remind you that
our terms are strictly 30 days nett and $   60Day
is more than 60 days overdue.

                        Yours faithfully
                        SAGESOFT PLC.,




                        Peter Walker
                        COMPANY ACCOUNTANT
                        ------------------
```

On the screen you will see a flashing text cursor. This cursor can be moved about by using the cursor control keys.

6   Use the various cursor control keys to move around the document.

7   Press ⌈Esc⌉ and a small window of options opens up.

8   Select **Abandon** and you are returned to the Stationery Layouts screen.

9   Repeat this procedure to view all the predefined documents that are available.

Complete this activity with the Stationery Layouts screen on display.

Ensure that the Stationery Layouts screen is on display.

1　Access the Text Editor and display the Account Letter OVERDUE.LET.

The top line of this screen contains the items:

Line:　　　which gives the screen line number that the cursor is on
Column:　　which gives the column number that the cursor is on
Ins Mode:　which indicates whether the mode is Insert On (1) or Insert Off (0)

2　Press Ins on your keyboard and you will see the Ins Mode change.

3　Ensure that the Insert Mode is on.

4　Use the cursor control keys to place the cursor on the **S** of **SAGESOFT** just beneath the Yours faithfully.

5　Press the Del key on your keyboard and you will notice that the S disappears and the rest of the letters move backwards so that the A is under the cursor.

This is the effect of deleting text using the Del key.

6　With the cursor over the letter **A** type:

Total

As you type you will see the word Total appear and the AGESOFT PLC., move to the right. This is because the Insert Mode is on so that when you type you insert text.

7　Turn the Insert Mode off.

8　Continue typing:

Bedrooms Ltd

Now you see that as you type you overwrite the AGESOFT PLC.,. This is because the Insert Mode is off and when you type you overtype.

There is a space missing between Total and Bedrooms.

9　Insert a space between Total and Bedrooms.

10　Continue editing until the bottom of the letter has been changed to:

```
Yours faithfully
Total Bedrooms Ltd.,



Bob Andrews
Company Accountant
------------------
```

11 Make sure that the Insert mode is off.

12 Move the cursor to the variable:

$ 60Day

13 Press F4 to reval a drop-down window in which all the variable options are displayed.

14 Move the highlight in the variable window until it is on the variable **90Day** and press Enter .

The variable **$ 60Day** is then replaced with the variable **$ 90Day**.

15 Press Esc and select to **Save** the document after which you are returned to the Stationery Layouts screen.

EXERCISE   1   Access the **Stationery Layouts** screen and open the **Invoices (Stock)** document named INVOICE.LYT.

At the head of this letter you will see the name and address of Sagesoft Plc.

2   Amend this document so that all references to Sagesoft are replaced by references to Total Bedrooms Ltd whose address is:

Slumber House
57 Halifax Road
Huddersfield
HD3 3DE

Notice that the list of variables accessed via the F4 key is different for this document.

3   When you have successfully edited the document save it and print it.

24   Value Added Tax

Value Added Tax, abbreviated to VAT, is an indirect tax levied on the sale of goods and services and is administered by Her Majesty's Customs and Excise. VAT is added to the value of goods and services supplied by individuals, partnerships and limited companies who are registered for VAT with HM Customs and Excise. The requirement for registration is dependent upon the size of the annual turnover and those organisations with an annual turnover less than the threshold are not required by law to register for VAT. Also certain businesses supplying exempt supplies are not required to be registered.

If a business is registered for VAT it must add VAT onto all its taxable supplies - the current rate is set at 17.5%. This is called the output tax. The business is entitled to deduct from its output tax any VAT that has been added onto its purchases of goods and services - its input tax.

If the output tax is greater than its input tax then the resulting difference must be paid over to HM Customs and Excise. If the input tax is greater than the output tax then the resulting difference can be reclaimed from HM Customs and Excise.

The normal method of calculating input and output tax uses the invoice date as tax point as the relevant date for deciding whether to include the item on a particular return.

24.1   Standard VAT accounting

Input tax is calculated from:

       Purchase invoices and credit notes
       Bank payments
       Cash payments
       Journal debits

Output tax is calculated from:

       Sales invoices and credit notes
       Bank receipts
       Cash receipts
       Journal credits

When the VAT Return has been calculated and accepted as correct the VAT Return is reconciled. This means that every transaction on the audit trail that has contributed to the current VAT Return is flagged, that is marked with an asterisk. A flagged transaction is automatically excluded from future VAT Return calculations.

If the VAT Return analysis does not agree with the closing balance of the VAT control account, it can be due to incorrect dates entered onto transactions or because you have corrupt data. The following reports will assist you in identifying and rectifying errors:

- The Transaction History for the VAT control account (code 2200) using the nominal activity option chosen via the **Nominal Ledger** screen. The items marked with a V on the VAT control account report should be included in the VAT Return.
- The Audit Trail.
- A copy of all the fixed transaction reports.
- A detailed VAT analysis report. Check the transactions listed at the end of the report against those on the fixed transactions reports and the VAT control account.

Assuming that you do not have data corruption there is usually an identifiable reason why a VAT Return will not reconcile and very often this can be traced to an incorrect date being entered at the time a transaction was entered into the system.

23.3   VAT cash accounting scheme

It has been possible since 1987 for certain small and medium sized businesses to opt for cash accounting. The business must have been registered for VAT for at least two years and have a turnover below a specified limit. Cash accounting means that VAT is accounted for on a cash received and cash paid basis rather than the usual basis of using the invoice date. The effect of using cash accounting is that output tax will not be paid over to HM Customs and Excise until the cash has been received from the debtor and input tax cannot be deducted until the creditor has been paid.

Input tax is calculated from:

> Purchase payments
> Bank payments
> Cash payments
> Journal debits

Output tax is calculated from:

Sales receipts
Bank receipts
Cash receipts
Journal credits

24.4   Reconciling the VAT Return

Because of the way VAT is calculated when the cash accounting option is used, the VAT control account which accumulates VAT from invoices and credit notes as they are entered into the system regardless of whether they have been paid or allocated will never agree with the results of the VAT Return Analysis. You are advised to reconcile the figures on your VAT Return Analysis reports with the following fixed transaction reports:

- Customer receipts
- Supplier payments
- Cash and bank payments
- Cash and bank receipts

Any taxable transactions not included on a VAT Return Analysis are flagged with an indicator to show that they have not been reconciled. For VAT cash accounting, only payments and receipts are flagged in this way.

24.5   EU VAT analysis

If you supply to or purchase goods from another state in the European Union (the European Community [EC] became the European Union [EU] on 1 November 1993), the VAT exclusive totals for sales and purchases, plus any related services such as transport costs, must be recorded on the VAT Return form.

In the Sage Sterling accounting system, the VAT analysis return includes boxes for the total value of all sales, purchases and related services to other member states of the European Union. In order to ensure that the correct values are accumulated in the appropriate fields, you should indicate which code(s) relate to EU transactions. This can be done by using the VAT Code Changes screen accessed via **VAT Code Changes** from the **Utilities** screen.

Ensure that the Financial Controller screen is on display.

1   Select the **Utilities** option to display the Utilities screen.

2   Select the **VAT Code Changes** option in the Utilities screen to reveal the VAT Code Changes screen:

Variable Tax Rates :

	0	1	3	5	6
T	0.000	17.500	0.000	0.000	0.000
T	0.000	17.500	0.000	0.000	0.000
T	0.000	17.500	0.000	0.000	0.000
T	0.000	17.500	0.000	0.000	0.000
T	0.000	17.500	0.000	0.000	0.000

The tax codes to the left can be changed to suit your needs. The first two should be set to zero and standard VAT.

Reserved Tax Rate Definitions:

2 VAT exempt transactions (set to a value of 0.000).
4 Sales to other EC countries (zero rated).
7 Zero rated purchases from other EC countries (set to match T0 code).
8 Standard rated purchases from other EC countries (set to match T1 code)
9 Non VAT transactions.

This screen can be used to amend the VAT rate if it is changed by the Government.

25 The Report Generator

We have already seen how to create reports based on the information stored in the three ledgers by accessing the Reports facility displayed in each ledger screen. We have also seen how to take advantage of predefined reports - in particular those that are created from information contained in the audit trail. In this chapter we shall learn how to create a new report based on information contained within the audit trail.

25.1 The Report Generator screen

Ensure that the Financial Controller screen is on display.

1. From the Financial Controller screen select the **Report Generator** option to display the Report Generator screen which lists a collection of report categories:

   Sales Ledger
   Purchase Ledger
   Nominal Ledger
   Management Reports
   Invoice Production
   Stock Control
   Sales Order Processing
   Purchase Order Processing

2. From the Report Generator screen select the **Sales Ledger** option to display the first of two Sales Ledger Report Generator screens.

In this first screen you will see a collection of predefined reports and we have already seen these used. What we wish to do is to create a new one.

25.2 Naming a new report

As you will see from the first Sales Ledger Report Generator screen the flashing text cursor is under the word **NAME**. This is where you enter the name of the report - this one will be called **SALES**.

1. Type in the **NAME** of the report as:

   SALES and press Enter to complete the entry.

Immediately, a prompt appears in the upper portion of the screen:

```
Do you want to : Run   Edit   Print   Delete
```

At the moment you have no report to Run, Print or Delete.

2   To create the report select **Edit**.

The highlight now moves under the heading **TITLE**.

3   Type in the **TITLE** as:

Sales Ledger Report for January 1995

When you complete this entry by pressing ⎡Enter⎤ the screen display changes to the second Report Generator screen:

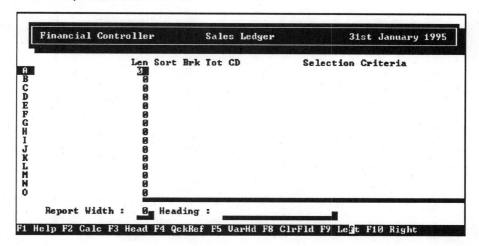

25.3 Viewing the second Report Generator screen

The details of the report's construction are to be entered into this second screen. Down the left-hand side of the screen are the letters **A, B, C, ...** and there is a highlight on the letter **A**.

1   Press ⎡**PgDn**⎤ a number of times.

You will see that the letters down the left-hand side range through **A** to **Z** and then **a** to **z** making 52 letters in all. The report will be created by listing variables against these letters thereby permitting up to 52 variables to form the report. To understand what is mean by a variable:

2   Press the function key ⎡**F4**⎤.

A small window is displayed in the right half of the screen. In this window you will see a list of variables - the first being **Account Ref.** These variables will form the headings of the report and are inserted into the report generator screen from this window.

3   Press PgDn three times and you will see the complete list of variables that are available.

4   Press PgUp three times to return the highlight to the top of the list of variables.

5   Press Esc to remove the window display.

6   Press PgUp until the highlight is back on the letter **A**.

Before you set about creating the report:

7   Press F1 and you will see a Help screen displayed.

The information in this screen is telling you the effects of the F4 and F3 function keys.

8   Press F1 again and the second Help screen gives you information concerning the labels **Len**, **Sort**, **Brk**, **Tot** and **CD** that are displayed across the top of the Report Generator screen.

Do not worry if they do not make too much sense at the moment. By the time you have generated your first report their meanings will become clear.

9   Press Esc and the Help screen disappears.

25.4   Creating a report

1   Ensure that the highlight is on the letter **A** and press the F4 function key.

The variable window now appears with a highlight on the first variable **Account Ref.**

2   Press Enter and this variable name now appears alongside the letter **A** in the Report Generator screen - the number **6** under **Len** represents 6 characters, being the length of the variable.

The highlight in the variable window has now moved to the next variable - **Account Name** - and the highlight in the Report Generator screen has moved down to the letter **B**. This is how variables are entered into the report.

3   Place the following variables in the report generator screen (you will have to move the highlight up and down the list of variables as they are not in the same order as the list required in the report):

Account Name
Analysis Code
Balance
Nominal A/C
Amount Paid
Amount Due
Payment Date

4   When these entries are complete press &boxed{Esc} to remove the variable window.

You now realise that the Nominal Account variable is not required. You need to remove it.

5   Place the highlight over the letter **E** alongside the Nominal Account variable and press &boxed{F4} to display the variable window.

6   Press &boxed{PgDn} until you see at the bottom of the list the words **Remove Field**.

7   Place the highlight over **Remove Field** and press &boxed{Enter}.

Immediately, the Nominal Account variable disappears and the following three variables move up a space to take its place. The report definition is almost complete. We have yet to consider those legends **Len**, **Sort**, **Brk**, **Tot** and **CD**. We shall do that later - for now look at the numbers listed under **Len**. **Len** stands for Length and the numbers represent the maximum numbers of characters that can appear under each variable heading.

8   Press &boxed{F3} and at the top of the screen you will see how the variable names will appear on the printed report.

You cannot see them all.

9   Press &boxed{F10} a number of times and you will see the list move to the left.

10   Press &boxed{F9} and the list moves back again.

11   Press &boxed{F3} to remove the display.

25.5   Running a report

Ensure that the second Report Generator screen is on display without the variable window.

 1   Press &boxed{Esc} and the prompt:

```
Do you want to : Save Edit Abandon
```

re-appears.

2   Select **Save** by typing **S** and the report definition will be saved to disk.

When this is complete you are confronted with the first Report Generator screen.

3   Press Enter and a prompt appears at the top of the screen:

```
Do you want to : Run Edit Print Delete
```

6   Select the default **Run** by pressing Enter .

You will then be confronted with a screen of defaults.

7   Accept all the defaults and send the report to the printer.

25.6   **Editing a report**

From the printout of the report you will now appreciate the role of the variables. Each variable forms a heading to the report and the various values of the variables that apply are listed beneath each heading.

From the appearance of the report you will also appreciate that the information it conveys is rather muddled. Some of the variable values are repeated, they are not in any coherent order and there are numbers without totals. You will now see how to improve this state of affairs.

Display the first screen of the report generator with the SALES report highlighted.

1   Press Enter and at the prompt select **Edit**.

The highlight moves to the **TITLE**.

2   You do not wish to edit this so press Enter to obtain the display of the second Report Generator screen.

The highlight is on the letter **A** again.

3   Use the cursor control keys to place the flashing cursor to the space beneath **Sort**.

4   Now press F1 again to reveal the Help display and then press F1 to display the second Help screen.

Read the description relating to Sort. You are going to want the Account Reference values to be listed in alphabetical order so you are going to want **1A** to be entered against this field under **Sort**.

5   Press Esc to remove the Help display and enter **1A** under **Sort** for the **Account Reference** variable.

6   Press **Enter** to complete your entry and the flashing cursor moves under **Brk**.

7   Read the Help information about **Brk** and then enter **L** in this space.

There will be a line break after each variable value.

8   Move the highlight to the **Balance** variable and place a **Y** under **Tot** so that for each Account Reference the Balance Values will be totalled.

Your report is now complete.

9   Press **Esc** and at the prompt select **Save**.

10   When the report has been saved press **Enter** and at the prompt select **Run**.

When your new report is printed you will appreciate the effect of what you have just done. On your new report you will see that the Analysis Code values are repeated unnecessarily. To avoid this re-edit the report and put a line break alongside Analysis Code.

Complete this activity with the Financial Controller screen on display.

25.7   Selection criteria

Selection criteria are instructions to the system to tell it what data to include in the report. The criteria are applied to the variables and the following symbols may be used:

=	equal to
!=	not equal to
<	less than
<=	less than or equal to
>	greater than
>=	greater than or equal to

AND and OR

The connectives AND and OR can be used to combine conditions. If two conditions are connected by AND then both conditions must be true for data to be selected. If two conditions are connected by OR then at least one of the conditions must be true for data to be selected. For example, the compound selection criterion for the variable **Amount - Net**:

(>= 1250 AND < 2500) OR =3000

will select only those transactions with a net value greater than or equal to 1250 and less than 2500 as well as those transactions with a value equal to 3000.

Wild cards

A wild card is a character that represents an undefined character or group of characters. There are two wild cards:

?   which represents a single undefined character
*   which represents a group of undefined characters in sequence.

For example, if the selection criterion applied to the variable **Tax Code** was:

T*

the tax codes selected would be all of them ranging from T0 to T99. However, if the selection criterion applied to the variable **Tax Code** was:

T?

the tax codes selected would consist only of those codes with a single number after the letter T. That is T0 to T9.

Specified text

Transaction variables containing specifed text can selected by using either:

$ or !$

For example, if the selection criterion applied to the variable **Sale/Purch. Ref** was:

$G

then only those customer or supplier records whose code contained a letter G would be selected, that is G001 for Gibbert Arms and G002 for George Hotel. If the selection criterion applied to the variable **Sale/Purch. Ref** was:

!$G

then only those customer or supplier records whose code did not contain a letter G would be selected.

Multi-company processing

Total Bedrooms have decided to create a subsidiary company called TB Stockholding that will look after all their stockholding facilities. The have also decided that the accounts of the new company will be looked after by Total Bedrooms Ltd.

The Sage Sterling Financial Controller accounting system possesses the facility to manage the data files of up to ten separate companies whilst using the same system programs. Each set of company data can be managed independently, though a special consolidation function is available to merge information from subsidiary companies into a single parent company file. This permits financial reporting at the parent company level based on information supplied from the subsidiaries. If preferred, however, separate companies can be managed without consolidation.

26.1 Adding a new company

The data files relating to a specific company are stored in their own collection of subdirectories on the hard disk.

When we first installed the Sage Sterling software the data files were stored in the **company0** subdirectory of the **sage** directory. The new company, TB Stockholding, will have its data stored in a new subdirectory of the **sage** directory called **company1**. To install a new company use will be made of a program called MULTICO.EXE that was installed when we first installed Sage Sterling.

 1   Leave the Sage Sterling Financial Controller and display the DOS prompt:

    C:\SAGE>

2   Type in the command:

    MULTICO and press Enter .

A screen display will appear telling you that up to ten companies can be installed.

3   Press any key to continue.

The system then sets about creating the new set of data files in a new subdirectory. During the installation you will be asked to enter the name and the address of the new company.

4   Enter the name and address of the new company as follows:

       Name   TB STOCKHOLDING LTD
  Address 1   SLUMBER LODGE
  Address 2   57 HALIFAX ROAD
  Address 3   HUDDERSFIELD
  Address 4   HD3 3DE

5   Accept the standard layout of the nominal ledger and all the neccessary data
     files are created.

When this process is complete a message is displayed:

```
*****   Installation of New Company Complete   *****

C:\SAGE>
```

26.2   Selecting and changing company

Once there is more than one set of company files the process of entering the Sage
Sterling Financial Controller is modifed. After you have accepted or amended the
date and entered a password a selection screen is displayed asking you which
company you wish to process.

1   Move the highlight to the company of your choice and press **Enter** .

You have then completed your selection and any further processing will be done in
that company. If at any time you wish to know the name of the company you are
processing then if you press **Shift-F8** the name will be displayed. To change
company you will first have to exit the Sage Sterling system and re-enter selecting
the new company.

2   Exit the Sage Sterling Financial Controller system.

3   Enter the Sage Sterling system and select the company TB Stockholding.

4   Create a customer account in TB Stockholding's accounts with code T001 in
     the name of Total Bedrooms.

5   Enter the receipt of £100,000.00 from Total Bedrooms as a bank receipt in the
     TB Stockholding accounts crediting the account 2300 Loans with the same
     amount.

6   Exit the Sage Sterling Financial Controller system.

7   Enter the Sage Sterling system and select the company Total Bedrooms.

8   Create a supplier account in Total Bedrooms' accounts with code TBS in the

name of TB Stockholding.

9   Make a bank payment of £100,000.00 from Total Bedrooms debiting the account 2300 Loans with tax code T0 to TB Stockholding.

Because we shall eventually be consolidating these two companies it is essential that the structure of their Nominal Ledgers be identical.

10   Amend the structure of the Nominal Ledger of TB Stockholding Ltd to be identical to that of Total Bedrooms. Refer to Chapter 2.

26.3   Consolidation

Consolidation is the process by which the data of one or more companies is merged to produce consolidated financial reports. The Sage Sterling Financial Controller accounting system permits the consolidation of the sets of accounts of a number of subsidiary companies into one single set of accounts of a parent company.

When the consolidation process is activated the parent company's nominal balances will be amalgamated with data from the consolidating subsidiary companies and any nominal accounts in the consolidating companies not present in the parent company will be created in the parent company's nominal ledger.

So far we have two companies, Total Bedrooms Ltd and TB Stockholding Ltd, and it may be tempting to think that because TB Stockholding Ltd was spawned from the profits of Total Bedrooms Ltd then Total Bedrooms Ltd is the parent company. This is not the case. Indeed at the moment there is no parent company; one has to be created.

1   Create a third company called TB Holdings Ltd using MULTICO.EXE where the company has the same address as the two subsidiaries.

Now we have three companies on the system, one parent and two subsidiaries. However, the Sage Sterling system does not know which is the parent company and which are the subsidiary companies. We have to define the parent and subsidiaries for the Sage Sterling system. To do this we make use of the text editing facilities available via the **Utilities** option in the Financial Controller screen.

2   Enter Sage and select any one of the three companies.

Ensure that the Financial Controller screen is on display.

3   Select the **Utilities** option to display the Utilities screen.

4   From the Utilities screen select the **Text Editor** option to display the Text Editor screen.

You will see a flashing text cursor in a box labelled **Filename**. We need to enter the name of a file here so that we can edit it in the main body of the screen. The names and the addresses of all three companies are contained in a file called COMPANY.

5   In the box labelled **Filename** enter the **Filename** as:

COMPANY

The screen then displays the three company names and addresses and the text cursor moves to the body of the screen.

6   Move the text cursor around the screen using the cursor control keys.

7   Place the cursor on the **N** of the word **Name** alongside TB Holdings Ltd and press ⎟**Enter**⎟.

The entire name and address moves down a line leaving a blank space above.

8   Place the cursor in the blank space and type in:

PARENT

This is how the parent company is designated within the system.

9   Repeat the above procedure for both Total Bedrooms and TB Stockholding but instead of **PARENT** type in:

SUBSIDIARY

Make sure your typing is accurate as this is essential to designate a subsidiary company and that each pair of company details are separated by a blank line. Another point that is essential is that in the list of companies in the COMPANY file the parent company must be the first one. If you find that this is not the case - and it will not be as the parent company was the third one formed and so is listed third - then you are going to have to perform some more editing. The easiest way to do this is to move the cursor to the first company on the list and change its name to "TB HOLDINGS LTD" (the double quotation marks are essential) and its status to PARENT. If necessary use the ⎟**Del**⎟ and ⎟**Ins**⎟ keys to delete and insert text. When you have done this change the name of the old "TB HOLDINGS LTD" to "TOTAL BEDROOMS LTD".

When you are satisfied that your entries are correct:

10   Press ⎟**Esc**⎟ and select the **Save** option.

The amended file is saved to disk and now the Sage Sterling Financial Controller knows which company is the parent and which are the subsidiaries.

The parent company has been created purely for the purposes of consolidating the accounts of the two subsidiary companies. As a consequence its account must be completely blank: there must be no transactions entered into it. Furthermore, the structure of its Nominal Ledger must be identical to the structure of the two subsidiary companies.

11 Amend the structure of the Nominal Ledger of TB Holdings Ltd to be identical to that of the other two companies. Refer to Chapter 2.

We are now ready to consolidate the accounts of the companies.

12 Ensure that you are processing within the parent company TB Holdings Ltd with the Financial Controller screen on display.

13 Select the **Utilities** option and from the Utilities screen select the **Data File Changes** option.

14 Select the **Rebuild Data Files** option and a message will be displayed describing what the process is about to do.

15 Press Enter and enter **No** at the prompt:

```
Do you have existing data?
```

When this process is complete:

16 Display the **Nominal Ledger** screen and select the **Consolidation** option.

Again a message is displayed telling you what the process is about to do.

17 Press Enter and the process will proceed returning you to the Nominal Ledger screen when it is complete.

18 Run the Profit and Loss and Balance Sheet Reports and create the Month End files to view the effect of the consolidation.

If any two nominal accounts coincide then their balances are totalled. If an account exists in a subsidiary's account that does not exist in the parent's accounts then a new account is created in the parent's accounts.

19 Check the nominal ledger of TB Holdings Ltd.

You will see that the account balances are identical to those of Total Bedrooms Ltd's nominal ledger except for the account 2300 Loans which has a credit of 100,000.00, this being identical to TB Stockholdings Ltd's account.

Appendices

A1 Default Nominal Ledger codes

Fixed Assets

0010	FREEHOLD PROPERTY
0011	LEASEHOLD PROPERTY
0020	PLANT AND MACHINERY
0021	P/M DEPRECIATION
0030	OFFICE EQUIPMENT
0031	O/E DEPRECIATION
0040	FURNITURE AND FIXTURES
0041	F/F DEPRECIATION
0050	MOTOR VEHICLES
0051	M/V DEPRECIATION

Current assets

1001	STOCK
1002	WORK IN PROGRESS
1003	FINISHED GOODS
1100	DEBTORS CONTROL ACCOUNT
1101	SUNDRY DEBTORS
1102	OTHER DEBTORS
1103	PREPAYMENTS
1200	BANK CURRENT ACCOUNT
1210	BANK DEPOSIT ACCOUNT
1220	BUILDING SOCIETY ACCOUNT
1230	PETTY CASH

Current Liabilities

2100	CREDITORS CONTROL ACCOUNT
2101	SUNDRY CREDITORS
2102	OTHER CREDITORS
2109	ACCRUALS
2200	TAX CONTROL ACCOUNT
2201	VAT LIABILITY
2210	P.A.Y.E.
2211	NATIONAL INSURANCE
2230	PENSION FUND
2300	LOANS
2310	HIRE PURCHASE
2320	CORPORATION TAX
2330	MORTGAGES

Financed By

3000	ORDINARY SHARES
3001	PREFERENCE SHARES
3100	RESERVES
3101	UNDISTRIBUTED RESERVES
3200	PROFIT AND LOSS ACCOUNT

Sales

4000	SALES TYPE A
4001	SALES TYPE B
4002	SALES TYPE C
4009	DISCOUNTS ALLOWED
4100	SALES TYPE D
4101	SALES TYPE E
4200	SALES OF ASSETS
4900	MISCELLANEOUS INCOME
4901	ROYALTIES RECEIVED
4902	COMMISSIONS RECEIVED
4903	INSURANCE CLAIMS
4904	RENT INCOME
4905	DISTRIBUTION AND CARRIAGE

Purchases

5000	MATERIALS PURCHASED
5001	MATERIALS IMPORTED
5002	MISCELLANEOUS PURCHASES
5003	PACKAGING
5009	DISCOUNTS TAKEN
5100	CARRIAGE
5101	DUTY
5102	TRANSPORT INSURANCE
5200	OPENING STOCK
5201	CLOSING STOCK

Direct Expenses

6000	PRODUCTIVE LABOUR
6001	COST OF SALES LABOUR
6002	SUB-CONTRACTORS
6100	SALES COMMISSIONS

6200	SALES PROMOTIONS	7701	OFFICE MACHINE MAINT.
6201	ADVERTISING	7800	REPAIRS AND RENEWALS
6202	GIFTS AND SAMPLES	7801	CLEANING
6203	P.R. (LIT. & BROCHURES)	7802	LAUNDRY
6900	MISCELLANEOUS EXPENSES	7803	PREMISES EXPENSES (MISC)
		7900	BANK INTEREST PAID

Overheads

7001	DIRECTORS SALARIES	7901	BANK CHARGES
7002	DIRECTORS REMUNERATION	7902	CURRENCY CHARGES
7003	STAFF SALARIES	7903	LOAN INTEREST PAID
7004	WAGES - REGULAR	7904	H.P. INTEREST
7005	WAGES - CASUAL	7905	CREDIT CHARGES
7006	EMPLOYERS N.I.		

Miscellaneous

7007	EMPLOYERS PENSIONS	8000	DEPRECIATION
7008	RECRUITMENT EXPENSES	8001	PLANT & MACHINERY DEPR.
7100	RENT	8002	FURNITURE/FIX/FITTINGS DP
7102	WATER RATES	8003	VEHICLE DEPRECIATION
7103	GENERAL RATES	8004	OFFICE EQUIPMENT DEPR.
7104	PREMISES INSURANCE	8100	BAD DEBT WRITE OFF
7200	ELECTRICITY	8102	BAD DEBT PROVISION
7201	GAS	8200	DONATIONS
7202	OIL	8201	SUBSCRIPTIONS
7203	OTHER HEATING COSTS	8202	CLOTHING COSTS
7300	FUEL AND OIL	8203	TRAINING COSTS
7301	REPAIRS AND SERVICING	8204	INSURANCE
7302	LICENCES	8205	REFRESHMENTS
7303	VEHICLES INSURANCE	9998	SUSPENSE ACCOUNT
7304	MISC. MOTOR EXPENSES	9999	MISPOSTINGS ACCOUNT

7400	TRAVELLING
7401	CAR HIRE
7402	HOTELS
7403	U.K. ENTERTAINMENT
7404	OVERSEAS ENTERTAINMENT
7405	OVERSEAS TRAVELLING
7406	SUBSISTENCE
7500	PRINTING
7501	POSTAGE AND CARRIAGE
7502	TELEPHONE
7503	TELEX/TELEGRAM/FACSIMILE
7504	OFFICE STATIONERY
7505	BOOKS ETC.
7600	LEGAL FEES
7601	AUDIT & ACCOUNTANCY FEES
7602	CONSULTANCY FEES
7603	PROFESSIONAL FEES
7700	EQUIPMENT HIRE

Sales/Purchase Ledger variables
Account Ref.
Account Name
Address 1
Address 2
Address 3
Address 4
Telephone Number
Contact Name
Analysis Code
Discount Code
Last Inv. Date
First Trans. No.
Last Trans. No.
Credit Limit
Turnover
Balance
Balance - Current
Balance - 30Day
Balance - 60Day
Balance - 90Day
Transaction No.
Type (Long)
Type (Short)
Nominal A/C
Department No.
Department Name
Transaction Date
Transaction Ref.
Details
Amount - Nett
Amount - Tax
Amount - Gross
Payment Date
Payment Ref.
Amount - Paid
Amount - Due
Tax Code
Tax Percentage

Paid (Yes/No)
Age of Trans.
Next Trans. A/C
Next Trans. N/C

Nominal Ledger variables
Account Ref.
Account Name
First Trans. No.
Last Trans. No.
Balance
Yearly Budget
Mth 1 to 12 Budget
Transaction No.
Type (Short)
Department No.
Department Name
Sales/Purch. Ref.
Transaction Date
Transaction Ref.
Details
Amount - Nett
Amount - Tax
Tax Code
Tax Percentage
Next Trans. N/C

Management Reports variables
Transaction No.
Type (Long)
Type (Short)
Sales/Purch. Ref.
Nominal A/C
Department No.
Department Name
Transaction Date
Transaction Ref.
Details
Amount - Nett

Amount - Tax
Amount - Gross
Payment Date
Payment Ref.
Amount - Paid
Amount - Due
Tax Code
Tax Percentage
Paid (Yes/No)
Next Trans. A/C
Next Trans. N/C

Stock Control variables
Stock Code
Stock Desc.
Category No.
Category Name
Sale Price
Cost Price
Units of Sales
Re-Order Level
Re-Order Qty
Discount A
Discount B
Discount C
Nominal Code
Nominal Name
Department
Department Name
Tax Code
Supplier Ref.
Supplier Name
Part Reference
Location
Qty in Stock
Qty on Order
Qty Allocated
Qty Sold MTH
Qty Sold YTD
Value Sold MTH
Value Sold YTD
Cost of Sale MTH
Cost of Sale YTD
Value of Stock
Last Sale
Last Purchase

Assembly Level
Transaction Type
Transaction Date
Reference
Description
Quantity
Quantity Used
Cost Price
Sale Price

Invoicing, Sales and Purchase Order variables
Invoice No.
Invoice Date
Sale A/C
Sales Name
Order No.
Order Date
Order A/C
Order Name
Address 1
Address 2
Address 3
Address 4
Telephone No.
Del. Name
Del. Address 1
Del. Address 2
Del. Address 3
Del. Address 4
Due Date
Order Taken By
Invoice/Credit
Customer No.
Allocate Status
Despatch Status
Notes 1
Notes 2
Notes 3
Global Nominal
Global Tax Code
Global Tax
Global Dept.
Global Desc.
Items Nett
Items Tax
Items Gross

Carriage Nett
Carriage Tax
Carriage Gross
Carriage Nominal
Carriage Tax Cde
Carriage Dept.
Total Cost
Total Nett
Total Tax
Invoice Total
Order Total
Settlement Days
Settlement DIsc.
Early Payment
Printed Flag
Posted Flag
Stock Code
Stock Desc.
Comment 1
Comment 2
Allocate Status
Despatch Status
Quantity
Quantity Alloc.
Quantity Ready
Quantity Desp.
Part Ref/Bin Loc
Unit Price
Units
Discount Rate
Cost Price
Discount
Nett Amount
Tax Amount
Gross Amount
Nominal Code
Nominal Name
Department
Department Name
Tax Code
Tax Value.

Index